P9-DYD-725
A
BOOK
IS A PRESENT
YOU CAN OPEN
AGAIN
AND
AGAIN
This Book Belongs To
Barbara Wolfson
8258 © Mary Engelbreit

EASY ENTERTAINING *with* MARLENE SOROSKY

BY THE SAME AUTHOR

Season's Greetings

The Dessert Lover's Cookbook

Marlene Sorosky's Year-Round Holiday Cookbook

Cookery for Entertaining

EASY ENTERTAINING *with* MARLENE SOROSKY

Photographs by Jeffrey Weir

1817

HARPER & ROW, PUBLISHERS, New York
Cambridge, Philadelphia, San Francisco
London, Mexico City, São Paulo, Singapore, Sydney

See photograph on previous page. Clockwise from top right: Appetizer platter with Cucumber Cups with Mock Crab, Miniature Frittatas in Whole Wheat Toast Cups, Lox and Cream Cheese Roll, Pepper Wedges with Tomatoes and Basil, Brie Quesadillas.

Photo credits appear on page 205.

 For information address Harper & Row, Publishers, Inc., 10 East 53rd Street, New York, N.Y. 10022. Published simultaneously in Canada by Fitzhenry & Whiteside Limited, Toronto.

FIRST EDITION

Designer: Goulet/Grann Art Direction
Copyeditor: Susan Derecskey

Library of Congress Cataloging-in-Publication Data
Sorosky, Marlene.
Easy entertaining with Marlene Sorosky.

Includes index.
1. Entertaining. 2. Cookery, American. 3. Menus.
I. Title.
TX731.S655 1988 641.5 87-45670
ISBN 0-06-181783-X

---

88 89 90 91 92 WAK 10 9 8 7 6 5 4 3 2 1

DEDICATION

To Hal,
who helps me live my dreams

ACKNOWLEDGMENTS

First and foremost, I am indebted to Susan Derecskey, my copy editor. She went over my recipes with such vigilance and thoroughness that her contribution to their accuracy is immeasurable. I thank you, Susan, for being so good at what you do. Because of your continued probing and questioning, you helped make me better.

My thanks also to Jeffrey Weir for his excellent photographs; Christine Goulet and Leslie Grann for their creative designs in the layout and format of the photographs and the book; Michael de Beneditto, for his beautiful food styling and great sense of humor; Joseph Montebello, Harper & Row's creative director, for his artistic input; and Pat Brown, my editor, for bringing these talented people together.

My appreciation also to Linda Annarino, a talented writer, for so generously offering her inspiration and wit; Edon Waycott, Frances Coleman, Carole Magness, Ellen Cline (and their families) for assisting with recipe development, testing and critiquing. They cooked the dishes in their homes and transported them to mine. Each of these women has stains in her car to prove it.

And last, but not least, a hug for Larry Ashmead and Connie Levinson at Harper & Row, and Maureen and Eric Lasher, my literary agents, for their continued support.

CONTENTS

INTRODUCTION

Ever since I can remember, I've wanted to be a teacher. When my friends were playing house, I was playing school. I began teaching cooking by accident. When my oldest daughter entered kindergarten, I used my home to demonstrate menus for entertaining to raise money for the PTA. The response was so extraordinary that soon I opened my own cooking school and cookware shop and began writing cookbooks.

To this day, I consider myself first and foremost a teacher, and a teacher's greatest desire is for the student to excel. To that end, the outstanding characteristic of all my recipes is that they are easy to follow and worth the effort.

Easy Entertaining is not a coffee table book. It's meant to be tattered and spattered in the kitchen, for every occasion from family breakfasts to formal dining. It is much more than a compilation of recipes. Each menu is composed with an internal structure beyond the obvious. On one side, ingredients are combined in new and exciting recipes, each tested countless times, not only by me, but by my students, friends and nonprofessional cooks. The dishes are then joined with others to complement taste, texture and appearance. People eat with all their senses, first with their eyes, so the plate must look beautiful.

On the other side, the menus are planned so that each one can be managed by one cook alone in the kitchen. I know, for every menu here has either been taught in class in its entirety or served in my home.

Each recipe in this book can be made at least partially in advance. Many can be frozen. There is a minimum of last-minute work, which makes these menus ideal for the busy or inexperienced cook.

To have everything ready when you need it takes some thoughtful planning. After you've chosen the dishes and read the menu hints on preparing them, make yourself a work sheet. List each recipe, how far in advance it can be made and on which day you plan to prepare it. If a dish can be frozen, plan to make it at a time you aren't doing too many other things. Don't feel compelled to complete the entire dish at one time. Often it's easier to divide a recipe by doing the initial preparation one day and assembling the dish the next. Go through each recipe and write down what will need to be done before serving. If it needs defrosting, list how and when. If it needs heating, for how long and at what temperature. All of this information is included in each recipe. Decide what time you plan to eat and make a timetable for everything you need to do.

An extra pair of hands to help in the kitchen is a nice bonus. Of course it's helpful if that person is experienced with cooking. If not, consider hiring someone to help arrange the plates, pour the water, stir the sauce and wash the dishes. Go over the routine with your helper, so he or she will know in advance what needs to be done.

It's my belief that nothing in cooking or entertaining is carved in stone. Even though each menu presented here was planned in depth from assembling the ingredients through execution in the kitchen, you should feel free to substitute and adapt as you like. Cooking is very much like fashion. By the time you add your own accessories and personality, the style is as much yours as the designer's.

Certainly it's easiest to plan a party around the plates, glasses and linens you have on hand. But don't be afraid to break out of the customary routine by doing something unusual. For a theme or ethnic party, look for inexpensive, colorful plates at outlet stores. Put together sets of dishes using one-of-a-kind plates, mix and match by using your regular dishes for coffee and dessert.

In place of white or pastel table linens, purchase a bold print from a fabric store or colorful sheets to cover your table. Napkin rings can be made from anything that ties or has a loop, such as antique keys, porcelain rings, colored twine with sprigs of fresh or silk flowers or pretty velvet or plaid ribbons.

Above all, the unwritten direction in each of my menus is, have fun. Entertaining is one of the most personal and treasured gifts we can give to others. When we open our homes and invite friends in, we open our hearts as well. It's my hope that *Easy Entertaining* will help fill your life and those dear to you with the warmth and love found only through the joy of giving.

Marlene Sorosky
Baltimore, Maryland
August 1988

PARTY PLANNING STRATEGY

Make guest list
Invite guests
Plan the menu
Write a timetable for food preparation
Prepare those dishes which can be frozen or made ahead
Purchase special decorations or accessories
Plan table settings: linens, dishes, glassware, silverware
Plan centerpiece
Plan serving pieces and utensils
Make shopping list: groceries, wine, florist, paper goods
Go over Entertaining Checklist

One or Two Days Before the Party

Shop
Set table
Prepare food
Defrost food as indicated in recipe

Day of Party

Final food preparation
Follow your timetable

Entertaining Checklist

Beverages

- ☐ Ice
- ☐ Ice tongs
- ☐ Ice bucket
- ☐ Cork screw
- ☐ Bottle opener
- ☐ Soft drinks
- ☐ Mixers
- ☐ Alcoholic beverages
- ☐ Wine
- ☐ Brandy and liqueurs
- ☐ Mineral or sparkling water
- ☐ Lemons, limes
- ☐ Olives, cherries, cocktail onions
- ☐ Coasters
- ☐ Cocktail napkins
- ☐ Nuts

Table Settings

- ☐ Table cloth or place mats
- ☐ Serving pieces, bowls, baskets, platters, and so on
- ☐ Glasses for wine, water and soft drinks
- ☐ Salt and pepper shakers
- ☐ Dishes
- ☐ Napkins
- ☐ Napkin rings
- ☐ Silverware
- ☐ Serving utensils
- ☐ Centerpiece
- ☐ Candles and matches
- ☐ Flowers
- ☐ Oasis floral sponge
- ☐ Place cards
- ☐ Party favors

Miscellaneous

- ☐ Coffee and decaffeinated coffee
- ☐ Tea
- ☐ Sugar and sugar substitute
- ☐ Cream or milk
- ☐ Salt and pepper
- ☐ Garnishes, parsley, watercress, mint
- ☐ Toothpicks
- ☐ Doilies
- ☐ Tissues
- ☐ Guest soap
- ☐ Guest towels in bathroom
- ☐ Hangers for guest closet
- ☐ Serving trays
- ☐ Ashtrays
- ☐ After-dinner mints

BEAUTIFUL BREAKFASTS AND BRUNCHES

Clockwise from top right: Sparkling Orange Juice, Rosemary Sausage Patties, Peanut Butter Streusel Muffins, Magic Strawberry Pancake Basket.

MENU

RISE AND SHINE BREAKFAST

Sparkling Orange Juice

Blueberry French Toast Cobbler
or
Magic Strawberry Pancake Basket

Make-Ahead Scrambled Eggs

Rosemary Sausage Patties

Peanut Butter Streusel Muffins (*Page 34*)
or
Banana Chocolate Chip Coffeecake (*Page 39*)

When you say "Good Morning" with an incomparable casserole of bubbly blueberries crowned with golden French toast, or a thin, crisp pancake shell brimming with strawberries and sour cream, you won't be the only one to rise and shine. Your reputation will soar. Although neither of these fruity entrees can be prepared completely ahead, they are both assembled very quickly. French Toast Cobbler is an ideal choice for a large crowd since it is easy to make and bake several casseroles.

Don't feel you have to serve Make-Ahead Scrambled Eggs with either of these entrees, as each of them stands beautifully on its own. Instead of filling the pancake basket with berries, use the Make-Ahead Scrambled Eggs, fruit, meat or fish salad or heap it high with colorful decorated eggs for a novel Easter brunch centerpiece. Some occasions for serving this breakfast menu are:

◇ Post-Tennis
◇ New Year's Day
◇ Easter Egg Hunt
◇ Mother's or Father's Day—Let the children help prepare a tray for breakfast in bed.

Sparkling Orange Juice

Begin your morning with sunshiny effervescence. Champagne may be substituted for mineral water, if you like. (See photograph, page 17.)

1 quart fresh orange juice, chilled
1½ quarts (6 cups) sparkling mineral water, chilled
Ice cubes or crushed ice
Fresh mint sprigs for garnish
1 orange, sliced, for garnish

In a large pitcher, stir orange juice and sparkling water together. Pour over ice in stemmed goblets. Garnish each with a sprig of mint and a slice of orange curled over the rim.

Serves 6 to 8.

Blueberry French Toast Cobbler

Batter-drenched French toast bakes to golden crispness atop bubbly blueberries, making an irresistible casserole. To save time in the morning, don't be afraid to soak the bread in the batter overnight. It will be puffed and soft, not at all soggy.

- 1 loaf (8 ounces) French bread
- 4 eggs
- ½ cup milk
- ¼ teaspoon baking powder
- 1 teaspoon vanilla
- 4½ cups fresh or frozen blueberries, not defrosted (about 1½ pounds)
- ½ cup sugar
- 1 teaspoon cinnamon
- 1 teaspoon cornstarch
- 2 tablespoons melted butter for brushing on top
- Confectioners sugar for sprinkling on top

Slice the bread diagonally into 10 to 14 slices about ¾ inch thick; place on a rimmed baking sheet (10½ × 15½ × 1 inch). In a medium bowl, whisk together the eggs, milk, baking powder and vanilla; slowly pour over the bread, turning to coat it completely. Cover with plastic wrap and let sit at room temperature for 1 to 2 hours or refrigerate overnight.

Before serving, preheat the oven to 450 degrees. Butter a 9 × 13-inch baking dish. Place blueberries, sugar, cinnamon and cornstarch in prepared dish; stir to coat berries. Place bread wettest side up on berries. Wedge slices in tightly, cutting some pieces to fit if necessary. (You may not use it all.) Brush tops of bread with melted butter. Bake in center of oven for 20 to 25 minutes or until the toast is golden and the berries are bubbling around the sides. Remove from oven and sift confectioners sugar over the top. Let sit 5 minutes before serving. To serve, lift toast onto plates, spooning blueberry sauce over the top.

Serves 6.

Magic Strawberry Pancake Basket

You'll be riveted to the oven window as you watch the batter rise magically into a basket. It will hold its shape until served. *(See photograph, page 17.)*

- Strawberry Sour Cream Filling (See below)
- 2 eggs
- ½ cup milk
- ¼ teaspoon salt, or to taste
- ½ cup all-purpose flour
- 1 tablespoon butter or margarine

Strawberry Sour Cream Filling

- 3 pints strawberries, stems removed and halved
- ½ cup sugar
- 2 cups (1 pint) sour cream
- ¼ cup (packed) golden light brown sugar

One to 2 hours before serving, prepare Strawberry Sour Cream Filling. Stir strawberries and sugar together; set aside. In a small bowl, stir sour cream and brown sugar together; refrigerate until ready to serve.

To make the pancake basket, place oven rack in center of oven and preheat to 450 degrees. In a small bowl, whisk eggs until combined. Whisk in milk, salt and flour. Put butter or margarine into a 9-inch deep-dish pie or quiche dish or 9-inch nonstick skillet. If the handle of the skillet is not ovenproof, wrap it in several layers of foil. Place in the oven for 1 to 2 minutes or until butter or margarine is melted and sizzling; quickly swirl to coat bottom and about 1 inch up sides of pan. Immediately pour in egg batter. Bake for 15 minutes. If the bottom puffs up, prick it with a fork. Reduce oven temperature to 350 degrees and continue baking for 8 to 10 minutes or until puffed and golden brown.

Remove from oven, lift out basket and place on a serving plate. Spoon strawberries in the center and top with sour cream. To serve, cut into wedges.

Serves 4 to 6.

Make-Ahead Scrambled Eggs

Perfect for a chafing dish. White sauce is the secret of keeping scrambled eggs soft and creamy for up to 30 minutes.

White Sauce (See below)
12 eggs
2 tablespoons butter or margarine
½ cup chopped ham, optional
1 green onion with top, sliced, optional

White Sauce

1 tablespoon butter or margarine
1 tablespoon all-purpose flour
½ cup regular or low-fat milk
½ teaspoon salt, or to taste
¼ teaspoon pepper

To make the White Sauce, in a small saucepan melt butter or margarine over low heat; stir in flour. Cook, stirring, for 1 minute; gradually whisk in milk. Cook, stirring constantly, until the mixture comes to a boil and thickens. Stir in salt and pepper. The sauce may be held at room temperature, covered with plastic wrap directly on its surface, for several hours. Reheat before using.

In a large bowl, whisk the eggs until foamy. Whisk in the white sauce. Melt 2 tablespoons butter or margarine in a large skillet. If using ham and green onion, sauté them for 2 minutes. Add eggs. Cook over low heat, stirring gently from time to time and lifting portions of coagulated eggs so that the uncooked egg can run underneath. If serving immediately, cook to desired doneness. If not, cook only until the eggs are barely set, but still very soft and moist. Remove to the top of a double boiler set over simmering water; cover and keep warm up to 30 minutes.

Serves 6.

Rosemary Sausage Patties

With a food processor and very little effort you can make your own lean sausage patties without any additives or preservatives. *(See photograph, page 17.)*

1 pound pork shoulder, cut into small cubes
1 pound veal stew meat, cut into small cubes
⅔ cup cracker meal
1 egg
2 teaspoons milk
½ teaspoon salt, or to taste
1 teaspoon dried rosemary
¼ teaspoon ground allspice
½ teaspoon dried sage
¼ teaspoon ground pepper
¼ teaspoon dried red pepper flakes
¼ cup parsley leaves
2 tablespoons butter or margarine
2 tablespoons vegetable oil

In a food processor fitted with the metal blade, process pork and veal until very finely chopped. Add cracker meal, egg, milk, seasonings and parsley leaves; process until well combined. Shape into 2½- to 3-inch patties. In a medium skillet, heat butter or margarine and oil over moderately high heat. Fry the patties in batches without crowding until golden brown and all pink is gone, about 3 to 4 minutes on each side. Drain on paper towels.

* The cooked patties may be refrigerated up to 2 days or frozen. Bring to room temperature and reheat at 450 degrees for 5 minutes or until heated through.

Makes 18 to 20 patties.

M E N U

GARDEN PARTY SUNDAY BRUNCH

Chilled Papaya and Champagne Soup

Fresh Spinach Frittata

Chicken Livers with Bacon and Apples

Eggplant, Zucchini and Tomato Tart

Orange Blossom Coffeecake (*Page 37*)
or
Spiraled Chocolate Yeast Coffeecake (*Page 38*)

This sophisticated brunch, resplendent with fresh fruit and vegetables, is as welcome on a frosty winter's morn as on a sweltering summer's day. Cold soups are often associated with warm weather, but Chilled Papaya and Champagne Soup in particular says "celebration." When papayas are not available, serve Bubbly Mixed Fruit Bowl (page 24), replacing the ginger ale with champagne. The beautiful Eggplant, Zucchini and Tomato Tart needs to be assembled and baked within several hours of serving, but because it begins with packaged puff pastry and the vegetables only need slicing, it goes together quickly.

Elaborate on the garden theme with a fresh vegetable centerpiece. Thickly line a wicker basket with leaves of curly Savoy cabbage or red-tip leaf lettuce. Heap it with Japanese eggplant, green onions, whole heads of garlic, zucchini, tomatoes and red, yellow and green peppers. Before your guests arrive, tuck in sprigs of parsley or mint. Suggested occasions for serving this festive menu are:

- **◇ Engagement Celebration**
- **◇ Family or School Reunion**
- **◇ Open House**
- **◇ Sweetheart Brunch—Invite one or two couples to join you for a celebration of love. Decorate the table with hearts and flowers.**

Chilled Papaya and Champagne Soup

One of the best fruit soups I've ever had. It sparkles in color and taste.

3 ripe papayas (about 1½ pounds each)
⅓ cup lime juice (about 2 limes)
¼ cup honey
1 cup orange juice
1 bottle (750 ml) champagne, chilled
1 kiwi, peeled and sliced, for garnish
6 small strawberries, hulled and cut in half, for garnish

Peel papayas, cut in half, scrape out seeds and cut flesh into small pieces. Puree in food processor with the metal blade until smooth, scraping sides as needed. Remove to a bowl and stir in lime juice, honey and orange juice. Cover and refrigerate until chilled.

∗ The soup may be refrigerated overnight, if desired.

Before serving, stir in 1 cup of the champagne. Serve in glass bowls, garnishing each with a slice of kiwi topped with 1 or 2 strawberry halves. At the table, pour a splash of champagne into each bowl.

Serves 6.

Fresh Spinach Frittata

Popeye would approve! This dish contains a high proportion of spinach to cheesy batter.

- 2 pounds fresh bulk spinach (about 10 ounces stemmed)
- 3 eggs
- ½ cup all-purpose flour
- 1 cup regular or low-fat milk
- ½ teaspoon salt, or to taste
- ¼ teaspoon pepper
- 1 teaspoon baking powder
- ½ teaspoon hot-pepper sauce, or to taste
- 1 pound jack cheese, shredded (about 4 cups)
- 3 tablespoons butter or margarine

Discard stems from spinach, wash and tear leaves into bite-size pieces; dry very well. Place oven rack in center of oven and preheat to 350 degrees. In a large bowl, whisk eggs until frothy. Whisk in flour until incorporated. Whisk in milk, salt, pepper, baking powder and hot-pepper sauce. Stir in cheese and spinach; there will be a lot compared to the amount of batter.

Place butter or margarine in a 9- or 10-inch quiche dish or 7 × 11-inch casserole; place in oven until melted. Pour spinach mixture into heated dish. Place on a baking sheet and bake for 45 to 55 minutes or until puffed and golden brown. A knife inserted in the center will not test clean. Cool 10 minutes. The frittata will fall as it cools. Cut into wedges or squares to serve.

∗ The frittata may be frozen. Defrost, covered, at room temperature and reheat, uncovered, at 350 degrees for 10 to 15 minutes or until heated through.

Serves 6 to 8.

Chicken Livers with Bacon and Apples

Sweet apples, smoky bacon and mellow wine combine with chicken livers for a sophisticated breakfast taste.

- ½ pound bacon, chopped
- 6 tablespoons (¾ stick) butter or margarine, divided
- 2 medium tart green apples
- 1 pound whole chicken livers
- ¼ cup all-purpose flour
- 3 tablespoons dry Marsala or Madeira wine
- 3 green onions with tops, chopped
- Salt and pepper to taste

In a large skillet, fry bacon until crisp; remove with slotted spoon and drain on paper towels. Discard all but 1 tablespoon drippings. Add 2 tablespoons butter or margarine to the pan. Peel, halve, core and thinly slice the apples. Sauté, stirring often until slices are crisp-tender; remove to a plate. Wash and dry livers; discard connective tissue and any greenish parts. If livers are large, cut them in half. Dip them in flour, coating lightly. Melt remaining 4 tablespoons butter or margarine in same skillet. Sauté livers over moderately high heat until browned on each side, about 5 minutes. Stir in wine, apples, bacon, and green onions. Cook, stirring gently, until heated through and livers are pink when cut into. Season to taste with salt and pepper.

∗ The mixture may be refrigerated overnight and reheated over moderately high heat before serving.

Serves 6.

Eggplant, Zucchini and Tomato Tart

This fresh vegetarian pizza with its overlapping rows of thinly sliced vegetables and light cheese filling atop storebought puff pastry is much simpler to make than anyone would think.

- 1 package (1 pound) frozen puff pastry, thawed until soft enough to roll, but still very cold
- 2 medium zucchini (¾ pound)
- 3 small tomatoes, preferably Italian plum
- 3 small eggplants, preferably Japanese, unpeeled (about ¾ pound)
- 2 cups ricotta cheese
- 2 tablespoons lemon juice
- 3 cloves garlic, minced
- ½ teaspoon salt, or to taste
- 2 cups shredded mozzarella cheese (about 8 ounces)
- ¼ cup olive oil
- 6 green onions with tops, chopped
- 2 teaspoons dried oregano
- 3 tablespoons fresh chopped basil or 1 tablespoon dried basil
- Freshly ground black pepper

On a lightly floured board, roll out the pastry into a 12 × 17-inch rectangle. Fit it into the bottom and up the sides of a 10½ × 15½ × 1-inch rimmed baking sheet (jelly-roll pan). Refrigerate while preparing the filling.

Place oven rack in bottom of oven; preheat to 425 degrees.

In a food processor fitted with the thin slicing blade or with a sharp knife, slice zucchini, tomatoes and eggplants into ⅛-inch slices; set aside. In a small bowl, stir together ricotta cheese, lemon juice, garlic and salt. Spread over bottom of pastry. Sprinkle with mozzarella. Arrange vegetables slightly overlapping in lengthwise rows over cheese, beginning and ending with a row of tomatoes. Fold edges of pastry over to form a rim. Brush vegetables and edges of pastry with the olive oil. Sprinkle the vegetables with green onions, oregano, basil and a liberal grinding of pepper. Bake for 25 to 30 minutes or until the vegetables are tender and the crust is lightly browned.

* The tart may be held at room temperature for several hours, if desired. Rewarm at 425 degrees for 7 to 10 minutes before serving.

Serve slices with side crust first, saving middle slices for second helpings.

Serves 8.

MENU

SLUMBER PARTY BREAKFAST

Bubbly Mixed Fruit Bowl

Over-Easy Omelet with International Variations

Pantry Pancakes

Honey Wheat Pancakes

Frothy Hot Chocolate

When my four children were growing up, I often whipped up weekend breakfasts far more elaborate than our usual daily fare. Those special moments we spent together before everyone headed off in different directions were well worth the extra time and effort. The recipes presented here are for some of the pancakes and omelets I have made for family breakfasts and birthday parties. There are far too many to comprise a menu; they merely suggest the range of possibilities.

Once you've mastered the technique for making omelets, let your imagination run wild with the fillings. For a large gathering, set out bowls with many different fillings and let your guests create their own favorite combinations.

If you want to see children eat leisurely, make Mickey or Minnie Mouse pancakes. Pour the batter into large rounds for the face with smaller rounds on the top for the ears. Before turning the pancakes, let the children make a mouth and eyes with chocolate chips or sliced maraschino cherries. Then sit back and watch each handmade pancake go down with a spoonful of giggles. Besides slumber parties, other occasions for serving pancakes and omelets might be:

◇ Camping Trip—Combine dry ingredients for pancakes and store in a plastic bag.
◇ Block Party Brunch—You provide the eggs for the omelets, and each neighbor brings a filling.
◇ Housewarming Party.

Bubbly Mixed Fruit Bowl

The fizz of ginger ale awakens fresh fruit to make a spirited nonalcoholic appetizer or dessert.

1 pear, peeled and cut into 1-inch chunks
1 teaspoon lemon juice
1 kiwi, peeled and sliced
¼ fresh pineapple, cut into chunks or 1 can (8¼ ounces) pineapple chunks, drained
1 orange, peeled and sectioned
1 cup red grapes, halved and seeded if necessary
1 banana, peeled and sliced
⅔ cup ginger ale, chilled

In a small bowl, toss the pear with lemon juice. In a medium bowl, gently toss the kiwi, pear, pineapple, orange and grapes together; cover with plastic wrap and refrigerate until chilled or up to 4 hours. Before serving, toss in banana. Spoon into 6 fruit dishes or stemmed goblets and pour ginger ale over each serving.

Serves 6.

Over-Easy Omelet

There's no such thing as a mundane omelet when inspiration for creative fillings comes from around the world.

3 eggs
Dash of salt
Butter or margarine
Desired fillings such as shredded cheese, chopped tomatoes, ham, green onions, avocado, smoked salmon, sautéed mushrooms, caviar, or fill as directed in the following recipes

In a small bowl, whisk the eggs and salt until combined; they do not need to be frothy. I prefer to use a nonstick skillet which measures 7 inches across the bottom, but any type of omelet pan will do. Melt 1 to 2 tablespoons butter over moderately high heat. If this is your week for dieting, use sparingly; if you're going for great taste, use more. When butter sizzles, pour in eggs. Tilt pan so eggs cover the bottom. Using a fork or narrow spatula, pull the cooked part of the egg into the center, then tilt the pan to allow the uncooked eggs to flow onto the bottom. When the omelet is done to your liking, spoon desired filling over the half of it that is opposite the handle of the pan. Slide the filled half onto a plate and fold the remaining half over to cover the filling.

Makes 1 omelet, serves 1 to 2.

French Brie Omelet

1 Over-Easy Omelet
½ teaspoon Dijon mustard
1 tablespoon chopped fresh tarragon or ¼ teaspoon dried tarragon
½ cup diced brie cheese (2 ounces)
½ small tomato, chopped (about 2 tablespoons)

Make Omelet as directed, whisking mustard and tarragon into the eggs. Fill with brie and tomato.

Makes 1 omelet, serves 1 to 2.

California Goat Cheese Omelet

½ small tomato, chopped (about 2 tablespoons)
1 green onion with top, finely chopped
1 ounce goat cheese such as montrachet (about 1 tablespoon)
1 Over-Easy Omelet

Measure 1 teaspoon of the tomato and green onion; set aside for the top. In a small bowl, stir together remaining tomato, green onion and goat cheese. Make Omelet as directed and fill with goat-cheese mixture. Top with reserved vegetables.

Makes 1 omelet, serves 1 to 2.

Oriental Seafood Omelet

2 tablespoons butter or margarine
2 mushrooms, sliced
2 green onions, finely chopped (2 heaping tablespoons)
⅓ cup bean sprouts, chopped
4 ounces flaked crab or small cooked shrimp
1½ teaspoons soy sauce
2 recipes Over-Easy Omelet

In a small skillet, melt the butter or margarine. Sauté mushrooms until soft. Remove pan from heat; stir in green onions, bean sprouts, seafood and soy sauce. Make Omelets as directed. Fill each one with half the filling.

Makes 2 omelets, serves 2 to 4.

Sicilian Mozzarella–Ham Omelet

1 Over-Easy Omelet
1 tablespoon chopped fresh basil or ½ teaspoon dried basil
Freshly ground pepper to taste
2 tablespoons chopped prosciutto or ham
½ cup shredded mozzarella cheese, divided
2 tablespoons chopped canned or fresh roasted red peppers or pimiento

Make Omelet as directed, whisking basil and pepper into the eggs. Fill with ham, half the cheese, red peppers or pimiento. Top with remaining cheese.

Makes 1 omelet, serves 1 to 2

Pantry Pancakes

I dubbed these fluffy pancakes "pantry" because they include basic ingredients on hand.

¼ cup All-Bran cereal
¾ cup regular or low-fat milk
1 egg, lightly beaten
2 tablespoons vegetable oil or melted butter
1 cup all-purpose flour
2 teaspoons baking powder
¼ teaspoon salt
2 tablespoons sugar
Melted butter for serving, if desired
Syrup for serving

In a small bowl, stir together bran, milk and egg. Let sit for 5 minutes. Stir in the oil or butter. In a medium bowl, stir together the flour, baking powder, salt and sugar. Stir in the milk mixture, mashing the bran lightly against the side of the bowl to break it up.

Heat a lightly greased griddle or skillet over moderately high heat. When hot, make 3-inch pancakes using about ⅛ cup batter for each. Cook until bubbles appear on the surface and underside is golden. Turn and brown on other side. Serve with butter and syrup, if desired.

Makes 12 to 13 pancakes, serves 3 to 4.

Variations:

Banana Pancakes

Slice 1 small, ripe banana into batter.

Blueberry Pancakes

Stir 1 cup fresh or frozen (not defrosted) blueberries into batter.

Chocolate Chip Pancakes

Stir 1 teaspoon chocolate extract and ½ cup chocolate chips into batter. Serve with melted butter and confectioners sugar or syrup.

Piña Colada Pancakes

Stir 1 can (8¼ ounces) crushed pineapple, well drained, ½ cup flaked coconut and 1 teaspoon coconut extract into batter.

Honey Wheat Pancakes

Brad Kreitler created these delicious pancakes. Beaten egg whites folded into the batter lighten the density of whole wheat.

1 cup whole wheat flour
2 teaspoons baking powder
¼ teaspoon salt
2 tablespoons melted butter or vegetable oil
1 cup regular or low-fat milk
2 eggs, separated
2 tablespoons honey
2 teaspoons sugar
Butter and syrup for serving, if desired

In a large bowl, stir together the flour, baking powder and salt. Whisk in butter or oil, milk, egg yolks and honey. With an electric mixer, beat egg whites until foamy. Add sugar and beat until stiff but not dry peaks form. Fold into flour mixture.

Heat a lightly greased griddle or skillet over moderate heat. When hot, make 3-inch pancakes using ¼ cup batter for each. Cook until bubbles appear on the surface. Gently turn and cook on other side until golden. Serve with butter and syrup, if desired.

Makes 12 to 14 pancakes, serves 3 to 4.

Variation:

Honey Wheat Pancakes with Toasted Pecans

Toast 1 cup chopped pecans at 350 degrees for 10 minutes. Cool and stir into batter with egg yolks.

Frothy Hot Chocolate

Winter warmth is blender easy.

2 ounces unsweetened chocolate, chopped
⅓ cup sugar
¼ teaspoon vanilla
Dash salt
¼ teaspoon cinnamon, optional
2½ cups hot regular or low-fat milk
Miniature marshmallows or large marshmallows cut in half

Place chocolate, sugar, vanilla, salt and cinnamon, if using, in blender container. Just before serving, add hot milk. Cover and blend until chocolate is melted. Pour into cups, top with marshmallows.

Makes 4 servings, about 5 ounces each.

M E N U

MEXICANA BUFFET BRUNCH

Tequila Sunrise

Fresh Tomato or Avocado Salsa
with Home-Fried Tortilla Chips
(*Pages 180 and 181*)

Fresh Fruit Sombrero with Margarita Dip

Fiesta Corn Tamale Torte

Blanco Cheese Enchiladas

Frosty Sherbet-Filled Citrus

Gather the gang together for this crowd-pleasing, fiesta-style party. Although I often serve this menu for brunch, the food is hearty enough for lunch or dinner and is very easy to manage.

When your guests arrive, greet them with a Tequila Sunrise or, if you prefer, Iced or Papaya Margaritas (page 158). Try your local party shop for a large sombrero that you can cram with fresh fruit and Margarita Dip. Cut the fruit a day ahead. Melons, pineapple, papayas, mangoes and oranges can be layered with damp paper towels and refrigerated, covered, overnight.

The novel Fiesta Corn Tamale Torte feeds a crowd with gusto. Blanco Cheese Enchiladas capped with crunchy vegetables rather than gutsy red sauce are great served with roast chicken or grilled fish. Such a generous menu needs a cool, refreshing dessert like Frosty Sherbet-Filled Citrus or Frozen Rainbow Yogurt Torte (page 126). Suggested occasions for serving this colorful brunch are:

◇ Cinco de Mayo
◇ Office Party
◇ Charity Group Fund-Raiser or Meeting
◇ Labor Day Patio Party

Clockwise from top right: Home-Fried Tortilla Chips, Fiesta Corn Tamale Torte, Tequila Sunrise, Blanco Cheese Enchiladas, Avocado Salsa.

Tequila Sunrise

What a way to greet the day! (See photograph, page 28.)

3 cups fresh orange juice
1 cup fresh lime juice
⅔ cup grenadine syrup
2½ cups tequila
2 egg whites
Crushed ice or ice cubes
2 oranges, sliced, for garnish

Place half the orange juice, lime juice, grenadine, tequila and egg whites in blender. Fill to 1 inch of the top with ice. Process until the mixture is slushy. Repeat with the second half of the ingredients. Pour into goblets or juice glasses. Garnish each glass with a slice of orange curled over the rim.

Makes 12 servings, about 6 ounces each.

Fresh Fruit Sombrero

Punch down the top of a sombrero and tuck a bowl of creamy Margarita Dip into the indentation. When melons and berries are out of season, substitute oranges, apples, bananas and pears.

Margarita Dip (See below)
1 small watermelon (about 6 pounds)
1 medium cantaloupe, honeydew or casaba melon
1 pound grapes, cut into clusters
2 papayas or mangoes, cut in half, peeled, seeded and sliced
1 quart strawberries
1 small pineapple, peeled and cut into wedges
3 kiwis, peeled and sliced
Fresh mint sprigs for garnish

Margarita Dip

2 packages (8 ounces each) cream cheese, at room temperature
½ cup confectioners sugar
5 tablespoons frozen margarita mix, defrosted
½ cup tequila
1 tablespoon lime juice

At least 2 hours before serving, prepare Margarita Dip. In a small mixing bowl with electric mixer, beat cream cheese and sugar until light and fluffy. Scrape down sides, add margarita mix, tequila and lime juice; mix on low speed until combined. Mix on medium speed for 30 seconds or until smooth. Refrigerate for at least 2 hours before serving. Serve with the fresh fruit.

* The dip may be refrigerated up to 1 week.

Cut melons in quarters and cut off peel. Slice fruit with knife or fluted cutter into serving-size pieces. Place a 24-inch sombrero on a platter; line brim with plastic wrap. Arrange each type of fruit in a section around it. Garnish with sprigs of mint.

Serves 16.

Fiesta Corn Tamale Torte

Made in a springform pan, this giant corn bread and chili torte boasts all the advantages of a casserole: it is assembled, refrigerated or frozen if desired and baked in the same pan. All you need to do is remove the sides of the springform and serve the torte. *(See photograph, page 28.)*

Meat Filling

- 2 tablespoons vegetable oil
- 1 medium onion, chopped
- 1 pound lean ground beef or ½ pound lean ground beef and ½ pound chorizo
- 4 large cloves garlic, minced
- 1 can (15 ounces) tomato sauce
- ¼ cup dry red wine
- 4½ teaspoons chili powder
- Salt and pepper to taste

Corn Bread

- 3 eggs
- 1 cup (½ pint) sour cream
- 1 cup milk
- 1 teaspoon sugar
- 1 can (7 ounces) green chili salsa
- 1¼ cups yellow cornmeal
- 1½ cups all-purpose flour
- 1 teaspoon baking powder
- 1 teaspoon baking soda
- 1 teaspoon salt, or to taste
- Several dashes hot-pepper sauce
- 1 can (12 ounces) corn with red and green peppers, drained
- 2 cups shredded jack cheese (about 8 ounces)

To make the Meat Filling, in a medium skillet heat oil over moderately high heat; sauté onion until soft. Add meat and garlic and cook, stirring with a fork to break up meat, until it loses its red color; pour off excess fat. Stir in tomato sauce, wine, chili powder and salt and pepper to taste. Cook over moderately high heat, uncovered, stirring often, until liquid has evaporated, about 15 to 20 minutes. Set aside to cool.

Meanwhile make the Corn Bread. In a medium mixing bowl, whisk the eggs until frothy. Whisk in sour cream and milk. Add sugar, salsa, cornmeal, flour, baking powder, baking soda, salt and hot-pepper sauce, whisking until combined. Stir in corn and cheese.

Preheat oven to 350 degrees. Generously butter the bottom and sides of a 9 × 3-inch or 10½ × 2-inch springform pan. Wrap the outside in foil. Pour half the cornbread batter into pan and spread evenly. Spoon meat over and spread gently to form an even layer. Top with remaining cornbread. Bake in center of oven for 75 to 85 minutes or until it is golden brown and a sharp knife inserted into the center comes out clean. Remove from oven and let sit at room temperature for 20 minutes before serving.

* The torte may be covered and refrigerated up to 2 days or frozen. Defrost at room temperature. Reheat, covered, at 350 degrees for 30 minutes or until heated through.

Before serving, go around edge of torte with a sharp knife and remove sides of springform. Place on serving platter and cut into wedges.

Serves 12.

Blanco Cheese Enchiladas

Three-cheese filling inside, shredded lettuce and radishes on top make these south-of-the-border favorites exceptionally creamy and light. Don't be surprised when you open the green chili salsa and find that it's red. (See photograph, page 28.)

3 green onions with tops, cut into 1-inch pieces
2 cups (1 pint) cottage cheese
1 cup shredded jack cheese (about 4 ounces)
1 cup grated parmesan cheese (about 4 ounces)
Several drops hot-pepper sauce
4 cans (7 ounces each) green chili salsa
12 flour tortillas (7 inches in diameter)
1 head iceberg lettuce, finely shredded
½ cup sliced black olives, drained
6 radishes, thinly sliced
3 limes, cut into wedges

To make the filling, in a food processor fitted with the metal blade, chop green onions. Add cottage cheese, jack cheese, parmesan cheese and hot-pepper sauce; process until well blended.

Pour half the salsa into the bottom of two 9 × 13-inch baking dishes. Pour the remainder into a shallow dish; use to dip tortillas, coating both sides. Spread 3 tablespoons filling over each tortilla and roll up. Place 6 rolls seam side down, ½ inch apart, in each baking dish. Pour remaining salsa over the top.

* The enchiladas may be refrigerated, covered, up to 2 days or frozen. Bring to room temperature before baking.

Preheat oven to 325 degrees. Bake, uncovered, for 8 to 12 minutes or until heated through and cheese is melted. Do not overbake or the enchiladas will fall apart. Garnish the tops with shredded lettuce, olives, and radishes. Serve each with a wedge of lime.

Makes 12 enchiladas.

Frosty Sherbet-Filled Citrus

Frozen orange and lemon shells rounded generously with matching flavored sherbet resemble the whole icy fruit.

6 small or 3 large oranges
6 medium lemons
3 quarts assorted fruit sherbet, orange, lemon, lime or pineapple
Mint sprigs for garnish, optional

If the oranges are large, cut them in half. Cut a small slice off one end of the fruit, so it sits flat. Cut a slice off the other end large enough so that you can fill the orange. Using a grapefruit knife and small spoon, scoop out the flesh; reserve for another use.

Fill shells with desired sherbet, mounding it over the top. Cover with foil and freeze.

* The fruit may be frozen up to 1 month.

Remove from freezer 5 to 10 minutes before serving. Top with a sprig of mint, if desired.

Serves 12.

RECIPES

MUFFINS AND COFFEECAKES

Chunky Applesauce Muffins

Donut-Hole Muffins

Peanut Butter Streusel Muffins

Corn Muffins with Bacon and Cheese

Jim Dodge's Bran Muffins

Best-Ever Sticky Buns

Orange Blossom Coffeecake

Spiraled Chocolate Yeast Coffeecake

Banana Chocolate Chip Coffeecake

Breakfasts and brunches don't need muffins or coffeecakes any more than dinners need desserts. Muffins offer more than great texture and taste. They are not necessary—just adored and delectable—and the batter couldn't be easier to make. Just remember not to overmix: it's supposed to be lumpy. All muffins freeze beautifully, but they should be rewarmed before serving.

You can now find muffin tins from giant sizes down to 1½-inch miniatures. All of my muffin recipes adapt to any size. Just reduce the baking time for smaller ones and increase it for larger. I enjoy making bite-size muffins, then offering an assortment in a bread basket. If you choose three different kinds, count on people taking one of each.

Coffeecakes can be considered bread or dessert. No rules apply—serve as varied an assortment as you like or highlight just one. (For notes on working with yeast, see The Bountiful Bread Basket on page 143.)

Chunky Applesauce Muffins

These muffins will be full of large apple pieces if you stir the chunky applesauce in by hand.

4 tablespoons (½ stick) butter or margarine, at room temperature
½ cup (packed) golden light brown sugar
1 egg
½ cup plain yogurt or sour cream
1 cup all-purpose flour
1 cup whole wheat flour
½ teaspoon salt, or to taste
3 teaspoons baking powder
½ teaspoon baking soda
1 teaspoon ground cinnamon
Scant ½ teaspoon ground allspice
1½ cups chunky applesauce
½ cup raisins

Topping

3 tablespoons sugar
½ teaspoon cinnamon

Grease 12 medium (2½-inch) muffin cups. Preheat the oven to 375 degrees. In a food processor fitted with the metal blade or in a mixing bowl with an electric mixer, process or beat butter or margarine and sugar until fluffy. Process or mix in egg and yogurt or sour cream. Add all-purpose and whole wheat flour, salt, baking powder, soda, cinnamon and allspice; pulse or mix until incorporated. Stir in applesauce and raisins. Divide batter among the muffin cups, filling them three-fourths full.

Make Topping by stirring sugar and cinnamon together; sprinkle over top of muffins. Bake for 20 to 25 minutes or until a toothpick inserted in the center comes out clean. Remove from oven and let sit for 5 minutes; remove by inserting tip of sharp knife into one side.

* The muffins may be held in an airtight container at room temperature for several days or frozen.

Makes 12 muffins.

Donut-Hole Muffins

Bite-size muffins coated with cinnamon sugar taste just like the missing donut hole.

1 egg
½ cup regular or low-fat milk
6 tablespoons (¾ stick) butter or margarine, melted
1½ cups plus 2 tablespoons all-purpose flour
¾ cup sugar
2 teaspoons baking powder
¼ teaspoon salt, or to taste
¼ teaspoon ground nutmeg

Topping

¼ pound (1 stick) butter or margarine
¾ teaspoon vanilla
1½ teaspoons cinnamon
¾ cup sugar

Preheat the oven to 400 degrees. In a food processor fitted with the metal blade or in a mixing bowl with an electric mixer, process or mix egg, milk and butter or margarine until well blended. Add flour, sugar, baking powder, salt and nutmeg; pulse or mix until incorporated. Spray 36 miniature 1½-inch muffin tins with nonstick vegetable-oil cooking spray. Spoon about ½ tablespoon batter into each cup, filling it about two-thirds full. Bake in center of oven for 15 to 20 minutes or until lightly browned and toothpick inserted in center comes out clean.

Meanwhile, make the Topping by melting butter or margarine with vanilla in a small skillet. In a small bowl, stir together cinnamon and sugar. When muffins come out of the oven, immediately remove from the tins by inserting the tip of a sharp knife along one edge. Roll muffins in butter and then in cinnamon-sugar mixture. Place on cooling racks until topping is set.

∗ The muffins may be held in an airtight container at room temperature for several days or frozen.

Makes 36 miniature muffins.

Peanut Butter Streusel Muffins

When Carole Magness, one of my recipe testers, tried these muffins, she returned the recipe with WOW DELICIOUS written boldly across the top. (See photograph, page 17.)

Peanut Butter Streusel

½ cup (packed) golden light brown sugar
2 tablespoons all-purpose flour
⅓ cup chunky or creamy peanut butter
3 tablespoons butter or margarine, melted
⅓ cup coarsely chopped roasted and salted peanuts

Muffins

4 tablespoons (½ stick) butter or margarine, at room temperature
½ cup sugar
1 egg
⅔ cup sour cream
1 teaspoon vanilla
1 cup all-purpose flour
½ teaspoon baking powder
½ teaspoon baking soda

Line 12 medium (2½-inch) muffin cups with cupcake papers. Preheat oven to 375 degrees. To make the Peanut Butter Streusel, in a food processor fitted with the metal blade or in a mixing bowl with an electric mixer, process or mix brown sugar, flour, peanut butter and melted butter or margarine until blended. Pulse or mix in peanuts and set aside.

To make the Muffins, cream butter or margarine and sugar in same processor or mixing bowl until light and fluffy. Process or mix in egg, sour cream and vanilla. Add flour, baking powder and soda; mix only until incorporated. Add ⅓ cup of the streusel and pulse once or twice or stir until marbled through the batter. Spoon into muffin cups, filling them about half full. Crumble remaining streusel over the tops; pat it lightly with your hands to help it adhere. Bake for 20 to 25 minutes or until a toothpick inserted in center comes out clean. Remove from oven and cool.

∗ Muffins may be held in an airtight container at room temperature for several days or frozen.

Makes 12 muffins.

Corn Muffins with Bacon and Cheese

As satisfying as cornbread and then some. For a great lunch or brunch dish, cut the muffins in half and smother with creamed chicken.

- 8 strips bacon
- 1 egg
- 1 cup regular or low-fat milk
- 4 tablespoons (½ stick) butter or margarine, melted
- 1 can (8¾ ounces) creamed corn
- 1 cup all-purpose flour
- 1 cup yellow cornmeal
- 3 tablespoons sugar
- 3 teaspoons baking powder
- ½ teaspoon salt, or to taste
- 2 dashes hot-pepper sauce
- 1½ cups shredded sharp cheddar cheese (about 6 ounces)
- Butter for serving, if desired

Preheat the oven to 400 degrees. Cut bacon into small pieces and cook until all fat is rendered. Remove bacon with a slotted spoon to paper towels to drain. In a medium bowl, whisk egg, milk and butter or margarine until blended. Stir in corn, flour, cornmeal, sugar, baking powder and salt. Add hot-pepper sauce, cheese and bacon, stirring until incorporated.

Grease 12 medium 2½-inch muffin cups. Spoon batter into tins, filling three-fourths full. Bake for 20 to 25 minutes or until toothpick inserted in center comes out clean and tops are lightly browned.

Cool 10 minutes and remove from tins. Serve warm with butter, if desired.

* Muffins may be held in an airtight container at room temperature up to 2 days or frozen. Reheat at 350 degrees until warm.

Makes 12 muffins.

Jim Dodge's Bran Muffins

If you've eaten breakfast at the Stanford Court Hotel in San Francisco, you've undoubtedly tasted these healthful muffins made by the hotel's pastry chef, Jim Dodge. They are testimony that wondrously good food can also be good for you.

- 3 cups unprocessed wheat bran
- 2 cups buttermilk
- ⅔ cup currants or snipped raisins
- 4 tablespoons (½ stick) butter or margarine
- ¼ cup sugar
- ⅓ cup molasses
- 2 eggs
- 1¼ cups all-purpose flour
- 1 teaspoon salt, or to taste
- 2 teaspoons baking soda

In a medium bowl, stir together bran, buttermilk and currants or raisins; set aside to soak for 10 minutes.

Grease 18 medium 2½-inch muffin cups. Preheat oven to 375 degrees. In a mixing bowl with the electric mixer, cream butter or margarine and sugar until well mixed. Add molasses and eggs and mix on low speed until blended. Add bran-buttermilk mixture and mix on medium speed for 1 minute. Add flour, salt and baking soda; mix on low speed until flour is incorporated. Increase speed to medium and beat for 5 minutes. Divide the batter among muffin cups, filling them almost to the top. Bake in center of oven for 15 to 20 minutes or until a toothpick inserted in center comes out clean. Remove from oven and let sit 5 minutes; remove from cups.

* The muffins may be held in an airtight container at room temperature for several days or frozen.

Makes 18 muffins.

Variation:

Pineapple Bran Muffins

Stir 1 can (8¼ ounces) crushed pineapple, well drained, into the batter after the flour has been incorporated.

Best-Ever Sticky Buns

Starch from the potatoes makes this dough amazingly easy to handle and exceptionally light textured. Rewarmed the next day, the buns will be as soft and moist as fresh from the oven. It's a good thing this recipe makes two pans full, because one batch never makes it to the table.

Dough

- 2 medium potatoes, peeled and cubed
- ⅓ cup sugar
- 6 tablespoons (¾ stick) butter or margarine, at room temperature and cut into small pieces
- 1 teaspoon salt, or to taste
- 1 egg, at room temperature
- 1 egg yolk
- 1 envelope dry yeast
- 4½ cups bread flour, plus additional flour for kneading and rolling

Filling

- 4 tablespoons (½ stick) butter or margarine
- ⅓ cup sugar
- 2 teaspoons cinnamon

Glaze

- ½ pound plus 4 tablespoons (2½ sticks) butter or margarine, melted
- 2 cups packed golden brown sugar
- ⅓ cup dark corn syrup
- 1 cup chopped walnuts (4 ounces)

To make the Dough, bring 2 cups water to a boil in a medium saucepan. Add potatoes and cook, covered, over moderate heat until tender when pierced with a knife. Drain, reserving 1 cup of the water. Mash potatoes and measure ⅔ cup; save remainder for another use. In a large bowl with an electric mixer, mix together the hot potatoes, sugar, butter or margarine, salt, lukewarm potato water, egg, egg yolk and yeast. Add flour and mix on low speed until incorporated. Mix on medium speed for 1 minute; the dough will be sticky.

Knead with a dough hook for 4 to 5 minutes or turn out onto a well-floured board and knead until smooth and elastic, 8 to 10 minutes. Transfer to a large oiled bowl, turn to grease all sides and cover loosely with a greased sheet of plastic wrap and a damp towel. Let rise in a warm place until doubled in bulk, about 1½ hours. Punch dough down and let rest 10 minutes.

While the dough rests, make the Filling by melting butter or margarine. In a small bowl stir sugar and cinnamon together. Set aside.

To make the Glaze, stir together the melted butter or margarine, brown sugar and corn syrup. Generously butter two 8- or 9-inch round cake pans. Pour half the glaze into the bottom of each pan. Sprinkle each with ½ cup nuts.

On a heavily floured surface, roll half the dough into a 10 × 16-inch rectangle, about ¼ inch thick. Brush with 2 tablespoons melted butter or margarine. Sprinkle with half the cinnamon sugar. Starting at a short end, roll up the dough as for a jelly roll. Repeat with second half in same manner. Cut each roll into ten ¾-inch slices. Arrange 10 slices in each prepared pan. Cover with a greased sheet of plastic wrap and a damp towel and allow to rise in a warm place until doubled in bulk, about 1 hour.

Preheat the oven to 350 degrees. Bake in center of oven for 25 to 30 minutes or until golden brown, rotating the pans half way through the baking time, if necessary. Remove from oven and let rest 5 minutes for the glaze to set, then invert onto serving platters. If some nuts stick to bottom of pan, loosen with spatula and spread over top. Serve warm or at room temperature.

* The buns may be wrapped in foil and kept at room temperature overnight or frozen. Defrost at room temperature. Reheat uncovered, at 350 degrees for 7 to 10 minutes or until warm.

Makes 20 buns.

Orange Blossom Coffeecake

A melt-in-your-mouth, buttery crumble cake lightly streaked with sugar and spice. It's great for afternoon coffees and teas, as well as breakfast.

Streusel

- ⅓ cup (packed) golden light brown sugar
- 1 teaspoon cinnamon
- 2 tablespoons grated orange peel

Cake

- ½ pound plus 4 tablespoons (2½ sticks) unsalted butter or margarine, at room temperature
- 1½ cups sugar
- 2 eggs, at room temperature
- 1 teaspoon vanilla
- 2⅔ cups all-purpose flour
- 3 teaspoons baking powder
- 1 teaspoon baking soda
- ¼ teaspoon salt, or to taste
- ¾ cup buttermilk
- ¼ cup frozen orange juice concentrate, thawed
- ½ cup orange marmalade, melted, optional

Generously butter a 12-cup bundt pan. Preheat oven to 375 degrees. To make the Streusel, in a small bowl stir together the brown sugar, cinnamon and orange peel; set aside.

To make the Cake, in a large mixing bowl with the electric mixer, cream butter or margarine and sugar until light and fluffy. Mix in eggs one at a time, beating well after each is added. Mix in vanilla; beat for 2 minutes. With mixer off, add flour, baking powder, soda and salt. Pour in buttermilk and orange juice concentrate. With mixer at low speed, mix until incorporated. Turn mixer to medium speed and mix 30 seconds.

Spread half the batter into the pan. Sprinkle with half the streusel. Using a knife, marble streusel through batter. Spread with remaining batter and top with remaining streusel, swirling it into the batter. Bake in center of oven for 35 to 45 minutes or until a toothpick inserted in center comes out clean. Immediately invert onto rack. Cool 15 minutes and if desired, brush melted marmalade over top and sides of cake. Let set until marmalade is firm.

* The cake may be held, covered, at room temperature up to 2 days or frozen.

Serves 12.

Spiraled Chocolate Yeast Coffeecake

Half of a rich yeast dough is flavored with chocolate. When the two halves are rolled up jelly-roll fashion, they rise into a stunning light and dark spiral.

Dough

- ⅓ cup warm water (105 to 115 degrees)
- 2 envelopes dry yeast
- 1 teaspoon plus ½ cup sugar, divided
- 3 eggs, at room temperature
- ¼ pound (1 stick) butter or margarine, melted and cooled slightly
- ¾ cup sour cream, at room temperature
- 1 teaspoon vanilla
- 1 teaspoon salt, or to taste
- 5½ cups all-purpose flour
- ½ cup semisweet chocolate chips, melted and cooled slightly

Filling

- 4 tablespoons (½ stick) butter or margarine, melted
- ¾ cup sugar
- 1½ teaspoons cinnamon
- ½ cup mini semisweet chocolate chips

Glaze

- 1 egg mixed with 1 teaspoon water

Pour water into a large electric mixer bowl; stir in yeast and 1 teaspoon sugar. Let stand 3 minutes or until foamy. Add ½ cup sugar, eggs, butter or margarine, sour cream, vanilla, salt and 3 cups flour. Beat at medium speed for 2 minutes. Mix or stir in as much of the remaining flour as needed to make a soft dough. Knead with dough hook for 3 minutes or turn out on a floured board and knead by hand for 6 to 8 minutes or until smooth. Transfer to a large, oiled bowl, cover loosely with an oiled sheet of plastic wrap and a damp towel. Let rise in a warm place until doubled in bulk, about 1½ hours.

Generously butter a 12-cup tube pan with a removable bottom. Punch dough down and remove a little less than half to a floured surface. Add melted chocolate to dough in bowl and mix with an electric mixer on low speed or by hand until incorporated. Roll white dough into an 8 × 18-inch rectangle. To

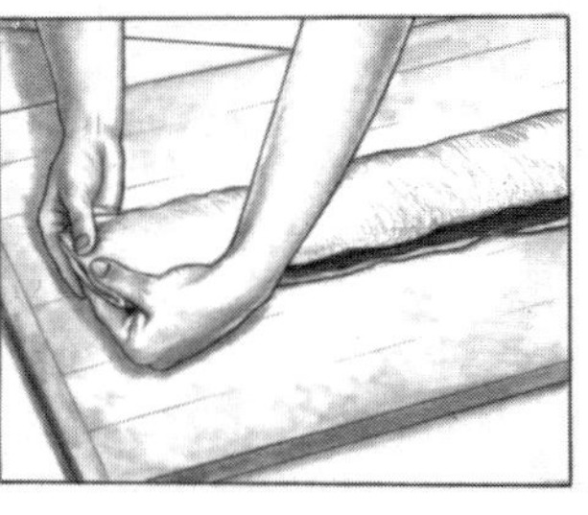

fill, spread with half the melted butter or margarine. Stir sugar and cinnamon together and sprinkle ¼ cup over the butter. On another floured surface, roll chocolate dough into an 8 × 18-inch rectangle. Place on top of white dough. Brush with remaining butter and sprinkle with ¼ cup cinnamon sugar and the chocolate chips.

Starting with a long end, roll up both doughs together tightly, jelly-roll fashion. Pinch ends closed. Place around the bottom of the prepared tube pan, seam side down, overlapping the ends. Drape a damp towel loosely over top of pan. Let rise in a warm place until doubled in bulk, about 1½ hours. The dough should be 1½ to 2 inches from the top of the pan. Brush top with egg glaze and sprinkle with remaining cinnamon sugar.

Preheat oven to 375 degrees. Place pan on a baking sheet and bake for 35 to 45 minutes or until well browned. Remove to a rack and cool to room temperature. To remove from pan, go around inside edges of cake with a sharp knife and lift off sides of pan. Then run knife around the tube and bottom and lift cake off.

∗ The cake may be tightly wrapped and held at room temperature for up to 2 days or frozen.

Serves 12.

Banana Chocolate Chip Coffeecake

This is my kind of coffeecake—it's like dessert! The crunchy streusel topping blankets a moist and rich banana cake that is sprinkled throughout with chocolate chips.

Streusel Topping

½ cup (packed) golden light brown sugar
¼ cup all-purpose flour
4 tablespoons (½ stick) butter or margarine, melted
½ cup chopped pecans or walnuts

Cake

¼ pound (1 stick) butter or margarine, at room temperature
1 package (8 ounces) cream cheese, at room temperature
1¼ cups sugar
2 eggs
2 very ripe bananas, mashed (1 cup)
1 teaspoon vanilla
2¼ cups all-purpose flour
2 teaspoons baking powder
1 teaspoon baking soda
¼ teaspoon salt, or to taste
¼ cup regular or low-fat milk
1 package (6 ounces) semisweet chocolate chips (about 1 cup)

To make the Streusel Topping, in a small bowl, stir together brown sugar, flour, butter or margarine and nuts until the mixture is thoroughly moistened; set aside.

Preheat the oven to 350 degrees. Grease a 12-cup tube pan with a removable bottom. To make the Cake, in a large bowl with the electric mixer on high speed, beat butter or margarine and cream cheese until smooth. Add sugar, beating until the mixture is light and fluffy, about 2 minutes. Mix in eggs, one at a time, beating well after each addition; mix in banana and vanilla. On low speed, mix in flour, baking powder, baking soda, salt and milk until incorporated, about 1 minute. Mix in chocolate chips. Pour batter into prepared pan.

Crumble streusel over top of cake. Bake in center of oven for 60 to 70 minutes or until a toothpick inserted in center comes out clean and top is deeply browned. Remove from oven and cool for 15 minutes. Remove sides of pan and cool cake completely. To remove the tube, go around inside edge of cake with a sharp knife; loosen the bottom with a knife or spatula. Lift cake off the tube.

* The cake may be held, well wrapped, at room temperature for several days or frozen.

Serves 12.

LEISURELY TO LUXURIOUS LUNCHEONS

Clockwise from top right: Ingredients for a Chinese Salad Bar, including tofu, sliced celery and waterchestnuts, Rice Noodles, Steamed Dumplings, chicken, shrimp, lettuce, mandarin oranges and cucumber strips, Fried Wonton Strips; Sesame Seed Cookies, Sesame Dressing.

M E N U

ORIENT-EXPRESS SALAD BAR

Chinese Salad Bar

Steamed Dumplings

Rice Noodles

Fried Wonton Strips

Red Ginger, Sesame, and Soy Lemon Dressings

Ginger Ice Cream Mold with Strawberry Sauce

Sesame Seed Cookies

When it's your turn to host that special-occasion luncheon, the Orient-Express Salad Bar is a striking way to go. If appropriate, announce the festivities with rice paper invitations attached to chopsticks sent out in mailing tubes. For a unique centerpiece, arrange flowers and chopsticks in a shallow container that fits into a wok. Put out bowls of fortune cookies for party favors.

Don't feel locked into my serving suggestions. If crab happens to be on special or if you like pineapple better than mandarin oranges, adjust the ingredients to your liking. All of the amounts listed will amply serve twelve. It looks skimpy to put out less, so plan on having some leftovers. Savory Steamed Dumplings are much more original than bread or rolls and every bit as wholesome.

For a simple dessert, stir candied ginger into vanilla ice cream—you won't find one that gets more raves. Suggested occasions for serving this buffet luncheon are:

◇ Baby or Bridal Shower
◇ Sweet Sixteen or Birthday Party
◇ Charity Group or Special Meeting
◇ Graduation

Chinese Salad Bar

Here's a colorful selection of ingredients for a make-your-own Chinese style salad buffet. Choose as many or as few of the ingredients as you like. The amounts listed will be enough for twelve people regardless of the assortment you choose to offer. (See photograph, page 41.)

3 pounds cooked medium-size shrimp
5 cups cooked chicken, torn into bite-size pieces
2 cans (11 ounces each) mandarin oranges, drained
1 cup chopped fresh cilantro
3 heads iceberg lettuce, washed, dried and thinly sliced into shreds
3 heads romaine lettuce, washed, dried and thinly sliced into shreds
2 cans (8 ounces each) water chestnuts, drained and sliced
1 package (1 pound) tofu, drained and cut into ½-inch cubes
3 ounces alfalfa sprouts (about 2 cups)
4 cucumbers, peeled, seeded and cut into matchstick strips
3 avocados, peeled, seeded and sliced
¼ pound bean sprouts, washed, dried and coarsely chopped
2 cups diagonally sliced celery
2 cups sliced green onions with tops (about 2 bunches)
2 cups coarsely chopped cashews or sliced almonds, toasted at 350 degrees until golden
1 recipe Steamed Dumplings (page 43)
1 recipe Fried Wonton Strips (page 43)
1 recipe Rice Noodles (page 44)
2 recipes Soy Lemon Dressing (page 44)
2 recipes Sesame Dressing (page 44)
1 recipe Red Ginger Dressing (page 44)

Steamed Dumplings

We tend to think of Chinese food as laborious. When you work with packaged wonton wrappers and a food processor, you'll be delighted how quickly these authentic-tasting dumplings go together. Serve them in place of rolls with a salad, as an appetizer or as part of a Chinese dinner. *(See photograph, page 41.)*

- 1 pound Chinese or Napa cabbage
- 1 piece (1 inch) fresh ginger, peeled
- 4 green onions, chopped into 1-inch pieces
- 1 pound ground pork
- ½ pound raw shrimp, shelled and deveined
- ¼ cup soy sauce
- 4 teaspoons dry sherry
- ¼ cup vegetable oil
- 1 package (16 ounces) wonton wrappers, 3 inches square

Dipping Sauce

- ¼ cup finely minced fresh ginger
- 6 tablespoons red wine vinegar
- 6 tablespoons soy sauce

Cut out core from cabbage. To wilt, either freeze overnight and defrost at room temperature for several hours; or blanch in a large pot of boiling water for 1 minute and drain. Wring out the leaves in a towel to remove excess water; coarsely chop. In a food processor fitted with the metal blade, mince ginger and green onions. Add pork and process until mixed. Add cabbage, shrimp, soy sauce, sherry and oil. Pulse until shrimp and cabbage are finely chopped, but not ground.

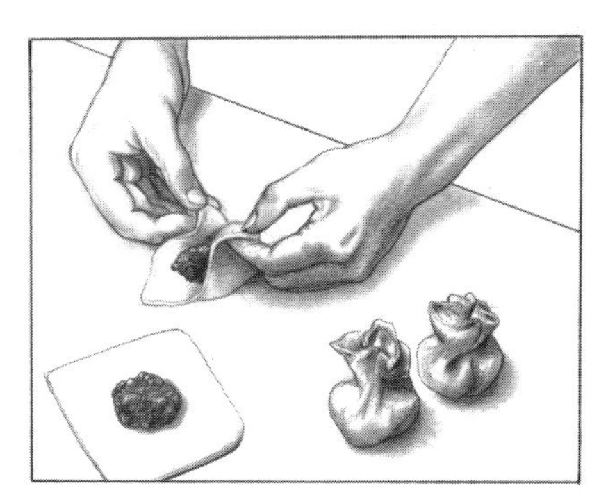

Shake or brush excess from off wonton wrappers and place 1 tablespoon filling in the center of each one. Pull the corners up to the center and press firmly together to seal. Fill a steamer or roasting pan with a rack with enough water to reach the bottom of the rack. Line the rack with cabbage leaves or a damp towel (not terry cloth); arrange the dumplings ¼ inch apart. Place the rack in steamer, cover and steam over boiling water for 15 minutes or until the pork is no longer pink when a dumpling is cut into.

Meanwhile, make the Dipping Sauce by stirring ginger, vinegar and soy sauce together.

* The dumplings will remain warm in a covered steamer off the heat for one hour. Or they may be refrigerated overnight or frozen. Bring to room temperature and resteam about 5 minutes or until heated through.

To serve as part of a buffet, drizzle dipping sauce over the dumplings. To serve as an appetizer pass the sauce separately for dipping.

Makes 48 dumplings.

Fried Wonton Strips

Use these in place of chow mein noodles for lighter texture and fresher flavor. *(See photograph, page 41.)*

- ½ package (16 ounces) wonton wrappers, 3 inches square
- Vegetable oil for frying

Cut the wonton wrappers into ¼-inch strips. Fill a wok or large skillet with 2 inches of oil and heat to 375 degrees. Fry strips in a single layer until golden on each side; turn and brown other side. Remove with slotted spoon or strainer to paper towels to drain.

* The strips may be stored in an airtight container for several days or frozen.

Serve warm or at room temperature. To rewarm, heat on baking sheets at 400 degrees for 3 minutes. Serve as part of a salad buffet or sprinkle over vegetables.

Serves 12 as part of a salad buffet.

Rice Noodles

If you've never watched rice noodles frying, you're in for a surprise. (See photograph, page 41.)

1 package (3¾ ounces) Chinese rice or cellophane noodles
Vegetable oil for frying

Separate the noodles into small bunches and break in half. Fill a wok or large skillet with 2 inches of oil and heat to 375 degrees. Add the noodles a handful at a time; as soon as they puff up, turn them over. Do not crowd in pan or they will not cook evenly. Remove with a slotted spoon or strainer and drain on paper towels. Serve at room temperature as part of a salad buffet or sprinkle over Chinese dishes.

✻ The noodles may be stored several days in an airtight container.

Serves 12 as part of a salad buffet.

Red Ginger Dressing

Red ginger is a specialty item available at oriental markets. This pungent pink dressing gives an original twist to spinach, chicken and seafood salads.

1 jar (12 ounces) Chinese preserved red ginger in syrup
½ cup vegetable oil
9 tablespoons red wine vinegar
1 tablespoon hot chili paste or several drops hot chili oil
1 tablespoon finely grated orange peel
2 tablespoons finely chopped fresh ginger

Pour ¼ cup red ginger syrup into a small bowl; cut ½ cup of the ginger into julienne strips. (Reserve the rest for another use.) Whisk oil, vinegar, chili paste or oil, orange peel and fresh ginger into syrup. Stir in red ginger.

✻ The dressing may be refrigerated for several weeks. Stir well before serving.

Makes about 2 cups.

Sesame Dressing

True, distinct sesame flavor comes from a golden brown oil made from toasted sesame seeds. Look for it in the oriental-foods section of your supermarket. (See photograph, page 41.)

¼ cup sesame seeds
⅓ cup white rice wine vinegar
2 teaspoons Dijon mustard
⅔ cup vegetable oil
¼ cup sesame oil
½ teaspoon salt, or to taste
Freshly ground pepper to taste

Toast sesame seeds in a small skillet over moderately high heat until lightly browned. In a medium bowl, whisk vinegar, mustard, vegetable and sesame oil, salt and pepper together.

✻ The dressing may be refrigerated up to 1 week.

Before serving, stir in sesame seeds.

Makes about 1 cup.

Soy Lemon Dressing

This sweet-and-sour dressing is typically found on Chinese chicken salad. It is also great over chilled asparagus.

2 tablespoons white rice wine vinegar
2 tablespoons lemon juice
1 tablespoon soy sauce
2 teaspoons dry mustard
1 tablespoon honey
½ cup vegetable oil
Salt and pepper to taste

In a medium bowl, whisk together the vinegar, lemon juice, soy sauce, mustard and honey. Slowly whisk in oil. Season to taste with salt and pepper.

✻ The dressing may be refrigerated up to 1 week. Bring to room temperature and stir well before using.

Makes about 1 cup.

Ginger Ice Cream Mold with Strawberry Sauce

Aromatic ginger does something wonderfully exotic to vanilla ice cream. Present it with miniature paper parasols—or lighted candles if this is a celebration—on a glossy strawberry sauce.

1½ quarts vanilla ice cream
4½ ounces crystallized ginger (⅔ cup chopped)

Strawberry Sauce
2 packages (10 ounces each) frozen strawberries in syrup, thawed
2 tablespoons lemon juice
½ teaspoon powdered ginger

Oil a 6-cup decorative mold or loaf pan or 12 individual molds; place in the freezer. Soften ice cream in a large bowl; do not let it melt. Meanwhile, in a food processor with the metal blade, chop the ginger into very small pieces. Stir it into the softened ice cream. Pour into prepared mold, cover with foil and freeze until firm.

* The mold may be frozen up to 2 months.

To make the Strawberry Sauce, place a strainer over a medium bowl. Using a wooden spoon, press thawed strawberries through the strainer, scraping the bottom often. Stir in lemon juice and ginger. Refrigerate until ready to serve or up to 2 days. Makes 2 cups.

Several hours before serving, dip the ice cream mold into warm water for a few seconds. Turn out onto a platter and return to freezer. Remove from freezer 10 minutes before serving. Slice and serve with strawberry sauce or spoon 2 to 3 tablespoons sauce onto each dessert plate, tilt the plate to coat the bottom and place ice cream in the center.

Serves 12.

Sesame Seed Cookies

Very buttery, very crisp and chock-full of golden brown sesame seeds, these are addictive. *(See photograph, page 41.)*

1 cup sesame seeds (6 ounces)
1½ cups (packed) golden light brown sugar
12 tablespoons (1½ sticks) butter or margarine, at room temperature
1 egg
1 teaspoon vanilla
1¼ cups all-purpose flour
¼ teaspoon baking powder
¼ teaspoon salt, or to taste

Preheat the oven to 350 degrees. On a small baking sheet or in a toaster oven, toast sesame seeds until golden, stirring occasionally, about 12 to 15 minutes; set aside until cool. In a food processor fitted with the metal blade or a mixing bowl with the electric mixer, cream sugar and butter or margarine until fluffy. Process or mix in egg and vanilla. Add flour, baking powder, and salt; pulse or mix on low speed until incorporated. Pulse or mix in sesame seeds.

Spray cookie sheets with nonstick vegetable-oil cooking spray. Drop 1½ teaspoons of batter about 2 inches apart onto prepared sheets. Bake for 8 to 10 minutes or until golden. Immediately remove to racks to cool.

* The cookies may be stored in an airtight container at room temperature for several days or frozen.

Makes about 70 cookies.

M E N U

HERE COMES THE BRIDE

Champagne Royale

Salmon Souffle Roll with Artichokes and Mushrooms

South Seas Chicken Salad
with Tropical Papaya Chutney

Marinated Vegetables in Raspberry-Walnut
Vinaigrette

Lemon Glazed Brioche with Lemon-Honey Butter
(*Page 150*)

Petite Raspberry Baked Alaskas
with Raspberry Sauce

For a variation on the usual bridal shower theme, send invitations for a shower called "That's Entertaining." Your gift can be the table centerpiece—an ice bucket or large salad bowl brimming over with candlesticks and candles, place mats rolled in napkin rings, linen napkins folded into elegant rosettes and the like. Tie place cards to champagne splits with lace ribbons for memorable party favors.

Although this shower or wedding menu is presented as a buffet, it adjusts easily to a sit-down affair as well. The two entrees, one hot and one chilled, can be served together or individually. For a sit-down event, cradle the chicken salad in small pineapple, cantaloupe or honeydew halves or wedges and place the accompanying condiments on the table. Other popular shower luncheon dishes include Salmon Stuffed with Spinach and Goat Cheese (page 105), Almond-Stuffed Trout (page 112) and Seafood Tourtière (page 173).

In case your freezer is not large enough to accommodate Petite Raspberry Baked Alaskas, the most exalted celebration cake I know is Chocolate Hazelnut Rhapsody (page 175). Write a special message in chocolate (see page 94).

Menu
CHAMPAGNE ROYALE
SALMON SOUFFLE ROLL
SOUTH SEAS CHICKEN SALAD

Champagne Royale

A royal treat for a majestic occasion. Open and pour the champagne just before serving. *(See photograph, page 46.)*

12 teaspoons Chambord or Crème de Cassis
2 bottles champagne, chilled
Fresh strawberries or raspberries

Pour 1 teaspoon Chambord or Cassis into each champagne glass. Fill with champagne. Place a fresh strawberry or several raspberries in the glass. Or, if desired, stir the ingredients together in a punch bowl.

Makes 12 servings.

See photograph on previous page. Clockwise from top right: Lemon-Glazed Brioche with Lemon-Honey Butter, Champagne Royale, Salmon Soufflé Roll with Artichokes and Mushrooms, Marinated Vegetables in Raspberry-Walnut Vinaigrette.

Salmon Soufflé Roll with Artichokes and Mushrooms **(See photograph, page 46.)**

I don't know what I like more about this elegant entree—that it's so pretty, tasty and unique or that it goes so easily from freezer to oven to table. Everyone else seems to like it too: You might want to make two rolls to be sure to have enough for seconds.

6 tablespoons (¾ stick) butter or margarine, divided
2 large shallots or ¼ onion, finely chopped
2 large cloves garlic, minced
3 tablespoons all-purpose flour
2 cups regular or low-fat milk
1 teaspoon salt, or to taste
¼ teaspoon white pepper
⅛ teaspoon ground mace
⅛ teaspoon ground nutmeg
5 egg yolks
7 ounces cooked salmon, fresh or canned, flaked and picked over for bones
6 egg whites, at room temperature

Artichoke and Mushroom Filling

1 can (15 ounces) artichoke bottoms, drained
½ pound mushrooms, coarsely chopped
¾ cup shredded jack cheese (about 3 ounces)
2 tablespoons lemon juice
¾ teaspoon dried dillweed or 1 tablespoon chopped fresh dill
Fresh sprigs of dill for garnish, optional
Lemon wedges for garnish, optional

To make the soufflé roll, grease a 10½ × 15½ × 1-inch rimmed baking sheet (jelly-roll pan). Line with parchment or waxed paper, letting 1 inch extend over each short end. Spray the paper with nonstick vegetable-oil cooking spray. Preheat the oven to 400 degrees.

In a medium saucepan, melt 3 tablespoons butter or margarine. Stir in shallots or onion and garlic; cook over low heat until soft. Stir in flour. Gradually add milk, whisking constantly over moderate heat until the mixture comes to a boil. Stir in salt, pepper, mace and nutmeg. Measure 1 cup sauce into a medium bowl; cover the remaining sauce with plastic wrap and set aside. Whisk the egg yolks into the 1 cup sauce until well blended. Stir in salmon.

In a large mixing bowl with the electric mixer, beat egg whites until stiff, but not dry, peaks form. Stir a dollop of whites into the salmon mixture; fold in the rest. Spread into the prepared pan. Bake for 14 to 16 minutes or until the top is golden and a toothpick inserted in the center comes out clean. Meanwhile, place a clean dish towel on a flat surface and spray it with nonstick vegetable-oil cooking spray. Go around sides of soufflé with a sharp knife, invert onto towel and remove the pan. Carefully peel off the paper by slowly pulling back on it. Don't be concerned if some of the soufflé comes off on the paper. Roll the soufflé in the towel, starting at a short end, and cool completely.

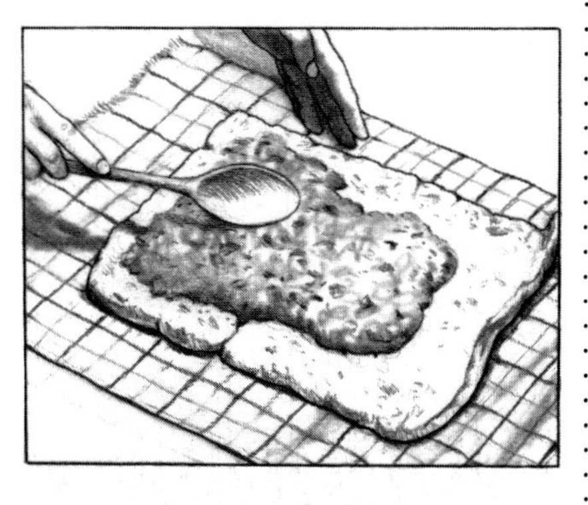

To make the Filling, coarsely chop 4 of the artichoke bottoms, reserving remainder for garnish. In a medium skillet, melt remaining 3 tablespoons butter or margarine. Sauté mushrooms and artichokes, stirring occasionally, until all the moisture has evaporated. Stir in the reserved sauce, cheese, lemon juice and dill. Unroll the soufflé, placing a short end in front of you. Spread with the filling, leaving 2 inches free on the side opposite you. Reroll the soufflé, beginning with the end in front of you. If it cracks, do not be concerned. If not serving immediately, wrap the roll in heavy foil.

* The soufflé roll may be refrigerated overnight or frozen up to 2 weeks. Defrost at room temperature. Before serving, bake, loosely covered with foil, at 400 degrees for 15 minutes or until heated through.

Using 2 large spatulas, remove to a platter. Garnish platter with artichoke bottoms filled with sprigs of dill and lemon wedges. Slice into ¾- to 1-inch-thick slices.

Serves 8 to 10.

Marinated Vegetables in Raspberry-Walnut Vinaigrette

A variety of cooked vegetables delicately coated in a walnut-oil marinade makes a colorful centerpiece on a buffet table. For a sit-down dinner, choose one type of vegetable, arrange it on lettuce-lined plates and serve as a first course salad. *(See photograph, page 46.)*

4 pounds fresh vegetables, such as asparagus, green beans, carrots, green or yellow squash
3 heads Boston, butter or curly endive lettuce, washed and leaves separated
1 cup chopped walnuts, toasted at 350 degrees for 10 to 12 minutes

Raspberry-Walnut Vinaigrette
⅓ cup raspberry vinegar
1 cup walnut oil
½ teaspoon sugar
2 large cloves garlic, minced
Salt and pepper to taste

Prepare the vegetables: Break tough ends off asparagus and peel lower half of the stalk with a vegetable peeler. Cut tips off green beans. Scrape carrots and cut into ¼ × 3-inch strips. Cut ends off squash and slice into ¼ × 3-inch strips.

Fill a large skillet with 1 to 2 inches of water. Add the asparagus and cook, covered, over moderate heat for 3 to 4 minutes or until crisp-tender. Remove with a slotted spoon and immediately run under ice water to stop the cooking. Cook remaining vegetables in the same manner. Green beans will take 3 to 4 minutes, carrots 8 to 10 minutes, squash 2 to 3 minutes. Drain the vegetables and place each type separately in a shallow dish. Cover with plastic wrap and refrigerate until chilled or overnight.

To make the Raspberry-Walnut Vinaigrette, whisk all the ingredients in a small bowl.

* The dressing may be refrigerated up to 5 days.

About 1 hour before serving, pour vinaigrette over each vegetable and marinate at room temperature, tossing once or twice to assure the vegetables are evenly coated. Line a basket or platter with lettuce leaves. Arrange vegetables on lettuce, keeping each type separate; sprinkle with chopped walnuts.

Serves 12.

South Seas Chicken Salad

I'm always looking for new recipes for chicken salad. With yogurt substituted for the more traditional mayonnaise and sour cream in the dressing, this tropical salad has a fresher, fruitier flavor and fewer calories than most. I prefer to make chicken salad from whole chickens, even precooked ones from the market. I find they retain their juices far better than individually cooked pieces.

1 large or 2 small pineapples
8 cups chopped cooked chicken from 4 whole cooked storebought chickens (about 1 pound each) or 10 cooked chicken breast halves (8 ounces each)
1 cup chopped green onions with green tops (about 1 bunch)
3 ounces bean sprouts, coarsely chopped (about 1 cup)
1 cup thinly sliced celery
4 medium oranges, divided into segments (about 1½ cups), or 2 cans (11 ounces each) mandarin oranges, drained

Chutney-Yogurt Dressing

⅓ cup Tropical Papaya Chutney (page 52) or storebought chutney, chopped
8 ounces pineapple, banana or spiced apple yogurt
2 teaspoons curry powder, preferably Madras
½ teaspoon salt, or to taste
White pepper to taste

For Serving

Large leaves or ferns for platter garnish
2 cups chopped peanuts or macadamia nuts, toasted at 350 degrees until golden
1 cup shredded coconut, toasted at 350 degrees until lightly golden
1½ cups chutney, chopped if pieces are large
1 cup raisins

Cut pineapple in half through the leafy frond, leaving the frond attached. Using a grapefruit knife, cut out the fruit. Cover the shells with plastic wrap and refrigerate. Cut the core from 1 of the pineapples and cut the fruit into chunks; measure 2 cups (reserve remainder for another use).

Before serving, in a large bowl, toss together pineapple, chicken, green onions, bean sprouts, celery and oranges. Cover and refrigerate until ready to use or overnight, if desired.

Make Chutney-Yogurt Dressing by stirring together the chutney, yogurt, curry powder, salt and pepper. The dressing may be refrigerated overnight.

Toss with dressing. Spoon into reserved pineapple shells, mounding the top. Place on a platter, garnish with leaves and accompany with small bowls of nuts, coconut, chutney and raisins.

Serves 12.

Tropical Papaya Chutney

These days any combination of vegetables and fruits accompanying a dish seems to be called a chutney, but there is nothing trendy about this recipe—it's been a favorite of mine for 25 years.

- 1 papaya, peeled, seeded and coarsely chopped (about 2 cups)
- 2 tart green apples, peeled, cored and coarsely chopped (about 1 cup)
- ½ cup (packed) golden light brown sugar
- ¼ cup golden raisins
- ¼ cup coarsely chopped green pepper
- ¼ cup chopped onion
- ⅓ cup white vinegar
- ¼ cup water
- 2 tablespoons lime juice
- 1 tablespoon chopped crystallized ginger
- 1 clove garlic, minced
- ½ teaspoon salt, or to taste
- ¼ cup slivered almonds

In a heavy deep saucepan, combine all the ingredients except the almonds. Cover and simmer over moderate heat for 30 minutes, stirring occasionally. Stir in the almonds. Cook, uncovered, over moderately low heat for 30 more minutes, stirring frequently to prevent sticking. Using a fork or potato masher, mash fruit slightly. Cool to room temperature. Store in the refrigerator up to 2 months or freeze.

Makes 2¼ cups.

Petite Raspberry Baked Alaskas

Chambord, a black-raspberry-flavored liqueur, is in three parts of this recipe. It's brushed on little shortcakes; whipped into meringue, turning it pastel pink; and then stirred into the raspberry sauce. Obviously, I really like it.

- 3 packages (4½ ounces each) shortcakes (12 cakes)
- ⅔ cup Chambord, divided
- 1 quart plus 1 pint raspberry sherbet or strawberry ice cream
- 9 egg whites, at room temperature
- ¾ cup sugar
- 2 recipes Raspberry Sauce (page 53)

Line 2 large baking sheets with foil. Place 6 cakes on each sheet; brush with ⅓ cup liqueur. Place a scoop of sherbet or ice cream onto each cake; place in freezer while preparing the meringue.

In a large mixing bowl with the electric mixer on high speed, beat egg whites until foamy. Beating continuously, add sugar, 1 tablespoon at a time, beating until the mixture is very stiff and shiny, like marshmallow cream. Beat in the remaining ⅓ cup Chambord. Spread meringue over ice cream and cake, making sure the ice cream is well covered. Return to freezer until ice cream is solid. Make Raspberry Sauce as directed.

Place rack in center of oven and preheat to 500 degrees. Bake one sheet of Alaskas at a time, for 2 to 3 minutes or until peaks are golden. Return to the freezer.

* Baked Alaskas may be frozen up to 5 days. Cover with foil after the meringue is hard.

To serve, place 2 to 3 spoonfuls of Raspberry Sauce on each dessert plate, turning the plate to coat the bottom. Place an Alaska in center. Pass remaining sauce.

Serves 12.

Raspberry Sauce

The frugal part of my conscience won't let me puree fresh raspberries. Fortunately, there's no need to when frozen berries and a splash of liqueur produce such a delicious sauce.

- 2 packages (10 ounces each) frozen raspberries in syrup, thawed
- ⅓ cup sugar
- ¼ cup Chambord

In a food processor fitted with the metal blade, puree raspberries and sugar. Place a medium-mesh strainer over a small bowl. Push raspberries through the strainer to extract as much juice and pulp as possible, scraping the bottom often; discard seeds. Stir in Chambord. Refrigerate until ready to serve.

∗ The sauce may be refrigerated up to 1 week.

Makes 1½ cups sauce.

M E N U

PACKING THE PICNIC BASKET

Overnight Iced Tea

Crusty Italian Picnic Loaf

Tuna Salad Turnovers

Ratatouille Quiche

Tortilla Roll-Ups

Marinated Vegetables on Skewers

Grandma's Sugar Cookies

Chocolate Chip Spice Crocodiles

Soft Ginger Cookies

Black and White Chocolate Chunk Cookies

Double Currant Bars (*Page 187*)

From a blanket on a grassy knoll to a box seat under the stars, wherever you're having your picnic, you'll find all these carefree offerings exceptionally easy to transport. Crusty Italian Picnic Loaf, a scooped-out bread layered with vegetables, cheese and omelets, Tuna Salad Turnovers and Ratatouille Quiche are all baked right before you leave. To help insulate them, wrap in foil first, then in several layers of newspaper. Tortilla Roll-Ups are great finger-lickin' sandwiches for the picnic basket or lunch box or, sliced thin, for the hors d'oeuvre tray.

Other portable entrees to consider are Eggplant, Zucchini and Tomato Tart (page 23), the crowd-pleasing Fiesta Corn Tamale Torte (page 31), Seafood Tourtière (page 173) or Pasta Salad with Fresh Tomato Pesto (page 125) (with cooked meat or seafood, if desired). If you prefer a potato, vegetable or leafy green salad to Marinated Vegetables on Skewers, pack the dressing separately and toss the salad before serving.

Clockwise from top right: Overnight Iced Tea, Marinated Vegetables on Skewers, Crusty Italian Picnic Loaf, Double Currant Bars, Chocolate Chip Spice Crocodiles, Black and White Chocolate Chunk Cookies.

Overnight Iced Tea

You don't even have to know how to boil water for this never-fail refresher. *(See photograph, page 54.)*

5 teaspoons loose tea, any variety
4 cups cold water
Honey or sugar to taste, if desired
Ice cubes
6 small sprigs fresh mint, optional
1 lemon, sliced, optional

Mix tea and water in a pitcher. Cover and let stand overnight. Strain tea through a fine strainer. Sweeten to taste, if desired. Fill thermos with ice to chill. Drain and fill with tea. Add mint sprigs and lemon slices, if desired. Serve over ice.

Makes 4 cups.

Crusty Italian Picnic Loaf

Omelets, spinach, mushrooms and mozzarella cheese are packed into a hollowed-out loaf of bread and then baked. What could be more perfect for transporting to a picnic than a meal in a bowl—a bread bowl, that is! *(See photograph, page 54.)*

1 round unsliced sourdough or French bread (1½ pounds), approximately 8 inches in diameter
3 tablespoons butter or margarine
2 cloves garlic, minced
6 eggs, divided
10 teaspoons vegetable oil, divided
4 tablespoons chopped green onions with tops, divided
About ¾ pound fresh bulk spinach, washed, stemmed, dried and torn into bite-size pieces (about 3 ounces stemmed)
2 cups shredded mozzarella cheese (about 8 ounces), divided
½ jar (7 ounces) roasted sweet red peppers, sliced
6 large fresh mushrooms, sliced

Using a serrated knife, cut top quarter off bread and reserve it. With your fingers, pull out inside of the bread, leaving a ½-inch shell. Melt butter or margarine with garlic and brush inside of loaf and top.

In a small bowl, whisk together 3 eggs. In a 6-inch skillet or omelet pan, heat 2 teaspoons oil over moderately high heat. Stir in 2 tablespoons green onion; sauté until soft, about 1 minute. Pour in eggs. With fork or spatula, pull edges of eggs toward the center and tilt the pan so the uncooked portion runs to the bottom of the pan. Cook until the top just begins to set. Slide omelet into hollowed-out bread. Heat 2 more teaspoons oil in same skillet, sauté remaining 2 tablespoons green onions. Whisk remaining 3 eggs and pour over onions, making a second omelet in the same manner as the first; remove from heat and set aside in the pan.

In a medium skillet, heat 3 teaspoons oil; sauté spinach over moderately high heat until it begins to wilt. Spread evenly over omelet in the bread. Sprinkle with half the mozzarella and arrange red pepper slices over cheese. In the same skillet, heat remaining 3 teaspoons oil and sauté mushrooms until barely tender. Spoon mushrooms over peppers; top with remaining cheese. Invert second omelet out of pan onto cheese. Replace bread top. Wrap the loaf in heavy foil.

∗ The loaf may be refrigerated overnight. Bring to room temperature at least 2 hours before baking.

Preheat the oven to 350 degrees. Place loaf on a baking sheet, open foil and bake, uncovered, for 20 to 25 minutes or until warm. Rewrap in foil to transport. To serve, remove top and slice loaf and top separately into wedges with serrated knife.

Serves 6 to 8.

Tuna Salad Turnovers

Everyone's favorite sandwich filling is wrapped in storebought puff pastry. Keep these turnovers in the freezer to pop in the oven when needed.

- 1 can (6½ ounces) tuna packed in water, drained
- 1 tablespoon chopped green onions with tops
- ¼ cup mayonnaise
- 2 eggs, hard-boiled and chopped
- Freshly ground pepper to taste
- 2 tablespoons lemon juice
- 1 package (1 pound) frozen puff pastry, defrosted until soft enough to roll, but still very cold
- ½ medium tomato, chopped (8 teaspoons)
- 8 thin slices avocado
- 1 cup shredded jack cheese (about 4 ounces)
- 1 egg, beaten with 1 tablespoon water, for glaze

In a medium bowl, stir together tuna, green onions, mayonnaise, eggs, pepper, and lemon juice. On a lightly floured board, roll half the pastry (1 sheet) into a 12-inch square. Refrigerate the remaining pastry. Cut into four 6-inch squares. Spoon 2 tablespoons tuna mixture in the center of each square, top with 1 teaspoon tomato, a slice of avocado and 2 tablespoons jack cheese. Brush edges of pastry with water. Fold one corner over to the opposite side, forming a triangle and enclosing the filling. Seal edges by pressing with tines of a fork. Repeat with remaining puff pastry. Brush tops of the triangles with as much egg glaze as needed to cover.

∗ The turnovers may be refrigerated, covered, overnight or frozen. Do not defrost before baking.

Place rack in bottom third of oven and preheat to 450 degrees. Place turnovers on a lightly greased rimmed baking sheet. Bake for 5 to 6 minutes, turn and bake 5 or 6 minutes more or until golden on each side. If frozen, bake for 25 to 30 minutes. Wrap in heavy foil to transport. Best served warm.

Makes 8 turnovers.

Ratatouille Quiche

The flaky base is a foolproof cream cheese pastry. It doesn't get tough when overhandled and can be simply pressed into the pan. A thick eggplant-tomato filling hidden beneath a cheesy custard topping comes as a surprise when the quiche is cut.

Flaky Pastry

- 12 tablespoons (1½ sticks) butter or margarine, cold and cut into 12 pieces
- 5 ounces cream cheese, cold and cut into small pieces
- 1½ cups all-purpose flour
- ¼ teaspoon salt, or to taste

Ratatouille Filling

- 6 tablespoons olive oil, divided
- 1 large onion, chopped
- 1 medium eggplant (about 1 to 1¼ pounds), peeled and diced into ¾-inch pieces
- 2 large cloves garlic, minced
- 1 can (28 ounces) whole tomatoes, drained and chopped
- 1 can (15 ounces) tomato sauce
- 2 tablespoons fresh chopped basil or 2 teaspoons dried basil
- ¼ cup chopped fresh parsley
- ½ teaspoon sugar
- 2 tablespoons Dijon mustard
- 2 cups shredded swiss cheese, (about 8 ounces)
- 2 whole eggs
- 1 egg yolk
- ½ cup heavy cream
- ¼ cup grated parmesan cheese

To make the Flaky Pastry, in a food processor fitted with the metal blade or in a mixing bowl with an electric mixer, pulse or mix butter or margarine and cream cheese until blended. Add flour and salt and mix until crumbly. Remove to a sheet of plastic wrap and shape into a flat disk. If necessary, refrigerate until cold enough to roll.

∗ The dough may be refrigerated up to 2 days or frozen.

Place oven rack on bottom rung and preheat oven to 375 degrees. On a lightly floured board, roll the pastry into a 13-inch circle. Fit it into an 11-inch tart pan with a removable bottom or a 9-inch pie dish. Or if desired, press the dough into bottom and up sides of pan with your fingers. Prick the bottom of the pastry with a fork at 2-inch intervals. Bake for 15 to 20 minutes or until the bottom is golden. Remove to a rack and cool.

∗ The pastry shell may be held at room temperature overnight or frozen. Bring to room temperature before filling.

To make the Ratatouille Filling, in a medium saucepan heat 2 tablespoons olive oil; sauté onion until soft. Add 2 more tablespoons oil; sauté eggplant over moderately high heat, stirring often until soft, adding additional oil as needed. Stir in garlic, tomatoes, tomato sauce, basil, parsley and sugar. Cook, uncovered, over moderately high heat, stirring occasionally until the mixture is thick and the liquid has evaporated, about 20 minutes.

∗ The filling may be refrigerated up to 5 days or frozen.

Preheat the oven to 375 degrees. Place oven rack in bottom third of oven. Spread mustard over bottom of pastry. Sprinkle with half the swiss cheese. Fill with eggplant mixture. In a medium bowl, whisk together the eggs, egg yolk and cream. Pour over eggplant, sprinkle with remaining swiss cheese and the parmesan cheese. (If using an 11-inch tart pan, you may have some cream mixture left over.) Bake for 20 to 30 minutes or until puffed and golden. Let rest at least 10 minutes before serving. To transport to a picnic, cool 30 minutes and wrap in a clean dish towel. The quiche can be served hot, warm or at room temperature.

Serves 8.

Tortilla Roll-Ups

Tortillas tend to dry out, so to roll them easily without cracking, be sure to start with a new package. These are deli sandwiches with a twist.

Turkey Filling (See below) or
Roast Beef Filling (See below) or
Smoked Salmon Filling (See below) or
Ham Filling (See below)
Flour tortillas (7½ inches)

Turkey Filling

3 tablespoons mayonnaise
1 tablespoon ketchup
4 thin turkey slices (about 4 to 6 ounces)
Salt and pepper to taste
⅓ cup shredded jack cheese
¼ avocado, pitted, peeled and chopped
1 cup shredded lettuce

Stir together the mayonnaise and ketchup; spread half over 1 tortilla. Cover with half the turkey. Sprinkle with salt and pepper. Cover with half the cheese, avocado and lettuce. Roll up tight and wrap in plastic wrap. Repeat with second tortilla and remaining ingredients.

Roast Beef Filling

3 tablespoons mayonnaise
1 tablespoon ketchup
4 thin slices rare roast beef (about 4 to 6 ounces)
2 tablespoons finely chopped green onions
2 tablespoons finely chopped peeled and seeded cucumber
⅓ cup shredded swiss cheese
½ cup alfalfa sprouts

Stir together mayonnaise and ketchup; spread half over 1 tortilla. Cover with half the roast beef. Sprinkle with half the green onions, cucumber, swiss cheese and sprouts. Roll up tight and wrap in plastic wrap. Repeat with second tortilla and remaining ingredients.

Smoked Salmon Filling

1 package (3 ounces) cream cheese with chives, at room temperature
4 ounces sliced smoked salmon
2 tablespoons finely chopped green onions
2 tablespoons finely chopped peeled and seeded tomato
2 tablespoons finely chopped peeled and seeded cucumber

Spread half the cream cheese over 1 tortilla. Cover with half the smoked salmon and sprinkle with half the green onions, tomato and cucumber. Roll up tightly and wrap in plastic wrap. Repeat with second tortilla and remaining ingredients.

Ham Filling

1 tablespoon mayonnaise
1 tablespoon Dijon mustard
4 slices thinly sliced ham
½ cup shredded cheddar or swiss cheese
2 tablespoons diced green chilies
¼ avocado, pitted, peeled and chopped

Stir mayonniase and mustard together. Spread half over 1 tortilla. Cover with half the ham. Sprinkle with half the cheese, chilies and avocado. Roll up tight and wrap in plastic wrap. Repeat with second tortilla and remaining ingredients.

Refrigerate all roll-ups for at least 1 hour or up to 4 hours. Before serving, cut each roll-up into 4 portions. To transport, rewrap in plastic wrap and then in foil.

Makes 2 tortilla roll-ups per filling.

Marinated Vegetables on Skewers

Any vegetable that tastes good raw, such as broccoli or cauliflower florets, zucchini, jícama or sliced carrots, can be substituted for those listed. What a fresh idea—salad on a stick. (See photograph, page 54.)

- Italian Mustard Vinaigrette (See below)
- 12 cherry tomatoes, stemmed
- 8 small mushrooms with tightly closed caps
- 1 piece (about 4 inches) cucumber, preferably hothouse or European
- ½ firm but ripe avocado, pitted and peeled
- 4 wooden skewers (9 inches)

Italian Mustard Vinaigrette

- 1 shallot or 1-inch piece onion, peeled
- 1 large clove garlic, peeled
- 1 tablespoon Dijon mustard
- 2 tablespoons red wine vinegar
- Dash of sugar
- ½ cup vegetable oil
- 3 tablespoons olive oil
- 2 tablespoons water
- Salt and pepper to taste

To make the Italian Mustard Vinaigrette, in a food processor fitted with the metal blade, chop shallot or onion and garlic until minced. Process in mustard, vinegar and sugar. With the machine running, slowly pour oil through the feed tube until the mixture is well blended and thickened. Add water and process until blended in. Season to taste. The dressing may be refrigerated up to 1 week.

Wipe tomatoes and mushrooms clean with a damp cloth. Cut cucumber into eight ½-inch pieces. Cut avocado in half and slice into eight ½-inch wedges. Beginning and ending with a tomato, alternate 3 tomatoes, 2 slices of avocado, 2 mushrooms and 2 cucumber pieces on each skewer. Place in shallow nonaluminum dish into which they fit comfortably. Pour enough dressing over to coat vegetables. Cover with plastic wrap. Refrigerate 2 to 8 hours, turning once or twice. To transport to picnic, wrap the skewers in plastic wrap and foil.

Serves 4.

Grandma's Sugar Cookies

Lots of sugar, lots of butter, lots of crunch make these old-fashioned favorites perfect for movable feasts. They're good and virtually indestructible.

- ¼ pound (1 stick) butter or margarine, at room temperature
- ¾ cup sugar
- 1 egg
- 1 teaspoon vanilla
- 1½ cups all-purpose flour
- ½ teaspoon baking powder
- ½ teaspoon baking soda
- ½ teaspoon nutmeg
- ¼ teaspoon salt, or to taste
- ⅓ cup plus 3 tablespoons sugar for rolling and sprinkling on top

Preheat the oven to 375 degrees. In a food processor fitted with the metal blade or in a small mixing bowl with an electric mixer, cream butter and sugar until fluffy. Beat in egg and vanilla. Add flour, baking powder, soda, nutmeg and salt. Pulse or mix on low speed until incorporated. Pinch off pieces of dough and shape into 1-inch balls. Roll in ⅓ cup sugar. Place on greased baking sheets 2 inches apart and flatten to ¼ inch with the bottom of a small glass dipped first in water and then in sugar.

Bake in center of oven for 10 to 12 minutes or until edges are lightly browned. If baking 2 cookie sheets in the same oven, rotate their positions half way through the baking time. Remove from oven and immediately sprinkle tops with remaining 3 tablespoons sugar. Remove to racks to cool.

* The cookies may be stored at room temperature in an airtight container for several days or frozen.

Makes about 36 cookies.

Chocolate Chip Spice Crocodiles

Small balls of delicately spiced dough are coated thickly with confectioners sugar to bake into crunchy, crackle-topped morsels. (See photograph, page 54.)

½ pound (2 sticks) butter or margarine, at room temperature
1⅓ cups (packed) golden light brown sugar
1 egg
1 teaspoon vanilla
2 cups all-purpose flour
1 teaspoon baking soda
1½ teaspoons cinnamon
1½ teaspoons ground ginger
½ teaspoon salt, or to taste
1 package (12 ounces) semisweet chocolate chips (about 2 cups)
1 cup chopped walnuts (about 4 ounces)
1 cup confectioners sugar for rolling

In a large mixing bowl with an electric mixer, cream butter and brown sugar until light and fluffy. Mix in egg and vanilla. Add flour, baking soda, cinnamon, ginger and salt, mixing on low speed until incorporated. Mix in chocolate chips and nuts.

Pinch off small pieces of dough and shape into 1-inch balls. If the dough is too sticky to work with, refrigerate until firm. Place balls on plates and refrigerate, covered with plastic wrap, for 2 to 3 hours or overnight.

Preheat oven to 350 degrees. Place oven rack in upper third of oven. Place confectioners sugar in a shallow bowl. Roll balls in sugar to coat thickly. Place on lightly greased baking sheets 2 inches apart. Bake for 10 to 12 minutes or until the tops look puffed, barely set and cracked. The cookies will be very soft but will firm up as they cool. Do not overbake or they will be dry. Let cool 2 to 3 minutes; remove to racks to cool.

* The cookies may be stored at room temperature in an airtight container for several days or frozen.

Makes about 72 cookies.

Soft Ginger Cookies

All the spice and sweetness of gingerbread are baked into these sugar-crusted cookies.

¼ pound (1 stick) butter or margarine, at room temperature
1⅓ cups sugar
1 egg
⅓ cup light molasses
3 tablespoons dark corn syrup
2 tablespoons regular or low-fat milk
4 cups all-purpose flour
2 teaspoons baking soda
2 teaspoons cinnamon
2 teaspoons ground ginger
1½ teaspoons ground cloves
Sugar for rolling

Preheat oven to 350 degrees. In a mixing bowl with an electric mixer, cream butter or margarine, sugar and egg until light and fluffy. Mix in molasses, corn syrup and milk. Add flour, baking soda, cinnamon, ginger and cloves, mixing until well blended. Pinch off small pieces of dough and shape into 1½-inch balls. Roll in sugar. Place 3 inches apart on ungreased baking sheets. Bake 12 to 14 minutes or until tops are puffed. Do not overbake or the cookies will not be soft. If baking 2 cookie sheets in the same oven, rotate their positions half way through the baking time. Cool cookies 1 to 2 minutes on baking sheets, then remove to racks to cool.

* The cookies may be stored at room temperature in an airtight container for several days or frozen.

Makes 40 cookies.

Black and White Chocolate Chunk Cookies

Pieces of rough white chocolate protruding through soft, dark chocolate create a mouthful of goodness with a rocky road effect. (See photograph, page 54.)

- ¼ pound (1 stick) butter or margarine, at room temperature
- ½ cup (packed) golden light brown sugar
- ½ cup granulated sugar
- 1 teaspoon vanilla
- ¼ teaspoon salt, or to taste
- ⅓ cup unsweetened cocoa powder
- 1 egg
- ½ teaspoon baking soda
- 1 cup all-purpose flour
- 6 ounces white chocolate, chopped into ½-inch pieces

Preheat the oven to 350 degrees. In a food processor fitted with the metal blade or in a small mixing bowl with an electric mixer, cream butter or margarine and both sugars until fluffy. Mix in vanilla and salt. Add cocoa and egg and mix until well blended. Mix in soda and flour until incorporated. Stir in white chocolate.

Drop 2 teaspoons of batter onto greased baking sheets about 2 inches apart. Bake for 10 to 12 minutes. The tops will look set, but the cookies will be very soft. Do not overbake; they will firm up as they cool. If baking 2 cookie sheets in the same oven, rotate their positions half way through the baking time. Remove from oven, let sit 1 minute and move cookies to racks to cool.

* The cookies may be stored in an airtight container at room temperature for several days or frozen.

Makes about 40 cookies.

MENU

DRESSED-UP SALAD LUNCHEON

Butter Lettuce Soup

Cheese-Crusted Rye Bread (*Page 144*)

Warm Chicken-Papaya Salad
with Orange-Ginger Dressing
or
Chilled Scallop Salad
with Citrus-Honey Dressing

Mandarin Orange Carrot Cake

Salads have come into their own with chic new styles. No longer composed merely of lettuce and tomatoes, contemporary salads include warm or cold ingredients artistically arranged on the plate.

If you make the Orange-Ginger Dressing and line the plates with lettuce ahead, then you need only stir-fry the chicken at the last minute for Warm Chicken-Papaya Salad. To double the recipe, sauté the chicken in batches rather than all at once. The scallops in Chilled Scallop Salad are actually "cooked" in the refrigerator. Cooking doesn't get any easier than this! Choose one or the other of these salads for lunch.

Other suitable main dish luncheon salads are Red Cabbage with Bacon and Goat Cheese (page 84), Sesame Spinach Salad with chicken or shrimp added (page 98), Cold Artichokes with Shrimp Salad (page 90) and Warm Spinach, Brie and Mushroom Salad (page 127).

A warm and tangy bread, like Cheese-Crusted Rye Bread (page 144) or Cheddar Garlic Twist (page 148), is an outstanding choice to complete the menu. Suggested occasions for this salad menu are:
◇ Card Party or Book Review Luncheon
◇ Charity Group or Business Meeting
◇ Reunion

Butter Lettuce Soup

It's surprising that this delicate and subtle lettuce cooks into such a tasty soup. For the smoothest texture, puree in a blender rather than a food processor.

4 tablespoons (½ stick) butter or margarine
1½ cups finely chopped carrots (about 4 large carrots)
1½ cups finely chopped green onions (about 2 large bunches)
2 medium white all-purpose potatoes (about 1 pound) peeled and cut into small cubes
1½ pounds Boston or butter lettuce (about 4 heads), cored and chopped
5 cups chicken broth
2 teaspoons bottled fines herbes
½ teaspoon dried dill
Salt and pepper to taste
¾ cup sour cream, at room temperature

In a medium soup pot, melt butter or margarine; sauté carrots and green onions until onions are soft. Add potato, cover and cook over moderately low heat, stirring often until potatoes and carrots are soft, 20 to 25 minutes. Stir in lettuce and chicken broth; simmer, uncovered, until vegetables are tender, about 10 minutes. Cool slightly. Puree in 2 batches in a blender or food processor with the metal blade. Mix in fines herbes, dill, salt and pepper.

* The soup may be refrigerated up to 2 days or frozen. It separates when defrosted but will smooth out when reheated.

Before serving, bring to a boil, lower heat and stir in sour cream. Do not boil. Adjust seasonings if necessary.

Serves 8.

Chilled Scallop Salad with Citrus-Honey Dressing

Striking concentric circles of scallops, avocado and oranges are drizzled with a refreshingly fruity oil-free dressing. Your guests would never guess the scallops were "cooked" in the dressing and not on the stove.

Citrus-Honey Dressing (See below)
1½ pounds scallops
3 oranges, peeled and sliced into rounds
1 head Boston or butter lettuce, leaves separated
2 bunches watercress (about 7 ounces), washed and stemmed
2 avocados, peeled, pitted and sliced

Citrus-Honey Dressing

Grated peel of 2 oranges
½ cup fresh lemon juice
½ cup orange juice
¼ cup honey
⅓ cup chopped green onion with tops
¾ teaspoon salt, or to taste
½ teaspoon celery seed
1 teaspoon hot chili oil or hot-pepper sauce, or to taste

To make the Citrus-Honey Dressing, in a medium bowl whisk all the ingredients together.

If the scallops are large, cut them horizontally into 3 or 4 slices. Place in a medium bowl (not aluminum). Pour about two-thirds of the dressing over and toss to coat. Cover and refrigerate for 5 hours or overnight, stirring once or twice. The acid in the dressing will cook the scallops. Place the orange slices in another bowl, pour on the remaining dressing, cover and refrigerate.

As close to serving as possible, line a platter or individual plates with lettuce leaves. Place a mound of watercress in the center. Using a slotted spoon, place the scallops on top of the watercress; discard scallop marinade. Remove the orange slices from the marinade and overlap them in a circle around the watercress. Arrange the avocado slices around the outer edge. Drizzle reserved marinade from the oranges over the avocado and watercress.

Serves 6.

Warm Chicken-Papaya Salad with Orange-Ginger Dressing

The contrast of cold papaya and warm chicken in a lightly spiced orange dressing makes a tantalizing salad. Inspired by Chinese cuisine, it is exquisite in color and taste, but it does require some last-minute cooking.

Orange-Ginger Dressing (See below)
8 skinless and boneless chicken breast halves (3 pounds net weight)
2 tablespoons soy sauce
1 large head Boston or butter lettuce, leaves separated
2 firm but ripe avocados, peeled, halved, seeded and sliced into thin wedges
3 firm but ripe papayas, peeled, halved, seeded and sliced into thin wedges
4 tablespoons sesame seeds
2 tablespoons vegetable oil

Orange-Ginger Dressing
1 piece (2 to 3 inches) fresh ginger, peeled and cut into 6 pieces
1 small green onion with top, cut into 1-inch pieces
6 fresh orange segments
½ cup white rice wine vinegar
½ cup orange juice
1 teaspoon dry mustard
1 heaping tablespoon jarred salsa jalapeña or hot picante salsa or ½ teaspoon hot-pepper sauce
1¼ cups vegetable oil
¾ teaspoon salt, or to taste
Freshly ground pepper to taste

To make the Orange-Ginger Dressing, in a food processor fitted with the metal blade, chop ginger; pulse in green onion. Add orange segments, vinegar, orange juice, dry mustard and salsa or hot-pepper sauce; process until blended. With motor running, slowly pour oil through the feed tube. Season with salt and pepper. The dressing may be refrigerated overnight, if desired.

Cut the chicken into strips about 2 inches long and ¾ inch wide. About 1 hour before serving, place in a glass bowl. Pour soy sauce over chicken, toss, cover and marinate for 1 hour. Arrange lettuce leaves on serving platter or individual plates. Dip avocado slices into the dressing and arrange alternately with papaya around the edges of the lettuce. The salad may be covered with plastic wrap and held at room temperature up to 1 hour.

In a wok or large skillet, toast the sesame seeds until lightly browned. Remove and set aside. Heat oil over moderately high heat until very hot; add chicken and sauté, stirring constantly, until cooked through, about 3 to 4 minutes. Remove from heat, pour dressing over and toss well. Spoon chicken into center of the lettuce leaves, drizzling some dressing over the avocado and papaya. Sprinkle sesame seeds over chicken and serve immediately.

Serves 8.

Mandarin Orange Carrot Cake

Once when making this cake I misread "4 carrots, shredded" and added 4 cups *shredded carrots. I realized my mistake while the cake was baking and thought I had ruined it. What a wonderful surprise to find the cake tasted and looked even better than before. In addition to having the goodness of whole wheat and honey, with all that vitamin A it now might also improve your eyesight.*

- 2 cups all-purpose flour
- 1 cup whole wheat flour
- 2 teaspoons baking soda
- 1 teaspoon salt, or to taste
- 1 teaspoon cinnamon
- 1¼ cups vegetable oil
- 1½ cups honey
- 3 eggs, at room temperature
- 4 cups shredded carrots (about 2 pounds)
- 2 teaspoons vanilla
- 1 tablespoon grated orange peel
- 1 can (11 ounces) mandarin oranges, well drained
- 1 cup raisins
- 1 cup shredded coconut

Fluffy Orange Frosting

- 1 package (8 ounces) cream cheese, a little colder than room temperature
- ¼ pound (1 stick) butter or margarine, a little colder than room temperature
- ¼ cup orange juice concentrate
- 1 cup confectioners sugar, sifted

Grease a 12-cup tube pan. Preheat oven to 350 degrees. In a large mixing bowl with the electric mixer on low speed, mix white and whole wheat flour, baking soda, salt and cinnamon. Mix in oil, honey and eggs until incorporated. Increase speed to medium and beat 2 minutes. On low speed, mix in carrots, vanilla, orange peel, mandarin oranges, raisins and coconut until combined. Beat at medium speed for 30 seconds.

Pour into prepared pan, smooth the top, and place on a baking sheet. Bake for 70 to 80 minutes or until a toothpick inserted into the cake comes out clean. Remove to a rack and cool 20 minutes; invert, remove pan and cool cake to room temperature.

To make the Fluffy Orange Frosting, in a small mixing bowl with the electric mixer, beat cream cheese and butter until light and fluffy. Mix in orange juice concentrate. Gradually mix in confectioners sugar, beating until light and fluffy. Spread over top and sides of cake. If frosting is soft, refrigerate until set. Remove from refrigerator 30 minutes before serving.

∗ The cake may be held at room temperature, uncovered, overnight or refrigerated for 2 days or frozen. Freeze, uncovered, until firm; then cover. Defrost, uncovered, at room temperature.

Serves 12 to 14.

INFALLIBLE FOWL

STAND-OUT SIT-DOWN CHICKEN DINNER

ONE TERRIFIC ONE POT CHICKEN

SUNDAY DINNER ALLA ROMANA

CELEBRATION CHICKEN BREASTS SUPREME

CRACKLING DUCK BY THE FIRESIDE

Stuffed Chicken Breast with Roasted Red Pepper Sauce, Angel Hair Pasta with Spinach and Pine Nuts, Buttermilk Crescent Rolls.

M E N U

STAND-OUT SIT-DOWN CHICKEN DINNER

Green Garden Vegetable Soup with Mozzarella Pesto

Buttermilk Crescent Rolls (*Page 146*)

Stuffed Chicken Breasts with Roasted Red Pepper Sauce

Angel Hair Pasta with Spinach and Pine Nuts

Caramel Apple Tart

Every cook has at least one tried-and-true dinner menu. Get ready to discover a new old favorite dinner, that's as at home on your finest lace cloth and china as it is on straw place mats and pottery.

The Green Garden Vegetable Soup is a delight year-round, but if you prefer a less filling starter, I would recommend the Romaine Salad with Papaya, Jícama and Toasted Pecans (page 132).

The meat for Stuffed Chicken Breasts with Roasted Red Pepper Sauce should be pounded thin. If you don't want to pound them yourself, ask the butcher to do it for you. You can stuff the breasts with cheesy zucchini filling weeks in advance, and put the better part of the work for this dinner behind you. Zucchini is so versatile, it will taste quite different in the filling than it does in the soup. If the last-minute preparation of Angel Hair Pasta with Spinach and Pine Nuts seems too hectic, substitute Parsley Rice Pilaf (page 106).

Reheat the scrumptious Caramel Apple Tart while you serve the coffee. Suggested occasions for serving this menu are:

- **◇ Birthday or Anniversary**
- **◇ Wedding Rehearsal or Engagement Party**
- **◇ Valentine's Day Dinner**
- **◇ Business Entertaining or Retirement Party**

Green Garden Vegetable Soup with Mozzarella Pesto

It's hard to believe this thick, creamy soup is made without the addition of cream or milk. A dollop of pesto in each bowl enhances the flavor and adds a splash of emerald green. Serve this terrific first course winter or summer, hot or cold.

4 tablespoons (½ stick) butter or margarine
1 large onion, chopped
3 pounds zucchini, sliced
6 cups chicken broth
1 package (10 ounces) frozen lima beans
1 package (10 ounces) frozen asparagus pieces or spears
1 package (10 ounces) frozen peas
Salt and pepper to taste

Mozzarella Pesto

3 cloves garlic, peeled
½ cup fresh basil leaves
¼ cup grated parmesan cheese
½ cup shredded mozzarella cheese
3 tablespoons olive oil

In a large soup pot, melt butter or margarine; sauté onion and zucchini until very soft, about 10 minutes, stirring occasionally. Add chicken broth and bring to a boil. Stir in lima beans, asparagus, and peas. Simmer, uncovered, for 20 to 25 minutes or until vegetables are soft.

Puree the mixture in batches in a food processor fitted with the metal blade or in a blender. Season to taste with salt and pepper.

To make the Mozzarella Pesto, mince garlic in a food processor with the metal blade. Scrape down sides, add basil and process until chopped. Add both cheeses and olive oil and mix until a thick paste is formed. Serve at room temperature.

* The soup may be refrigerated up to 2 days or frozen. The pesto may be tightly covered and refrigerated up to 1 week or frozen.

Before serving, bring soup to a simmer. Ladle into soup bowls and top each with a spoonful of pesto, allowing your guests to stir in their own. Pass additional pesto, if desired.

Serves 10 to 12.

Stuffed Chicken Breasts with Roasted Red Pepper Sauce

With a spiral of zucchini-flecked filling and luxuriant red pepper topping, these chicken breasts make a truly jewel-like presentation. (See photograph, page 67.)

3 small zucchini (about 12 ounces)
½ teaspoon salt, or to taste
2 shallots or ¼ onion, peeled
2 cloves garlic, peeled
1½ packages (4 to 5 ounces each) garlic and spice cheese, such as Rondelé, Alouette or Boursin
¾ cup grated parmesan cheese (about 3 ounces)
12 large boneless and skinless chicken breast halves, pounded very thin (6 to 8 ounces each)
Salt and pepper
4 tablespoons (½ stick) butter or margarine, melted
Paprika

Roasted Red Pepper Sauce

4 large or 8 small red bell peppers
¼ cup raspberry or red wine vinegar
¼ cup dry red wine
2 teaspoons cornstarch
1 cup chicken broth
Salt and pepper to taste

To make the stuffing, shred zucchini in a food processor fitted with the shredding disk. Place in a colander in the sink, sprinkle with salt, toss with your hands and let stand for 30 minutes. Squeeze a handful at a time in a kitchen towel to remove excess moisture. In the same processor workbowl, process shallots or onion and garlic until minced. Mix in both cheeses and the zucchini.

Place chicken breasts on a flat surface, shiny or skin side down. Sprinkle with salt and pepper. Spoon 2 tablespoons stuffing over each breast; spread evenly. Fold one end over, turn in the sides and roll up to enclose the filling. Skewer closed.

∗ The breasts may be wrapped tightly and refrigerated overnight or frozen for up to 2 weeks. Bring to room temperature before baking.

For the Roasted Red Pepper Sauce, roast the peppers. Line a shallow roasting or broiler pan with foil. Broil peppers 4 inches from the broiler flame, turning with tongs until the outside is black and charred and the inside is soft, 25 to 30 minutes. Place in a paper bag or dish towel and set aside for 20 minutes. Scrape off peel under running tap water. Cut out core and rinse out all seeds. Dry lightly and puree in a food processor fitted with the metal blade.

∗ The puree may be refrigerated for several days or frozen. Makes 1 cup.

To make the sauce, bring vinegar and wine to a boil in a medium saucepan. Boil over high heat until reduced to ¼ cup; remove from heat. Dissolve cornstarch in chicken broth and whisk into reduced vinegar and wine mixture. Return to heat and bring to a boil, whisking constantly. Stir in red pepper puree. Season to taste with salt and pepper. The sauce may be held covered at room temperature for several hours.

Before serving, preheat oven to 400 degrees. Place chicken breasts in a shallow roasting pan without crowding. Brush tops with butter or margarine. Sprinkle with paprika. Bake, uncovered, for 25 to 30 minutes; after the first 15 minutes, baste once or twice. Remove skewers; place breasts on serving plates. Measure ¼ to ½ cup of the pan drippings into the red pepper sauce. Bring to a boil and spoon some across the center of each breast. Pass remaining sauce.

Serves 8; makes 12 breasts.

Angel Hair Pasta with Spinach and Pine Nuts

The huge mound of spinach, which takes so long to wash, cooks down to a handful in very few minutes. When Frances Coleman was testing this recipe for me, her family ate the first batch before she could get it out of the house, so she had to make another one for me. (See photograph, page 67.)

- 1 cup pine nuts
- ½ cup olive oil
- 4 very large cloves garlic or 8 small cloves, minced
- ¾ teaspoon dried red pepper flakes
- 3 pounds fresh bulk spinach, stemmed, washed, dried well and coarsely chopped (about 18 ounces stemmed)
- ¾ pound angel hair pasta (cappellini)
- 4 tablespoons (½ stick) butter or margarine
- ½ cup grated parmesan cheese
- Salt and pepper to taste

In a wok or large skillet, sauté pine nuts until golden. Remove and set aside. Heat oil in same pan; sauté garlic and red pepper flakes for 1 minute; remove from heat.

Before serving, bring a large pot of salted water to a boil. Cook pasta until tender to the bite (al dente). Reheat oil with garlic; add spinach and toss over high heat until wilted, 2 to 3 minutes; do not overcook or it will stick together. Stir in butter or margarine. Drain pasta well. Place in a large bowl, add spinach mixture, parmesan cheese and pine nuts; toss well. Season to taste with salt and pepper. Serve immediately.

Serves 8.

Caramel Apple Tart

Storebought puff pastry encases buttery, caramel-soaked apples. Mom's apple pie was never like this.

- 1 package (1 pound) frozen puff pastry, defrosted until soft enough to roll, but still very cold

Caramel Sauce

- 1 cup sugar
- ½ cup water
- ¾ cup heavy cream
- 3 tablespoons butter or margarine

Apple Filling

- 6 large tart cooking apples (about 3 pounds)
- 4 tablespoons (½ stick) butter or margarine
- ⅓ cup sugar
- 1 tablespoon all-purpose flour
- 1 egg lightly beaten with 1 teaspoon water for glaze

On a lightly floured board, roll half the pastry (1 sheet) into a 13-inch square; transfer to an 11-inch tart pan with a removable bottom. Press pastry into bottom and sides of pan; trim edges even with the top rim. Refrigerate pastry-lined pan and remaining pastry while preparing the sauce and filling.

To make the Caramel Sauce, combine sugar and water in a heavy medium size saucepan. Cook over moderately high heat, without stirring, until mixture turns golden brown; be careful not to let it burn. Immediately remove from heat and slowly stir in cream. The sugar will harden, but stirring will smooth it out. Stir in butter or margarine until melted.

Place oven rack in lowest position. Preheat oven to 425 degrees. To make the Apple Filling, peel, halve, core and thinly slice the apples. Heat butter or margarine in a large skillet over moderately high heat. Sauté apples, turning often, until barely tender, about 5 to 8 minutes. Remove from heat and sprinkle with sugar and flour, stirring until coated. Pour hot apples with their juices into pastry-lined pan. Measure ½ cup warm caramel sauce and pour over apples. (Reserve remaining sauce; it may be refrigerated up to 2 weeks. Reheat in microwave or top of double boiler before using.)

Roll remaining pastry and cut a 12-inch circle; cut a 1-inch circle out of the center. Place over apples; press onto rim of pan and trim edges even with rim. Brush top lightly with egg glaze. If desired, reroll scraps of pastry, cut into decorations and place on top; brush with egg glaze.

Place tart on a baking sheet and bake for 30 to 40 minutes or until the top is deep golden brown. The top crust will have pulled away from the sides. Remove from oven and cool 10 minutes. To keep the sides from sticking, place the tart on a bowl smaller than the tart pan, carefully lower the sides and then raise them back in place. Let the tart cool in the pan for at least 30 minutes before serving.

* The tart may be held covered at room temperature overnight or frozen. Before serving bring to room temperature and reheat, uncovered, at 425 degrees for 5 to 10 minutes or until hot.

To serve, remove sides of tart pan. Spoon warm sauce over each slice.

Serves 8.

MENU

ONE TERRIFIC ONE POT CHICKEN

Seven Greens Salad

Drop Biscuits with Chives (*Page 145*)

Whole Roast Lemon Chicken with Vegetables

Chocolate Fudge Pound Cake

Crisp Whole Roast Lemon Chicken makes an ideal old-fashioned Sunday dinner for family and guests. Cooking chicken whole, rather than in pieces, produces the most succulent meat, because all the juices stay inside where they belong, and while the chicken roasts, it bastes and flavors the vegetables and potatoes beneath. Then when it's time to clean up, there's only one pan to wash!

This ample dish needs only a green salad, served either first or alongside, to complete the menu. Everyone loves sublime Chocolate Fudge Pound Cake, but if you want a lighter dessert, try the Frozen Rainbow Yogurt Torte (page 126) instead. Suggested occasions for serving this menu are:
- ◇ **After Work Get-together**
- ◇ **Vacation Slide Show**
- ◇ **Before the Recital**
- ◇ **Pre-Theater Dinner**
- ◇ **Mother's Day Surprise**
- ◇ **Post-Sporting-Event Dinner**

Seven Greens Salad

Toss together some new "designer" greens with some popular old favorites and you've turned over a new leaf in salads.

1 bunch arugula (about 2 ounces)
1 head romaine (about ¾ pound)
1 head limestone, Boston or butter lettuce (about 4 ounces)
1 small head radicchio (about 3 ounces)
½ head chicory or curly endive (about 4 ounces)
1 bunch watercress (about 5 ounces), stems removed
2 heads Belgian endive (about 6 ounces), sliced ½-inch thick

Vinaigrette

¼ cup raspberry vinegar
¾ cup walnut oil
½ teaspoon sugar
1 large clove garlic, minced
Salt and pepper to taste

Wash and dry arugula, romaine, limestone lettuce, radicchio, chicory and watercress; tear into bite-size pieces. Add Belgian endive and wrap in paper towels and a plastic bag; refrigerate until ready to serve or overnight.

To make the Vinaigrette, whisk all ingredients together in a small bowl.

* The dressing may be refrigerated for up to 5 days.

Before serving, place greens in a large bowl. Toss with as much vinaigrette as needed to moisten the greens. Season with salt and pepper to taste.

Serves 8.

Whole Roast Lemon Chicken with Vegetables

A whole lemon bakes in the cavity of a chicken roasting atop a panful of vegetables. When the chicken is done to crisp golden goodness, the lemon is squeezed over it, adding a fresh zesty tang.

2 chicken fryers (about 3 pounds each)
2 large lemons
2 teaspoons salt, or to taste
1 teaspoon pepper
1 tablespoon dried oregano
4 cloves garlic, minced
½ cup olive oil, divided
2 medium onions, sliced ⅓ inch thick
4 stalks celery, sliced ¾ inch thick on the bias
4 carrots, peeled and sliced ¾ inch thick
6 medium baking potatoes, cut into 2-inch cubes (about 2½ pounds)
⅔ cup fresh lemon juice (from 3 to 4 lemons)
⅔ cup chicken broth

Pat inside and outside of chickens dry; discard excess fat. Using a two-tined fork, pierce the lemons at ¼-inch intervals. Place a lemon in the cavity of each chicken and close the cavity with metal skewers.

Preheat oven to 500 degrees. In a small bowl, stir salt, pepper, oregano, garlic and ¼ cup olive oil into a paste. Rub the mixture over both chickens. Distribute onions, celery, carrots and potatoes in the bottom of a large shallow roasting pan. Place chickens on top of the vegetables, breast side up. Stir together the lemon juice, chicken broth, and remaining ¼ cup olive oil; pour over chicken and vegetables. Bake, uncovered, for 20 minutes. Turn the chickens over and roast, back side up, for 20 more minutes, basting the vegetables every 10 minutes. Reduce heat to 450 degrees and turn the chickens breast side up. Cook for an additional 20 minutes, basting vegetables and chicken twice. The chicken is done when the drumsticks wiggle easily.

Remove pan from oven and place the chickens on a cutting board. Let rest for 10 to 15 minutes and then remove the lemons from the cavities. Using kitchen shears, cut the chickens into quarters. Arrange chicken pieces and vegetables on a platter. Cut the lemons in half and squeeze lemon juice over all. Skim pan juices and serve over chicken and vegetables, if desired.

Serves 8.

Chocolate Fudge Pound Cake

Try to imagine a pound cake so chocolaty it melts in your mouth. That's exactly what this one does. It combines the density of pound cake with the richness of fudge. If you prefer to omit the glaze, dust the top with confectioners sugar.

- 7 ounces semisweet chocolate, chopped
- 3 ounces unsweetened chocolate, chopped
- ½ pound (2 sticks) butter or margarine, at room temperature
- 2 cups sugar
- 4 eggs
- 2 teaspoons vanilla
- 3 tablespoons brandy or water
- 2¼ cups all-purpose flour
- ½ teaspoon salt, or to taste
- 1 teaspoon baking soda
- 1¼ cups buttermilk

Chocolate Glaze, optional

- 4 ounces semisweet chocolate, chopped
- 6 tablespoons (¾ stick) butter or margarine
- 2 teaspoons light corn syrup
- 1 teaspoon water

Heavily grease a 12-cup bundt pan; set aside. Preheat oven to 350 degrees. To make the cake, place both chocolates in top of a double boiler over simmering water or in a microwave; stir until melted and smooth. Set aside to cool slightly.

In a large mixing bowl with an electric mixer, cream butter or margarine and sugar until light and fluffy. Mix in eggs one at a time, beating after each addition. Mix in chocolate, vanilla and brandy or water. In a small bowl stir together flour, salt and baking soda. With mixer on low speed, alternately add flour in fourths and buttermilk in thirds, beginning and ending with the flour. Pour into prepared pan. Bake in center of oven for 1 hour or until a toothpick inserted in the center comes out clean. Remove to rack and cool 10 minutes. Invert to remove from pan, and cool at least 20 minutes before frosting.

Meanwhile make Chocolate Glaze, if desired, by melting chocolate and butter or margarine in a small saucepan or microwave. Remove from heat and stir in corn syrup and water. If too thin, let sit until it thickens slightly. Pour warm glaze over top of cake, allowing it to drip down the sides. If the glaze is too thick, reheat slightly. Let cake sit several hours before serving.

* The cake may be covered and held at room temperature for several days or frozen. Freeze, uncovered, until glaze is solid, then wrap in heavy foil. Defrost, uncovered, at room temperature.

Serves 12.

M E N U

SUNDAY SUPPER ALLA ROMANA

Fresh Fennel, Green Bean and Tomato Salad

Ricotta Cheese Herb Rolls (*Page 147*)

Italian Chicken and Sausage Stir-Fry
or
Turkey Piccata

Spaghetti with Roasted Garlic Sauce

Cappuccino Nut Torte

Espresso Ice Cream

With so many enticing intermingled flavors, Italian Chicken and Sausage Stir-Fry has long been a favorite of mine, and requests for it never seem to stop. Turkey Piccata was created because I always found it difficult to duplicate at home the exquisitely sautéed veal dishes I had in fine Italian restaurants. Switching to thinly sliced breast of turkey solved the problem.

Coordinating a dinner with two stove-top dishes, each requiring last-minute attention, can be a delicate operation. Rather than juggle both dishes at the same time, finish one and let it sit while you attend to the other. I suggest you save both these entrees for less formal occasions where you can cook them at the last minute and prepare the plates in the kitchen.

The crunchy Fresh Fennel, Green Bean and Tomato Salad can be totally prepared ahead. While eating the salad, bring a large pot of salted water to a boil for the Spaghetti with Roasted Garlic Sauce. Plain white or brown rice or Parsley Rice Pilaf (page 106) may be substituted for the pasta.

Cappuccino Nut Torte, crunchy, nutty and spiked with chocolate and coffee, is a lofty ending to an Italian meal. So is the creamy frozen Praline Cassata (page 157).

Fresh Fennel, Green Bean and Tomato Salad, Italian Chicken and Sausage Stir-Fry.

OF FRANCE
DE CECCO
FILIPPO
MUSTARD

Fresh Fennel, Green Bean and Tomato Salad

If you haven't tried fresh fennel yet, by all means do so now with this salad. Its clean taste and crunch add refreshing character to green beans, tomatoes and toasted walnuts. When served warm, this same colorful mélange becomes a marvelous vegetable side dish. *(See photograph, page 74.)*

- 6 tablespoons red wine vinegar
- 1 tablespoon Dijon mustard
- ½ pound green beans, cut into 1½-inch diagonal pieces
- 2 small or 1 large fennel bulb (about 1½ pounds)
- ¾ cup walnut oil
- ¾ cup walnut halves and large pieces
- 3 cloves garlic, minced
- 3 cups seeded and chopped tomatoes, Italian preferred (about 4)
- ⅓ cup chopped fresh basil or 1 tablespoon dried
- 2 heads Boston or butter lettuce, leaves washed and separated
- Salt and pepper to taste

In a small bowl, whisk together vinegar and mustard. Fill a medium saucepan with water, bring to a boil and cook the green beans 1 minute; drain and run under cold water. Cut a thin slice off top and root end of fennel and discard. Slice the bulb into ¼-inch slices and then into 1-inch pieces. You should have about 2 cups.

In a large skillet, heat the walnut oil over moderate heat; sauté walnuts until they begin to brown. Add fennel and garlic; cook, stirring constantly, until fennel begins to soften, 2 to 3 minutes. Remove from heat. Stir in tomatoes, green beans, vinegar-mustard and basil.

* The salad may be held at room temperature for 8 hours or refrigerated overnight. Bring to room temperature before serving.

Serve on lettuce leaves.

Serves 6.

Italian Chicken and Sausage Stir-Fry

This intriguing recipe combines Chinese techniques with Italian ingredients and is one I use frequently. It's easy enough to make for the family, sophisticated enough for company. *(See photograph, page 74.)*

- 4 boneless and skinless chicken breast halves
- ¼ cup soy sauce
- 4 tablespoons olive oil
- 2 medium zucchini, cut into ⅓ × 1½-inch strips (about ¾ pound)
- ½ pound hot Italian sausages
- ¼ pound sweet Italian sausages
- 1 teaspoon cornstarch
- ⅓ cup chicken broth
- ¼ cup dry white wine or imported dry vermouth
- 3 cloves garlic, minced
- 1 jar (7 ounces) roasted sweet red peppers or pimientos, drained and cut into strips
- Several drops hot chili oil or hot-pepper sauce

Cut chicken breasts across into ½-inch slices. Place in a bowl or heavy plastic bag and pour soy sauce over. Marinate at room temperature for 1 to 2 hours.

Meanwhile, in a wok or large skillet, heat olive oil over high heat. Sauté zucchini 3 to 4 minutes or until lightly browned, but still crisp; remove with slotted spoon Cook sausages over moderate heat, turning until they are cooked through and well browned. Remove to a cutting board and discard all but 2 tablespoons of the pan drippings. Cut the sausages into ¼-inch slices and set aside.

* The recipe may be held at room temperature 1 to 2 hours at this point.

Drain the chicken and pat dry. Heat reserved 2 tablespoons sausage drippings; sauté chicken over high heat for 2 to 3 minutes or until browned. Remove pan from heat. Dissolve cornstarch in broth and stir the mixture, the wine or vermouth and garlic into the pan. Return to heat and bring to a boil, stirring constantly. Stir in zucchini, red peppers or pimiento, sausages and chili oil or hot-pepper sauce to taste. Cook, stirring constantly, until chicken is cooked through, 2 to 3 minutes. Serve immediately.

Serves 6.

Turkey Piccata

If it looks like veal and it tastes like veal, then your guests automatically assume it must be veal. Thinly sliced breast of turkey doesn't dry out as easily, it's more economical—and just as delicious.

- 3 cloves garlic, peeled
- ½ cup loosely packed parsley leaves
- 1 tablespoon grated lemon peel
- 3 anchovy fillets
- ½ cup all-purpose flour
- ½ teaspoon salt, or to taste
- ⅛ teaspoon pepper
- 1¼ pounds boneless turkey breast, sliced into 8 very thin slices
- 2 tablespoons butter or margarine
- 3 tablespoons olive oil
- ⅔ cup dry white wine or imported dry vermouth
- ⅔ cup beef broth
- 2 tablespoons lemon juice
- ½ teaspoon cornstarch dissolved in 1 tablespoon water
- 1 lemon, thinly sliced

In a food processor fitted with the metal blade, chop garlic. Add parsley, lemon peel and anchovy and process until finely minced; set aside.

Combine flour, salt and pepper in a shallow dish. Dip both sides of the turkey slices into the flour; pat it with your hands to remove the excess. In a large skillet, heat butter or margarine and 2 tablespoons of the olive oil until sizzling. Sauté half the turkey slices over high heat until lightly browned on each side, about 2 minutes. Remove to a platter, add more oil if needed and repeat with remaining turkey.

Stir the wine, beef broth, lemon juice and reserved parsley mixture into the pan drippings. Bring to a boil, stirring constantly and scraping up all of the brown bits clinging to the bottom of the pan. Remove from heat and stir in the dissolved cornstarch. Return to heat and simmer, stirring constantly, until the sauce thickens.

* The turkey slices and sauce may be held, separately, covered, at room temperature for up to 2 hours.

Stir lemon slices into sauce and simmer for 2 minutes. Return turkey to pan, cook over moderately high heat, basting with sauce until heated through, about 2 minutes. Serve each slice of turkey with a slice of lemon and some sauce.

Serves 8.

Spaghetti with Roasted Garlic Sauce

The aromatic nutty flavor of roasted garlic elevates any savory dish. Creamed into butter, then melted over pasta and sprinkled with parmesan cheese, it reaches its crowning glory.

- 2 large heads garlic (about 4 ounces each), with the largest cloves available, unpeeled
- 2 tablespoons olive or vegetable oil
- 2 large cloves garlic, peeled
- ¼ pound (1 stick) butter or margarine, at room temperature
- ¼ cup heavy cream
- Salt and freshly ground pepper to taste
- ¾ pound spaghetti
- ½ cup grated parmesan cheese
- Grated parmesan cheese for serving

Preheat oven to 350 degrees. Separate unpeeled garlic into cloves and place in a pie dish; drizzle with oil and toss until coated. Bake for 20 to 25 minutes, stirring once or twice, until garlic is lightly browned and feels soft when lightly pressed with fingers. Remove from oven and cool slightly. Peel away the skin or scrape each clove out of the skin.

In a food processor fitted with the metal blade, mince raw garlic. Add butter and roasted garlic; mix until pureed. It will not be smooth.

* Roasted garlic butter may be refrigerated up to 3 days or frozen.

Before serving, heat garlic butter over low heat in a small saucepan. Stir in cream; simmer, stirring, for 2 to 3 minutes. Season with salt and lots of pepper. Meanwhile, cook spaghetti until tender to the bite (al dente). Drain, transfer to a large bowl and toss with roasted garlic butter and parmesan cheese. Serve immediately, passing additional cheese.

Makes 6 side dish servings.

Cappuccino Nut Torte

Graham-cracker crumbs and pecans replace flour in this easy-to-make, cake-like, chocolate-flecked extravaganza.

- 1¾ cups graham-cracker crumbs
- 1½ cups very finely chopped pecans (about 6 ounces)
- 1 package (6 ounces) semisweet chocolate chips (about 1 cup)
- 2 teaspoons baking powder
- 5 egg whites, at room temperature
- 1 tablespoon instant coffee granules
- 1½ cups sugar
- 2 teaspoons vanilla

Chocolate Cappuccino Frosting

- ½ cup heavy cream
- ¾ teaspoon instant coffee granules
- 1 package (6 ounces) semisweet chocolate chips (about 1 cup)

Preheat oven to 350 degrees. Grease and flour a 9-inch springform pan. In a medium bowl, stir together crumbs, pecans, chocolate chips and baking powder; set aside. In a large bowl with an electric mixer, beat egg whites and instant coffee until soft peaks form. Gradually add sugar, beating constantly until the mixture is stiff like marshmallow cream. Mix in vanilla. Fold dry ingredients into whites. Spoon into prepared pan, spreading the top evenly. Bake 40 minutes or until the top is crusty and feels firm to the touch. Remove from oven and run a knife around edge; remove sides of pan, but leave cake on springform bottom. Cool to room temperature.

To make the Chocolate Cappuccino Frosting, in a medium saucepan over moderate heat, bring cream and instant coffee just to a boil. Remove from the heat; whisk in chocolate chips until melted and smooth. Place cake on rack set over a sheet of waxed paper. Spoon hot frosting over top, spreading around the sides. Allow to sit several hours for frosting to set. Serve at room temperature.

* The torte may be held, uncovered, at room temperature overnight or frozen. Freeze, uncovered, until frosting is solid, then cover tightly. Defrost, uncovered, at room temperature.

Serves 8 to 10.

Espresso Ice Cream

Coffee lovers can multiply their after-dinner pleasure with a scoop of mellow, full-bodied espresso ice cream.

3 cups half and half
½ cup freshly ground Italian or French roast coffee
6 egg yolks, at room temperature
⅔ cup sugar

Bring half and half to a simmer in a small saucepan. Remove from heat and stir in espresso. Let the grounds steep for 18 to 20 minutes, stirring occasionally.

Meanwhile, in a small mixing bowl with an electric mixer, beat egg yolks and sugar until light and lemon colored. Strain the half and half through a fine mesh strainer lined with cheesecloth into a heavy deep saucepan. Reheat the half and half until very hot to the touch; mix a small amount into the egg yolks. Return to saucepan and cook over moderate heat, stirring constantly until mixture is thick enough to leave a path on a wooden spoon when you run a finger along it. Do not boil. Transfer to a bowl, cover and refrigerate until well chilled.

* The custard may be refrigerated, well covered, for up to 2 days, if desired.

Pour cold coffee mixture into ice-cream maker and freeze according to manufacturer's directions. Serve immediately or transfer to a bowl, cover and freeze.

Makes 1 quart.

MENU

CELEBRATION CHICKEN BREASTS SUPREME

Mushroom and Goat Cheese Tartlets

Chicken Breasts in Triple Mustard Sauce

White and Wild Rice Pilaf

Wine-Glazed Cherry Tomatoes

Black Satin Fudge Cake with White Chocolate Custard Sauce

Take out your most lavish table setting and prepare for a shimmering candlelit evening. Gather up all the candle holders you've got. Place the tallest in the center of the table and arrange the shorter ones on each side, tapering down the length of the table. Fill each with the same color candle. If you refrigerate the candles several hours before lighting, they'll burn slower and drip less. Drape fern, shiny leaves or holly around the base of the candlesticks and tuck in tiny bouquets of fresh blossoms.

Sometimes I enjoy serving Mushroom and Goat Cheese Tartlets with drinks in the living room, eliminating the need for a first course at the table. Cold Artichokes with Shrimp Salad (page 90) or Mixed Greens with Fried Goat Cheese (page 111) may be served instead, if desired. Before your guests arrive, quickly sauté the chicken breasts, being careful not to cook them all the way through. Prior to serving, complete the sauce and reheat the chicken in it. If you don't have an extra pair of hands in the kitchen, you may want to substitute oven-baked Minted Peas in Tomato Cups (page 91) for the Wine-Glazed Cherry Tomatoes. Suggested occasions for serving this menu are:

◇ Anniversary or Engagement Party
◇ New Year's Eve
◇ Business Entertaining

Mushroom and Goat Cheese Tartlets

You would expect to be served this elegant first course at a most distinguished restaurant, yet it's surprisingly easy to prepare at home. The marvelous variety of mushrooms now available gives them an intriguing woodsy flavor. Serve warm, rather than piping hot, so the goat cheese barely melts.

Flaky Pastry

- 12 tablespoons (1½ sticks) butter or margarine, cold and cut into 12 pieces
- 5 ounces cream cheese, cold and cut into 5 pieces
- 1½ cups all-purpose flour
- ¼ teaspoon salt, or to taste

Mushroom Filling

- 1 ounce dried mushrooms, shiitake, porcini or cèpes
- Boiling water
- 4 tablespoons (½ stick) butter or margarine
- 4 tablespoons olive oil
- 2 cloves garlic, minced
- ¼ pound fresh oyster mushrooms, coarsely chopped
- ¼ pound fresh shiitake mushrooms, coarsely chopped
- ½ pound fresh button mushrooms, coarsely chopped
- Salt and pepper to taste
- 2 tablespoons chopped fresh tarragon or 2 teaspoons dried tarragon
- 2 ounces goat cheese, such as montrachet, cold and cut into ½-inch pieces
- 8 sprigs fresh tarragon for garnish, optional

To make the Flaky Pastry, in a food processor fitted with the metal blade or in a mixing bowl with an electric mixer, mix the butter or margarine and cream cheese until blended. Add flour and salt and mix until crumbly. Remove to a sheet of plastic wrap and shape into a flat disk. The dough may be refrigerated up to 2 days, if desired.

Divide the pastry into 8 equal portions. Press each evenly into the bottom and up the sides of eight 4-inch tart pans with removable bottoms. Prick the bottoms with a fork and refrigerate for at least 30 minutes.

Place oven rack on bottom rung and preheat the oven to 350 degrees. Place tart pans on a baking sheet and bake for 20 to 25 minutes or until lightly golden. Remove from oven and cool completely.

∗ The shells may be covered and held at room temperature overnight or frozen. Defrost at room temperature.

To make the Mushroom Filling, soak dried mushrooms in boiling water to cover for 30 minutes, stirring once. Drain, squeeze dry, cut off stems and coarsely chop mushrooms. In a large skillet over moderately low heat, melt butter or margarine and oil; sauté dried mushrooms for 6 to 8 minutes, stirring often. Add garlic and fresh mushrooms and sauté over moderately high heat, stirring often, until tender, about 5 to 8 more minutes. Stir in tarragon. Remove from heat and cool slightly. Gently stir in goat cheese; do not let it melt. Spoon the filling into tart shells.

∗ The tarts may be held, covered, at room temperature several hours or refrigerated overnight. Before baking, bring to room temperature.

Before serving, preheat oven to 350 degrees. Bake tarts, uncovered, for 5 to 7 minutes or until warm. Garnish the center of each with a sprig of fresh tarragon, if desired.

Serves 8.

Chicken Breasts in Triple Mustard Sauce

This is an easy two-step stovetop dish. First the chicken is poached in wine and seasonings. Then cream is added and the liquid is reduced to a luxuriant, coat-the-spoon sauce.

4 large whole chicken breasts, boned, skinned and split (about 4 pounds net weight)
Salt and pepper
Paprika
1 tablespoon butter or margarine
2 tablespoons vegetable oil, divided
1 tablespoon whole-grain mustard
1 tablespoon Dijon mustard
1 teaspoon dry mustard
½ cup imported dry vermouth or dry white wine
1 cup heavy cream, at room temperature
Salt and white pepper to taste

Sprinkle the top of each chicken breast with salt, pepper and paprika; rub into meat. In a large skillet, heat butter or margarine and 1 tablespoon of the oil over moderately high heat. Cook half the chicken breasts top side down until golden brown, about 4 minutes. Using tongs, turn and cook until springy to the touch and well browned, 4 to 5 more minutes. Remove to a platter, cover loosely with foil and if serving immediately, put in a very slow oven (200 degrees). Repeat with remaining breasts, adding 1 tablespoon oil; reserve pan juices.

In a small bowl, stir the 3 mustards together. Stir vermouth or wine into the drippings in the skillet. Bring to a boil over moderately high heat, scraping up any brown bits sticking to the bottom of the pan. Stir in the mustards. When incorporated, whisk in the cream.

* The chicken and sauce may be prepared 1 hour ahead and kept covered, separately, at room temperature, if desired.

Bring the sauce to a boil, whisking often until it is thick enough to coat a spoon, about 3 minutes. If it reduces too much, thin with a little cream or wine. Season to taste with salt, pepper and additional mustard, if desired. Return chicken to sauce and cook, turning, until heated through. Spoon some sauce over each piece when serving.

Serves 8.

White and Wild Rice Pilaf

Because wild rice takes longer to cook, start it first and then add the white rice and seasonings to the same saucepan. This is so easy and much tastier than anything you can buy packaged.

6 ounces wild rice (about 1 cup)
4 cups chicken broth
4 tablespoons (½ stick) butter or margarine
2 medium onions, finely chopped (about 1½ cups)
1½ cups long-grain white rice
3 tablespoons soy sauce
¾ cup coarsely chopped canned water chestnuts
¾ cup chopped parsley

In a deep saucepan, bring wild rice and chicken broth to a boil. Cover, reduce heat to moderately low, and simmer for 35 minutes. Meanwhile, in a medium skillet melt butter or margarine; sauté onions until soft. Stir onions, white rice, soy sauce and water chestnuts into wild rice and broth. Cover and cook over moderately low heat until all the liquid is absorbed, 15 to 20 minutes. Remove from heat and let sit, covered, for 5 minutes. Stir in parsley.

* The pilaf may be refrigerated for up to 2 days. Reheat, covered, in a glass dish in the microwave or at 350 degrees, stirring occasionally until hot, about 15 minutes.

Serves 8.

Wine-Glazed Cherry Tomatoes

Use this glistening dish wherever color and interest are needed to perk up a menu. Be sure your tomatoes are at room temperature and cook them very briefly so they retain their shape.

6 tablespoons butter or margarine
2 tablespoons sugar
1 teaspoon seasoned salt
¼ teaspoon pepper
2 tablespoons chopped fresh basil or 2 teaspoons dried basil
½ cup dry red wine
1½ pounds cherry tomatoes, stemmed and at room temperature

In a medium skillet, melt butter or margarine. Stir in sugar, salt, pepper, basil and wine. Bring to a boil over high heat, reduce heat and cook, uncovered, until reduced by half, about 5 minutes. Just before serving, stir in tomatoes and cook over high heat, tossing and turning until they are well glazed and heated through, about 2 minutes. Serve immediately, spooning over any remaining glaze.

Serves 8.

Black Satin Fudge Cake with White Chocolate Custard Sauce

Tantalizing combinations of warm and cool, black and white, fudgy and creamy are a chocolate fan's fantasy.

1 recipe White Chocolate Custard Sauce (page 83)

Fudge Cake
½ pound (2 sticks) butter or margarine
6 ounces unsweetened chocolate
6 ounces semisweet chocolate
5 eggs, at room temperature
1 cup sugar, divided
⅓ cup light corn syrup

Make White Chocolate Custard Sauce as recipe directs. Refrigerate until ready to use.

Preheat oven to 350 degrees. To make the Fudge Cake, butter a 9- or 9½-inch springform pan. Cut a circle of waxed paper or parchment to fit the bottom; butter the paper. Wrap outside of pan in foil to keep the batter from seeping out as the cake bakes.

In a medium saucepan over low heat or in a microwave oven, melt butter or margarine with all the chocolate, stirring until melted; set aside to cool slightly.

In a large mixing bowl with an electric mixer, beat eggs with ½ cup sugar on high speed until light and fluffy, about 5 minutes. Meanwhile, in a small saucepan, stir together corn syrup and remaining ½ cup sugar. Bring to a boil over moderate heat; transfer to a heatproof glass measuring cup. Slowly pour hot sugar syrup in a thin, steady stream into the eggs, beating with the mixer on medium speed. On low speed, mix in chocolate until incorporated. Pour into prepared pan.

Place the springform in a shallow roasting pan; place in oven and pour in about 1 inch of hot water. Bake for 45 minutes or until a toothpick inserted in the center comes out clean. Do not overbake, as the cake will firm up as it cools. Remove from water and cool on rack for 30 minutes. If serving immediately, invert onto serving plate. If not, invert onto a sheet of heavy foil.

* The cake may be held, covered, at room temperature up to 2 days or frozen. Before serving, reheat at 350 degrees for 10 minutes or until warm. Using spatulas, transfer to serving plate.

To serve, spoon a small amount of sauce onto center of each dessert plate, rotating the plate so sauce covers the bottom. Place a slice of warm cake in the center. Pass remaining sauce.

Serves 10 to 12.

White Chocolate Custard Sauce

White chocolate does more than flavor this rich sauce—it adds silky smoothness.

- 7 egg yolks, at room temperature
- 2 tablespoons sugar
- 1 teaspoon cornstarch
- 2¼ cups milk
- 6 ounces white chocolate, preferably Tobler Narcisse, finely chopped
- 2 tablespoons light Crème de Cacao

In a large bowl with an electric mixer on medium speed, beat egg yolks and sugar until very thick and light colored, about 3 minutes. Mix in cornstarch.

Meanwhile, in a heavy deep saucepan, heat milk until small bubbles appear around the sides. Remove from heat and stir in chocolate until smooth. Gradually stir about 1½ cups of the milk-chocolate mixture into yolks to warm them, then pour the yolk mixture into the chocolate. Cook over medium-low heat, stirring constantly with a wooden spoon, until the custard thickens slightly. It is done when you can run your finger down the back of the spoon and a path remains in the custard for several seconds. Do not let it boil.

Remove from the heat and immediately pour through a strainer into a metal bowl to cool quickly. Stir occasionally until cool. Stir in Crème de Cacao. Cover and refrigerate until ready to use.

* The sauce may be refrigerated for up to 2 days.

Makes 2½ cups sauce.

MENU

CRACKLING DUCK BY THE FIRESIDE

Red Cabbage Salad with Bacon and Goat Cheese

Crisp Roasted Duck

Black Cherry, Orange Chutney or
Apple Ginger Sauce

Sweet Potatoes Anna

Lemon Mousse Cheesecake

For many years I tried unsuccessfully to cook duck at home. My mouth watered in anticipation of crisp, deeply browned skin and tender, juicy meat. I baked, broiled, boiled and steamed. I even combined the methods, but to no avail. Whenever I got the craving for duck, I headed for a restaurant.

But this die-hard duck lover didn't give up. Finally I hit on a foolproof formula: refrigerate the duck (uncovered) for one or two days to dry out the skin, then bake it in a very hot oven (500 degrees) for about 55 to 60 minutes, removing the fat as it accumulates. Once the duck is cool, quarter it and refrigerate the pieces overnight. Reheat before serving.

It's fun to serve duck with a variety of fruit sauces. Warm them, each in its own serving dish, in the microwave. Red cabbage, duck's longtime partner, is offered here in a lively new guise. Lightly warmed in a glistening vinaigrette with bacon and goat cheese, it makes a positively smashing salad. Sweet Potatoes Anna is a lovely dish, with golden slices of yam arranged in a spiraled petal design. Baked with butter and cheese, they have a pure, sweet taste. Suggested occasions for serving this menu are:

◇ Business Entertaining
◇ New Year's Eve Dinner
◇ Welcome Home

Red Cabbage Salad with Bacon and Goat Cheese

Once while vacationing, I had a dish so memorable I couldn't wait to get home to recreate it. The crimson of cabbage, crunch of bacon and tang of goat cheese join forces in an exceptional salad. It's great as a first course or for lunch.

1 small head red cabbage (about 1 pound)
1 pound sliced bacon, diced
5½ ounces goat cheese, such as montrachet, crumbled

Dressing
¼ cup reserved bacon drippings
½ cup vegetable oil
2 cloves garlic, minced
¼ teaspoon pepper
¼ cup red wine vinegar

Remove core from cabbage. Shred cabbage with thin or medium slicing blade of food processor or a sharp knife; place in a large bowl. Fry bacon until crisp, drain and add to cabbage. Reserve ¼ cup drippings for the dressing. Add goat cheese to cabbage and toss well.

To make the dressing, whisk together bacon drippings, oil, garlic, pepper and vinegar in a small saucepan.

∗ Both the salad and dressing may be refrigerated overnight. Bring salad to room temperature 1 hour before serving.

In a small saucepan, heat dressing until hot. Pour over as much dressing as needed to coat the cabbage, toss well and serve immediately.

Serves 6.

Crisp Roasted Duck

Roasting duck in a very hot oven is the best method I've found for producing succulent meat, a minimum of fat and very crisp skin. Buy the duck several days ahead to allow time for the skin to dry out before roasting. Serve with one or more of the fruity sauces.

2 ducks (4 to 6 pounds each)
Black Cherry, Orange Chutney or Apple Ginger Sauce (page 84)

If the ducks are frozen, defrost at room temperature. Place in shallow roasting pan and refrigerate, uncovered, for 1 to 2 days to dry out the skin. Bring to room temperature at least 2 hours before roasting. Preheat oven to 500 degrees. Remove giblets and pull out any fat from cavities. Prick skin with a skewer or fork at ½-inch intervals all over the breast and legs. Choose a roasting pan about 1½ to 2 inches deep which will hold the ducks without crowding them; line it with 2 layers of heavy foil.

Place ducks breast side down on rack in pan. Roast a 4- to 5-pound duck for 25 minutes, a 5- to 6-pound duck for 30 minutes. Remove fat from pan. Turn breast side up and continue roasting for 30 more minutes, removing fat every 10 to 15 minutes. The skin should be very crisp and deep golden brown.

Remove ducks to a carving board and let rest at room temperature for at least 30 minutes. Cut the ducks in quarters with kitchen shears by first cutting along the breast bone. Then cut along each side of the back bone, removing about a ¾-inch strip of bones. Cut each half in half again. If desired, pull or cut away some of the smaller bones.

* The ducks may be held at room temperature for several hours or refrigerated, loosely covered, overnight. Bring to room temperature. Reheat on rimmed baking sheets, uncovered, at 425 degrees for 15 minutes or until sizzling and the skin is recrisped.

Serve with desired sauce or a selection of sauces.

Serves 6 to 8.

Sweet Potatoes Anna

I had some reservations about making this dish a day ahead, so to be on the safe side, I made another one just before dinner. When I turned them out, I forgot which was which and never could tell them apart!

3 pounds sweet potatoes or yams (about 3 medium)
¼ pound (1 stick) butter or margarine, melted, divided
⅓ cup grated parmesan cheese, divided
Salt and pepper to taste

Place rack on bottom rung of oven. Preheat oven to 425 degrees. Using a food processor with a thin slicing blade or a sharp knife, slice yams into slices ⅛ inch thick. Line the bottom of a 9-inch cake pan with a circle of aluminum foil. Pour in 1 tablespoon butter or margarine and swirl to coat the bottom of the pan. Arrange a layer of yam slices closely overlapping in a spiral pattern, covering the bottom of the pan. Drizzle the potatoes with 1 tablespoon butter or margarine, 1 tablespoon parmesan cheese, and salt and pepper. Repeat layers of potatoes, butter or margarine, parmesan cheese, salt and pepper until all potatoes are used. Drizzle top with any remaining butter or margarine. Cover pan with foil and press down firmly on potatoes with your hands to compress them.

Bake, covered, on bottom rack for 30 minutes; uncover and bake 30 to 35 more minutes or until potatoes are brown and crisp on top and around the edges.

* When cool, the potatoes may be refrigerated, covered, overnight. Bring to room temperature and reheat, uncovered, at 425 degrees for 10 minutes or until sizzling around the sides.

Remove from oven and let stand 5 minutes. Go around sides of the pan with a sharp knife, place a serving plate over the top and invert. Cut into wedges to serve.

Serves 6.

Black Cherry Sauce

½ bag (1 pound) frozen dark sweet cherries (1¼ cups)
¼ cup plus 2 tablespoons gin, divided
1 jar (12 ounces) cherry preserves
½ cup beef broth
½ cup dry red wine
1 tablespoon plus 2 teaspoons cornstarch

Place cherries in a medium bowl; pour over ¼ cup gin, cover and marinate at room temperature several hours or overnight. Drain cherries, reserve liquid in a deep saucepan. Stir cherry preserves and beef broth into the liquid. Bring to a boil and cook over moderately high heat until the liquid is reduced by about half, 10 to 15 minutes. Stir in wine and remove pan from heat. Dissolve cornstarch in remaining 2 tablespoons gin. Stir into sauce, return to heat and cook, stirring constantly, until sauce comes to a boil and thickens slightly. Stir in reserved cherries.

∗ The sauce may be refrigerated up to 2 days.

Serve warm or at room temperature over duck.

Makes 2½ cups.

Orange Chutney Sauce

1 jar (about 8 ounces) peach or mango chutney
¼ cup orange juice
1 tablespoon honey

In a small saucepan over moderately low heat, stir all the ingredients together until heated through. The sauce may be served warm or at room temperature.

Makes about 1 cup sauce.

Apple Ginger Sauce

1½ cups frozen apple juice concentrate, thawed but not diluted
¾ cup dry white wine or imported dry vermouth
1½ cups beef broth
2 small tart green apples, peeled, halved, cored and cut into ¼-inch slices
¼ cup finely chopped crystallized ginger
1 tablespoon plus 1 teaspoon cornstarch
3 tablespoons calvados or brandy

In a deep saucepan, combine apple juice, wine or vermouth and broth. Boil over moderately high heat until reduced by half, about 15 minutes. Add apple slices and ginger and cook until apples are tender, 4 to 6 minutes. Remove pan from heat. Dissolve cornstarch in brandy; stir into sauce. Return to heat and cook, stirring until thickened.

∗ The sauce may be refrigerated overnight.

Serve warm or at room temperature over duck.

Makes 2½ cups.

Lemon Mousse Cheesecake

Neither a true mousse nor a true cheesecake, this is an ultra-lemony, feather-light combination of both. Prepare to make this a classic in your repertoire.

Crust

- 43 vanilla wafers (about 6 ounces, 1¼ cups crumbs)
- ¼ cup sugar
- 4 tablespoons (½ stick) butter or margarine, melted

Lemon Filling

- 3 packages (8 ounces each) cream cheese, at room temperature
- 1½ cups sugar, divided
- ⅓ cup all-purpose flour
- 6 egg yolks
- ¾ cup fresh lemon juice (about 4 lemons)
- 4 egg whites, at room temperature
- 1 tablespoon grated lemon peel
- Confectioners sugar for sprinkling on top

Butter a 9 × 3- or 10½ × 2-inch springform pan and wrap the outside in foil. Preheat oven to 325 degrees. To make the Crust, crush wafers in a food processor fitted with the metal blade. Pulse in sugar and butter or margarine and press in bottom of pan.

To make the Lemon Filling, in a large mixing bowl with an electric mixer, beat cream cheese until fluffy. Gradually add 1¼ cups sugar, mixing until light and fluffy. Mix in flour and egg yolks; beat for 1 minute. With mixer at low speed, slowly mix in lemon juice.

In a separate mixing bowl with clean beaters, beat egg whites until foamy; gradually add remaining ¼ cup sugar, beating until stiff peaks form. Fold whites and lemon peel into the lemon mixture. Pour over crust, smoothing the top. Place cake pan in a shallow roasting pan and place in oven. Pour about 1 inch of hot water into roasting pan. Bake for 55 to 65 minutes or until the top of the cake is well puffed and golden. Remove to a rack and cool to room temperature; the cake will sink as it cools. Cover with plastic wrap and freeze overnight before serving.

* The cake may be frozen for up to 2 months.

Cut with a sharp knife while frozen, dipping it into a glass of hot water and wiping it clean before cutting each slice. Defrost overnight in the refrigerator. Before serving, remove sides of springform pan. Sift confectioners sugar over the top.

Serves 10 to 12.

MARVELOUS MEATS

PARTY WRAPPED FILLETS IN PHYLLO

PIQUANT PORK FOR WINTER WARMTH

IMPERIAL STROGANOFF CHINOISE

Clockwise from top right: Phyllo-Wrapped Fillets of Beef, Minted Peas in Tomato Cups, Chocolate Strawberry Carousel, Cold Artichokes with Shrimp Salad, Brioche Rolls.

MENU

PARTY WRAPPED FILLETS IN PHYLLO

Cold Artichokes with Shrimp Salad

Brioche Rolls (*Page 148*)

Phyllo-Wrapped Fillets of Beef

Minted Peas in Tomato Cups

Chocolate Strawberry Carousel

Phyllo-Wrapped Fillets of Beef are a magnificent entree for a birthday, anniversary party or special occasion for any number of people, and they are easy to make. You can find frozen phyllo in most supermarkets. If possible, though, buy it fresh from an Italian or Middle Eastern market; it is much easier to handle. The fillets can be frozen already wrapped and ready for the oven and the Minted Peas in Tomato Cups refrigerated a day ahead, leaving minimal last-minute work. Cold Artichokes with Shrimp Salad are stunning, but Green and Orange Salad (page 117) or Butter Lettuce Soup (page 63) are also excellent choices for a first course.

Chocolate Strawberry Carousel is a showstopper dessert, whether served undecorated or with your own message written across the top in chocolate. Suggested occasions for serving this menu are:

◇ Wedding Rehearsal or Wedding Dinner
◇ Birthday or Anniversary
◇ Valentine's Day Dinner
◇ Business Entertaining

Cold Artichokes with Shrimp Salad

Cooked chilled artichokes are opened out to hold a creamy shrimp salad. The salad is also excellent served as a first course over ice or on lettuce leaves. (See photograph, page 89.)

8 artichokes
½ lemon
2 tablespoons olive oil
1 teaspoon lemon juice
½ teaspoon salt, or to taste
Lemon wedges for garnish

Shrimp Salad

1½ cups sour cream
3 tablespoons white wine vinegar
1 tablespoon prepared horseradish
1 teaspoon Dijon mustard
½ cup chopped peeled and seeded cucumber
¼ cup finely chopped green onions with tops
1 heaping tablespoon chopped fresh dill or 1 teaspoon dried dill
¾ pound cooked medium shrimp, cut in half
Salt to taste

Slice 1 inch off the top of each artichoke. Cut off stems to make a flat base; pull off tough or discolored leaves from around the base. With kitchen scissors, snip off the thorny tips of each leaf. Rub the base and all cut surfaces with lemon to prevent discoloring.

Pour 2 inches of water into a wide nonaluminum saucepan or roaster that will hold the artichokes comfortably in one layer. Add oil, lemon juice and salt. Bring to a boil, add the artichokes, cover and cook over moderate heat for 35 to 50 minutes or until their bases are easily pierced with the tip of a sharp knife. Remove from water and drain upside down on paper towels. Cover and refrigerate several hours or overnight.

Gently spread open the top leaves of each artichoke and with a spoon, remove and discard the fuzzy choke from its center. Return to refrigerator until ready to serve.

To make the Shrimp Salad, stir the sour cream, vinegar, horseradish and mustard together in a medium bowl. Stir in cucumbers, green onion, dill and shrimp. Season to taste. Cover and chill several hours or overnight for flavors to blend.

Before serving, place each artichoke on a plate and with your fingers, gently spread open the leaves. Fill the center with Shrimp Salad. Garnish with lemon wedges.

Serves 8.

Minted Peas in Tomato Cups

Here's a beautiful vegetable dish with no last-minute work. (See photograph, page 89.)

8 small to medium tomatoes
1 bag (1 pound) frozen petite peas, defrosted
3 tablespoons fresh chopped mint
¼ teaspoon salt, or to taste
Pepper to taste
3 tablespoons butter or margarine, melted

Slice ¼ inch off the top of each tomato. With a small paring knife or grapefruit knife, scoop out insides, leaving a shell. Invert on paper towels to drain.

In a medium bowl, stir together peas, mint, salt, pepper and butter or margarine; do not be concerned that the butter coagulates. Spoon approximately 3 tablespoons of the peas into each tomato shell. Place in a shallow baking dish.

* The tomatoes may be covered with foil and refrigerated overnight. Bring to room temperature before baking.

Preheat oven to 375 degrees. Bake, covered, for 15 minutes or until heated through.

Serves 8.

Phyllo-Wrapped Fillets of Beef

These crisp, golden phyllo packages will pique your guests' curiosity. Inside are juicy, pink steaks smothered with three kinds of onions, mushrooms and green peppercorns. *(See photograph, page 89.)*

Leek and Green Peppercorn Stuffing (See below)
8 filet mignon steaks, 1½ inches thick (6 to 7 ounces each)
Salt and pepper
2 tablespoons butter or margarine
2 tablespoons vegetable oil
1 pound phyllo, approximately 12 × 16 inches, defrosted if frozen (about 16 sheets)
½ pound (2 sticks) butter or margarine, melted

Leek and Green Peppercorn Stuffing

2 pounds leeks (about 4)
1 large yellow onion, peeled and cut into eighths
1 bunch (about 8) green onions with tops, chopped into 1-inch pieces
4 tablespoons (½ stick) butter or margarine
1 pound fresh mushrooms, quartered
4 teaspoons green peppercorns packed in brine or dried green peppercorns soaked in hot water for 5 minutes, drained and lightly crushed
Salt to taste

To make the Leek and Green Peppercorn Stuffing, cut green off leeks and discard. Cut a small slice off root end, then cut leeks in half lengthwise; wash each leaf. Cut into 1-inch pieces and place in a food processor fitted with the metal blade. Add yellow and green onions; pulse until chopped. In a large skillet, melt 4 tablespoons butter or margarine; sauté leek-onion mixture until soft, stirring occasionally. Coarsely chop mushrooms in food processor and add to skillet. Cook over moderate heat, stirring frequently, until all the liquid is absorbed, about 10 minutes. The onions and mushrooms should be soft; set aside to cool. Stir in green peppercorns and salt to taste.

Sprinkle steaks lightly with salt and pepper. Melt 2 tablespoons butter or margarine with oil in a large skillet. Quickly brown steaks over high heat for 1½ minutes on each side.

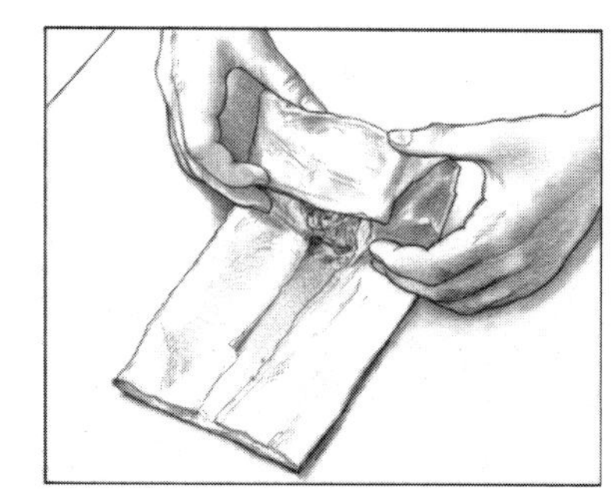

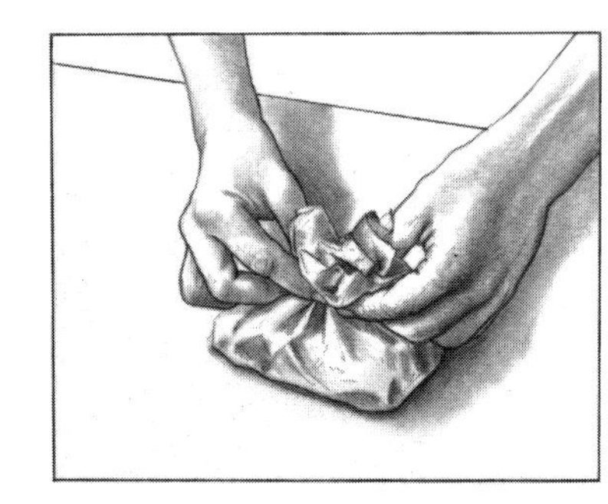

Place 1 sheet of phyllo on a work surface; keep remaining phyllo covered with a sheet of waxed paper and a damp towel. Brush the sheet lightly with melted butter or margarine and fold it in half. Turn the phyllo so that a narrow end faces you. Place a steak about 3 inches from the end. Spread top of meat with about 2 tablespoons stuffing. Fold the narrow end over, fold in the sides and then roll up. Remove a second sheet of phyllo and cut it into a 12-inch square; butter lightly. Place wrapped steak, stuffing side up, in the center. Bring ends to the middle, gently squeeze them together and then pull them up and out to resemble a money bag. Brush top and sides lightly with butter. Repeat with remaining steaks.

* The wrapped steaks may be refrigerated overnight. They may be frozen up to 2 weeks. Defrost, uncovered, in refrigerator overnight. Bring to room temperature 2 hours before baking.

Before serving, preheat the oven to 400 degrees. Place steaks at least 2 inches apart on buttered rimmed baking sheets. Bake 15 minutes for rare, 17 minutes for medium rare and 20 minutes for medium. If baking 2 sheets in 1 oven, rotate their positions half way through the baking time.

Serves 8.

Chocolate Strawberry Carousel

The crust here is a big chocolate cookie baked right onto the bottom of the pan. Strawberry halves encircle the sides and whole berries dot the bottom. A rich, velvety chocolate mousse covers all. This is an absolutely spectacular dessert, with or without a chocolate message on top. (See photograph, page 89.)

Crust

- 1/3 cup chopped pecans
- 1/2 cup sugar
- 2 tablespoons unsweetened cocoa
- 2 tablespoons all-purpose flour
- 2 egg whites, unbeaten
- 1/2 teaspoon vanilla
- 1/4 cup seedless strawberry jam

Filling

- 1 pound semisweet chocolate, chopped
- 2 eggs, at room temperature
- 4 egg yolks, at room temperature
- 1/4 cup Chambord liqueur or Crème de Cacao
- 6 egg whites, at room temperature
- 1/4 cup confectioners sugar
- 1 cup heavy cream
- 2 pints fresh strawberries

To make the Crust, preheat oven to 425 degrees. Place rack in center of oven. Remove sides of 9-inch springform pan and generously butter the bottom. In a food processor fitted with the metal blade, finely grind the pecans and sugar. Transfer to a bowl and stir in the cocoa and flour. With a wooden spoon, stir in egg whites and vanilla; the batter will be very runny. Using the back of a spoon or spatula, spread the batter to cover bottom of springform. Place on a baking sheet and bake for 12 to 13 minutes or until the edges look crisp and pull away from rim of the pan. Remove from oven and if necessary, trim the crust even with pan edge, using a sharp knife. Cool completely. Spread with jam and reattach sides of springform.

To make the Filling, melt chocolate in top of double boiler over hot water or in bowl in microwave. Remove from heat and cool 10 minutes. With wooden spoon, stir in whole eggs, one at a time; the mixture

(continued)

will be stiff. Stir in egg yolks and liqueur. In a large mixing bowl with an electric mixer, beat egg whites until soft peaks form. Beat in confectioners sugar 1 tablespoon at a time, mixing until stiff peaks form. In a separate bowl, whip cream until soft peaks form; do not beat stiff. Fold chocolate into the cream until blended. Fold into whites.

To assemble the carousel, cut a small slice off stem end of each berry; slice 10 to 12 of them in half through the stem end. Place these around the edges of the crust, pointed side up, cut sides against the sides of the pan. Arrange remaining whole berries over bottom of crust, about ½ inch apart. Pour chocolate mixture over the berries. Smooth top and if desired, make design with tines of a fork or cake-decorating comb. Refrigerate several hours.

* The carousel may be refrigerated overnight.

Before serving, remove sides of springform.

Serves 10 to 12.

To write a message in chocolate on a cake:
Write your message in pencil first on a sheet of waxed paper, making sure it will fit the cake. Set the paper on a baking sheet or tray that fits into your freezer. Melt 4 to 6 ounces chocolate chips in a microwave or in the top of a double boiler. Fit a pastry bag with a #1 or #2 writing tip and fill with the melted chocolate. Trace over your pencil writing with even strokes. Freeze 5 minutes or until firm. Remove from the freezer and pipe a second layer of chocolate directly on top of the first. Freeze until firm or keep covered in the freezer indefinitely. Several hours before serving, carefully peel waxed paper back from the writing, handling the chocolate as little as possible. Position on cake and refrigerate until serving.

MENU

PIQUANT PORK FOR WINTER WARMTH

Carrot-Ginger Soup

Peanutty Roast Loin of Pork

Stir-Fry Broccoli

Creamy Potato Gratin

Cranberry-Pear Cobbler

Pork is increasing in popularity because it has a lower fat content and it cooks quicker than it used to. Peanutty Roast Loin of Pork becomes exceptionally tasty and tender after sitting for 24 hours in a soy-pineapple marinade. When you stir peanut butter and red-pepper flakes into the marinade, it becomes a thick, pungent sauce.

Start the meal off with either Carrot-Ginger Soup or Sesame Spinach Salad (page 98), then add a side dish of Creamy Potato Gratin. Its silken creaminess beautifully offsets the pork's spiciness. Stir-Fry Broccoli provides fresh color and crunch. Put the garlic into the cold oil. While the pork and potatoes are baking, it can sit for hours, waiting for you to turn it on.

If you have some time a couple of hours before serving, make the Cranberry Pear Cobbler. You should keep in mind, however, that the pears must be peeled and sliced and the pastry rolled right before the dessert is put in the oven. If necessary, it can be made earlier and reheated at 375 degrees for 7 to 10 minutes. Ginger Spice Layer Cake with Applesauce Cream (page 101) is a great make-ahead alternative. Suggested occasions for serving this menu are:
◇ Business Meeting
◇ Après Ski
◇ New Cook's First Dinner
◇ Academy Awards Supper

Carrot-Ginger Soup

With their lovely orange color and ready availability, carrots are a natural for making into bright, sunny soups. Their sweetness is highlighted by the spiciness of ginger.

- 4 tablespoons (½ stick) butter or margarine
- 1 medium onion, chopped (about 1 cup)
- 2 tablespoons finely minced fresh ginger
- 6 cups chicken broth
- 8 large carrots, peeled and finely chopped (about 2 pounds)
- Salt to taste
- ¼ teaspoon white pepper
- ¼ teaspoon ground nutmeg
- ½ teaspoon sugar
- ½ cup sour cream
- Sour cream for garnish
- ¼ cup chopped chives or green onion tops for garnish

In a medium soup pot, melt butter or margarine; sauté onion and ginger over moderate heat until soft. Stir in chicken broth and carrots. Cover and cook over moderately low heat until the vegetables are very soft, about 1 hour. Cool slightly and puree in batches in a blender or food processor fitted with the metal blade.

* The soup may be refrigerated up to 2 days or frozen.

Before serving, bring the soup to a simmer; season to taste with salt, pepper, nutmeg and sugar. Stir in sour cream; heat gently but do not allow to boil. Ladle into soup bowls, garnishing each with a dollop of sour cream and a sprinkling of chives or green onions.

Serves 6.

Peanutty Roast Loin of Pork

The U.S. Department of Agriculture now recommends cooking pork to an internal temperature of 160 degrees (rather than the old standard of 170 degrees) for optimum flavor, tenderness and juiciness. For a juicy, succulent roast, follow these new guidelines. Use a meat thermometer to be on the safe side.

- 1 boneless pork loin roast, about 3 pounds
- ¼ cup lemon juice
- 3 tablespoons soy sauce
- 6 cloves garlic, minced
- 1 teaspoon sugar
- 3 tablespoons pineapple juice
- Scant ½ teaspoon dried red-pepper flakes
- 3 tablespoons creamy peanut butter
- 1 tablespoon hot water, if needed

Place roast in a nonaluminum baking dish into which it fits snugly. In a small bowl, stir together lemon juice, soy sauce, garlic, sugar and pineapple juice; pour over pork. Cover with plastic wrap and marinate in the refrigerator overnight, turning once.

Remove from refrigerator and let stand at room temperature for about 1 hour. Preheat oven to 375 degrees. Pour marinade into a small saucepan and set aside. Dry the roast with paper towels and place in a shallow roasting pan. Bake for 1 hour 15 minutes to 1 hour 30 minutes or until a meat thermometer registers 155 degrees. Remove from oven and let rest 15 minutes. The internal temperature will rise about 5 degrees to 160 degrees.

Meanwhile, stir red-pepper flakes into the marinade; bring to a boil. Remove from heat and whisk in peanut butter until smooth. The sauce will thicken as it cools. If it becomes too thick, stir in 1 tablespoon hot water before serving. Carve meat into thin slices and serve with sauce.

Serves 6.

Stir-Fry Broccoli

Peeled and thinly sliced broccoli stalks cook right along with the florets and become just as tender and tasty.

2 pounds fresh broccoli
3 tablespoons vegetable oil
2 cloves garlic, minced
Salt and pepper to taste

Cut florets from broccoli. Peel the stalks with a vegetable peeler; slice them into ¼-inch pieces. Bring a large saucepan of water to a boil. Blanch florets and stems until the color brightens and they are slightly tender, about 2 minutes. Drain and rinse with cold water to stop the cooking. Dry with paper towels.

∗ The broccoli may be refrigerated overnight.

Before serving, heat oil in a large skillet or wok over moderately high heat. Sauté garlic until soft, about 1 minute. Add broccoli and sauté, stirring and tossing, until heated through and crisp-tender, about 2 minutes. Season to taste with salt and pepper.

Serves 6.

Creamy Potato Gratin

Sliced potatoes drenched with cream and cheese bake until they absorb every drop of rich goodness.

6 medium all-purpose potatoes (about 2½ pounds)
Salt and white pepper
⅔ cup shredded swiss cheese (about 2½ ounces)
¾ to 1 cup heavy cream

Peel the potatoes, dropping them into a bowl of cold water to cover. With the thin slicing blade of a food processor or a sharp knife, slice them ⅛ to ¼ inch thick. Place in a bowl of cold water for 5 to 10 minutes.

Preheat the oven to 375 degrees. Heavily butter a shallow 2- to 3-quart gratin dish or 9 × 13-inch casserole. Dry the potatoes well with paper towels. Overlap half the potatoes in lengthwise rows in the bottom of the dish. Sprinkle lightly with salt, pepper and half the cheese. Repeat second layer of potatoes in same manner; sprinkle with salt, pepper and remaining cheese. Pour ¾ cup cream over the top. Bake, uncovered, in center of oven for 40 minutes. If serving immediately continue baking for 15 to 20 minutes more or until the top is golden brown and the potatoes are tender.

∗ If desired, the gratin may be baked for 40 minutes and then covered and held at room temperature for up to 3 hours. Before serving, pour an additional ¼ cup cream over the top and bake at 375 degrees, uncovered, for 15 to 20 minutes more or until golden brown.

Serves 6.

Cranberry-Pear Cobbler

Don't limit cobblers to summer fruits. Tart red cranberries contrast with luscious sweet pears in a beautiful, warm winter dessert.

Pastry

- 1¾ cups all-purpose flour
- ½ teaspoon salt, or to taste
- ⅓ cup vegetable shortening, chilled in freezer until firm
- 5 tablespoons butter or margarine, cold and cut into 5 pieces
- 4 tablespoons ice water

Filling

- 1½ cups sugar
- ¼ cup all-purpose flour
- ¼ teaspoon ground allspice
- ⅛ teaspoon ground cardamom, optional
- 1 bag (12 ounces) cranberries (3½ cups berries)
- 4 medium pears, peeled, halved, cored and sliced ¼ inch thick
- 1 tablespoon butter or margarine, cut into small pieces
- Vanilla ice cream for serving, if desired

To make the Pastry, in a food processor fitted with the metal blade or in a medium bowl with a pastry blender or finger tips, combine flour and salt. Add shortening and butter or margarine; pulse or mix until the mixture resembles coarse meal. Sprinkle ice water over and mix just until the pastry holds together when pinched between your fingers. Do not form into a ball. Flatten into a disk, wrap in plastic wrap and refrigerate while preparing the filling or overnight, if desired.

To make the Filling, in a medium bowl stir together sugar, flour, allspice and cardamom, if using. Add cranberries and pears; toss until combined. Pour into buttered 7 × 11-inch glass baking dish or 4- to 5-cup gratin dish. Sprinkle butter or margarine over fruit.

Preheat oven to 400 degrees. On a lightly floured board, roll out pastry about 1 inch larger than the baking dish and approximately ⅓ inch thick. Place over fruit; press against the sides of the dish to form a border and seal the edges. Cut three 2-inch slits in top to allow steam to escape. Bake for 35 to 45 minutes or until the pastry is lightly browned and fruit is bubbling. The pastry will shrink from the sides. Cool 15 to 20 minutes before serving. Serve warm with ice cream, if desired.

Serves 6 to 8.

M E N U

IMPERIAL STROGANOFF CHINOISE

Sesame Spinach Salad

Oriental Beef Stroganoff

Noodles with Toasted Parsley Bread Crumbs

Pea Pods with Cashews

Ginger Spice Layer Cake with Applesauce Cream

Oriental Beef Stroganoff is old-fashioned Stroganoff enlivened with a wonderful ginger flavor. Complemented with a host of Chinese-inspired accompaniments, it spans the generation gap. It's perfect for a large, homey, casual affair.

I doubt I've ever made a single recipe of the Stroganoff. It's not much more work to double it and have an extra dinner in the freezer. The most time-consuming task is slicing the meat, so I ask the butcher to do it for me.

If desired, serve Sesame Spinach Salad with the entree. If you make the menu in its entirety, reheat the Stroganoff in the oven while the Noodles with Toasted Parsley Bread Crumbs and Pea Pods with Cashews are on top of the stove. Parsley Rice Pilaf (page 106) or White and Wild Rice Pilaf (page 81) are both excellent alternatives to the noodles.

Fragrant Ginger Spice Layer Cake with Applesauce Cream freezes completely frosted, making it a grand choice for parties. I like to serve it on Thanksgiving, right along with my pumpkin pie. Suggested occasions for serving this menu are:
◇ Graduation or Family Reunion
◇ Bringing Dinner to Friends or New Neighbors
◇ Open House
◇ Vacation Slide Show Dinner
◇ Bon Voyage Dinner

Sesame Spinach Salad

Pungent oriental sesame oil and sweet rice wine vinegar enliven a salad of spinach, cucumber and radish strips. My daughter, Cheryl, is always experimenting by adding different meats and shellfish to turn this into a main dish.

¾ pound bulk spinach (about 3 ounces stemmed)
1 hothouse or European cucumber, unpeeled, or 2 regular cucumbers, peeled and seeded
12 radishes
6 ounces fresh bean sprouts (about 2 cups), washed and dried

Dressing
2 tablespoons sesame seeds
3 tablespoons white rice wine vinegar
1 teaspoon Dijon mustard
⅓ cup vegetable oil
2 tablespoons sesame oil
¼ teaspoon salt, or to taste
Pepper to taste

Wash and dry spinach, remove stems. Bunch leaves together and slice across into ½-inch strips. Wrap in damp paper towels and a plastic bag and refrigerate for several hours or overnight. Cut cucumber into 2-inch pieces; cut each piece into matchstick strips. Cut ends off radishes, slice ¼ inch thick and then into ¼-inch strips. Coarsely chop the bean sprouts into 1-inch pieces. Refrigerate vegetables in a plastic bag or covered bowl until chilled or overnight.

To make the Dressing, toast sesame seeds in a small skillet over moderately high heat or in a toaster oven at 350 degrees for 15 minutes or until lightly browned; set aside. In a small bowl, whisk together the remaining ingredients. The dressing may be refrigerated for up to 2 days.

Before serving, toss spinach, cucumber, radishes and bean sprouts in a large bowl. Add as much dressing as needed to moisten, toss well and serve. Sprinkle each serving with toasted sesame seeds.

Serves 6.

Oriental Beef Stroganoff

It takes American imagination to incorporate Chinese flavors into a Russian classic. Stirring sour cream into pungent ginger, soy sauce and garlic brings the dish back to its origins.

- 1½ ounces dried mushrooms
- 2 cups boiling water
- 4 tablespoons (½ stick) butter or margarine
- 3 tablespoons vegetable oil
- 2 pounds top sirloin, sliced in ¼-inch-thick strips
- 3 onions, chopped
- 5 tablespoons minced fresh ginger
- 6 cloves garlic, minced
- ⅔ cup dry sherry
- 1½ cups beef broth
- ⅓ cup soy sauce
- ¼ teaspoon ground pepper
- ½ pound large fresh mushrooms, sliced
- 1 green pepper, cut into 1-inch squares
- 1 teaspoon cornstarch
- 1 cup sour cream

Soak dried mushrooms in boiling water for 30 minutes or longer, stirring occasionally. Meanwhile, in a large wide saucepan or deep skillet, heat butter or margarine and oil over high heat until sizzling. Sauté meat in batches until browned on all sides; remove with slotted spoon to a dish and set aside. Reduce heat to moderate. Add onions, ginger and garlic and sauté until the onions are soft.

Squeeze the liquid from the dried mushrooms over a small bowl and reserve. Cut the mushrooms into thin strips, discarding the stems. Strain the liquid through a fine strainer and add it and the mushrooms to the onions. Stir in sherry, broth, soy sauce and pepper. Stir in the meat with its juices and bring to a boil. Reduce heat to a simmer, cover and cook, stirring occasionally, for 1 hour. Uncover and cook for 45 more minutes or until the meat is tender.

* The Stroganoff may be refrigerated overnight or frozen. Defrost at room temperature. Reheat on top of the stove or at 350 degrees for 30 minutes, stirring occasionally, until heated through.

Before serving, stir in the sliced fresh mushrooms and green pepper. Simmer 10 to 15 minutes or until they are tender. In a small bowl, stir the cornstarch into the sour cream; stir into meat. Bring to a simmer and serve; do not boil.

Serves 6 to 8.

Noodles with Toasted Parsley Bread Crumbs

When you make your own bread crumbs, you can vary the flavors by using egg, wheat or rye bread.

- 2 slices day-old bread, crusts removed
- ¼ pound (1 stick) butter or margarine
- 2 tablespoons chopped fresh parsley
- Salt and pepper to taste
- 1 package (12 ounces) medium egg noodles

To make bread crumbs, process bread in a food processor fitted with the metal blade; you should have 1 cup crumbs. Melt butter or margarine in a small skillet; stir in parsley and crumbs. Sauté over moderately high heat until golden brown. Season with salt and pepper.

∗ The crumbs may be held at room temperature overnight, refrigerated for several days or frozen. Reheat in skillet or microwave before using.

Before serving, cook noodles until tender to the bite (al dente). Drain and place in a shallow bowl or on individual plates. Sprinkle crumbs over the top and serve immediately.

Serves 6.

Pea Pods with Cashews

Blanch the snow peas first, then all you need to do is quickly sauté them in a minimum amount of oil before serving.

- 1 pound snow peas
- 1 teaspoon plus 1 tablespoon vegetable oil, divided
- ½ cup coarsely chopped cashews
- Salt and pepper to taste

Wash pea pods, trim ends and pull off strings. Blanch in a pot of boiling water for 1 minute; drain. Dry on paper towels.

∗ The pea pods may be refrigerated overnight.

In a medium skillet or wok, heat 1 teaspoon oil. Sauté nuts over high heat, stirring constantly, until golden; remove to a small bowl. Before serving, heat 1 tablespoon oil in same skillet or wok; sauté pea pods until hot. Stir in cashews. Season to taste with salt and pepper.

Serves 6.

Ginger Spice Layer Cake with Applesauce Cream

In this heavenly harvest creation, a fragrant cinnamon-apple whipped cream is sandwiched between thin layers of spice cake. The traditional, homey goodness of gingerbread is dressed up enough to suit your fanciest dinner.

Ginger Spice Cake

- ½ cup vegetable oil
- 1 cup light molasses
- 1 cup sugar
- 2 eggs
- 2 cups all-purpose flour
- 1 teaspoon salt, or to taste
- 1 teaspoon ground cloves
- 1 teaspoon ground nutmeg
- 2 teaspoons ground cinnamon
- 1 tablespoon ground ginger
- 1 teaspoon baking soda
- 1 cup boiling water
- Cinnamon for sprinkling on top

Applesauce Cream

- 1 cup heavy cream
- 2 tablespoons confectioners sugar
- ½ teaspoon ground cinnamon
- 1 cup applesauce

Grease a 10½ × 15½ × 1-inch jelly-roll pan. Line with heavy foil, leaving 2 inches extending over the short ends; grease the foil. Preheat the oven to 350 degrees.

To make the Ginger Spice Cake, in a large bowl with a wooden spoon, stir together oil, molasses, sugar and eggs. Stir in flour, salt, cloves, nutmeg, cinnamon and ginger; the mixture will be very stiff. In a small bowl, dissolve baking soda in boiling water. Slowly stir into batter. Pour into prepared pan and bake for 20 to 30 minutes or until a toothpick inserted in the center comes out clean. Remove from oven and cool 10 minutes. Remove cake from pan by lifting the foil ends. Place on a flat surface and cool completely. Cut cake lengthwise into 3 strips, each 5 inches wide.

* The cake may be wrapped in foil and held at room temperature overnight or frozen. Defrost at room temperature.

To make the Applesauce Cream, whip cream in a small mixing bowl with an electric mixer until thick. Add confectioners sugar and cinnamon and beat until stiff peaks form. Fold in applesauce.

Place 1 cake layer on a serving platter. Spread a fourth of the cream over the cake layer, top with a second layer and spread with a third of the remaining cream. Top with third cake layer and spread remaining cream over top and sides. Sprinkle cinnamon lightly over the top. Refrigerate until ready to serve. Slice with a serrated knife.

* The cake may be refrigerated overnight or frozen. Freeze, uncovered, then wrap in foil when firm. Defrost, uncovered, on serving platter in the refrigerator.

Serves 10 to 12.

DECIDEDLY DIVINE DINNERS

SEABORNE TREASURES

SALMONCHANTED EVENING

MARDI GRAS SHRIMP CREOLE

TROUT STRUTS ITS STUFF

Salmon Stuffed with Spinach and Goat Cheese, Cucumber Vichyssoise.

M E N U

SALMONCHANTED EVENING

Cucumber Vichyssoise

Crisp Garlic French Rolls (*Page 144*)

Salmon Stuffed with Spinach and Goat Cheese

Parsley Rice Pilaf

Celestial Souffléd Cheesecake

Next time you spy whole fresh salmon at your fish market, plan a party. Salmon Stuffed with Spinach and Goat Cheese makes a stunning centerpiece, especially if you're able to purchase a whole fish. The spinach goat cheese stuffing can be multiplied for any size fish.

I poach fish in the oven, using my largest roasting pan, rather than on top of the stove because the temperature is more constant. If your roaster doesn't have a lid, cover it tightly with heavy foil. There is no need for any last-minute anxiety or frantic rush with this entree. You can allow 15 to 30 minutes extra time after cooking. Standing gives the juices time to settle, and serving the fish lukewarm won't diminish its goodness one bit.

Although this menu is designed for a sit-down dinner, the fish is an outstanding choice for a luncheon or supper buffet. Complete it the day before and refrigerate, covered, overnight. Bring to room temperature and garnish several hours before serving. Accompany it with Marinated Vegetables in Raspberry-Walnut Vinaigrette (page 50) and Pasta Salad with Fresh Tomato Pesto (page 125).

If the weather feels too chilly for Cucumber Vichyssoise, replace it with hot, velvety Butter Lettuce Soup (page 63). Suggested occasions for serving this menu are:

◇ Birthday or Anniversary Party
◇ Wedding Rehearsal or Wedding Celebration
◇ Business Entertaining

Cucumber Vichyssoise

This frosty, pastel green soup is worthy of your most elegant glass bowls or shrimp cocktail glasses nestled in crushed ice. (See photograph, page 103.)

- 3 medium baking potatoes (about 2 pounds)
- 4½ cups chicken broth
- 1½ cups firmly packed watercress leaves
- 6 green onions with tops, coarsely chopped (about ¾ cup)
- ⅓ cup chopped fresh dill
- 2 small hothouse or European cucumbers, peeled, or 3 regular cucumbers, peeled and seeded (about 2¼ pounds)
- 1 teaspoon sugar, or to taste
- ¾ teaspoon salt, or to taste
- White pepper to taste
- ½ cup plain yogurt
- Plain yogurt and fresh chopped dill for garnish

Peel and chop the potatoes into ½-inch pieces. In a deep saucepan, bring chicken broth, potatoes and watercress to a boil. Reduce heat and simmer, partially covered, over moderate heat until soft, 15 to 20 minutes. Meanwhile, in a food processor fitted with the metal blade, chop green onions and dill until minced. Coarsely chop cucumber, add to processor and process until pureed. Scrape down sides and process until smooth, about 1 minute. Transfer to a large nonaluminum bowl. When potatoes are tender, use a slotted spoon to transfer them and watercress to same food processor workbowl. Add ½ cup of the broth and process until smooth. Remove to bowl with cucumber; stir in remaining broth, seasonings and yogurt. Refrigerate until chilled.

∗ The vichyssoise may be refrigerated overnight.

Serve chilled, garnishing each serving with a dollop of yogurt and a sprinkling of chopped dill.

Serves 8.

Salmon Stuffed with Spinach and Goat Cheese

This is an entree of the grandest scale. Although the finished dish looks like a huge amount of labor, actually your fish man works the hardest. (See photograph, page 103.)

- 1 whole or center-cut salmon (4 to 6 pounds)
- 3 pounds fresh bulk spinach, washed, stems removed (about 1 pound stemmed)
- 3 tablespoons butter or margarine
- ¼ cup finely chopped shallots or onion
- ½ cup chopped fresh basil or 2 tablespoons dried basil
- ¼ cup finely chopped fresh chives or green onion tops
- 4 ounces goat cheese
- ⅓ cup sour cream
- Salt and ground pepper to taste
- 1½ cups imported dry vermouth or dry white wine
- 2 tablespoons lemon juice
- 2 lemons, thinly sliced, for garnish
- Fresh sprigs basil or parsley, for garnish

Have the fish man butterfly the salmon and remove the center bone. Wipe inside with paper towels and remove any small bones with tweezers. Wipe outside.

To make the stuffing, cook spinach in a small amount of water until soft and wilted. Drain, squeeze dry and chop by hand or in a food processor fitted with the metal blade. In a large skillet, melt the butter or margarine; sauté shallots or onion until soft. Stir in spinach. Remove pan from heat and stir in basil, chives, goat cheese, sour cream and salt and pepper to taste. Cool to room temperature.

∗ The stuffing may be refrigerated overnight.

Spread stuffing over half the salmon, then fold the other half over to enclose the filling. Spray a large sheet of foil with nonstick vegetable-oil cooking spray and place fish on it. To determine the cooking time, measure the height of the fish by holding a ruler perpendicular against it at its thickest point. The salmon should be cooked 20 minutes per measured inch for the first 2 inches and 15 minutes for each additional inch. For example, a fish measuring 3 inches high will cook for 55 minutes. Transfer salmon to a large shallow roasting pan, allowing the foil to extend past the fish at each end for handles. Bend the foil up around the fish to hold in the juices.

∗ The fish may be refrigerated, covered, up to 8 hours. Bring to room temperature 2 hours before baking.

Preheat oven to 350 degrees. Pour vermouth or wine and lemon juice over the salmon. It should come 1 inch up the sides of the fish. Cover the pan with a lid or heavy foil and bake the fish, determining the cooking time as described above. The fish is done when the flesh looks opaque when flaked with the tip of a sharp knife. Use the foil handles to lift the fish from the pan. Discard the juices. With a sharp knife, scrape off the skin. Invert the fish onto a platter, scrape the skin from the other side. Garnish with slices of lemon interspersed with basil or parsley sprigs. Serve hot, warm or at room temperature. If desired, the fish may be refrigerated overnight and brought to room temperature 2 hours before serving.

Serves 8 to 12, allowing ½ pound per person.

Parsley Rice Pilaf

A toaster oven is ideal for roasting pine nuts; you can keep an eye on them and they brown evenly.

- 4½ cups chicken broth
- 3 tablespoons butter or margarine
- 2¼ cups long-grain white rice
- 1½ cups finely chopped fresh parsley
- 1 cup pine nuts, toasted at 350 degrees for 12 minutes or until golden

In a medium saucepan over high heat, bring chicken broth and butter or margarine to a boil, stirring until dissolved. Add rice; cover, reduce heat to medium-low and simmer for 20 to 25 minutes or until all the liquid is absorbed and the rice is tender. Remove from heat.

∗ The pilaf may be made up to 2 days ahead and refrigerated or frozen. Reheat, covered, in microwave or in the oven at 350 degrees, stirring occasionally, until hot, about 15 minutes.

Before serving, stir in parsley and pine nuts.

Serves 8 to 10.

Celestial Souffléd Cheesecake

Every day for at least a month, testing and tasting this cake was part of my daily routine. Getting a light-as-air cheesecake to bake with a cake layer rising to the top was quite a feat.

- 3 packages (8 ounces each) cream cheese, at room temperature
- 1 cup plus 2 tablespoons sugar, divided
- ¼ cup all-purpose flour
- 1 teaspoon baking powder
- ½ teaspoon baking soda
- 1 tablespoon lemon juice
- 2 teaspoons vanilla
- 3 egg yolks, at room temperature
- 1 whole egg, at room temperature
- 1 cup sour cream, at room temperature
- 4 egg whites, at room temperature
- Confectioners sugar for sprinkling on top

Preheat oven to 425 degrees. Lightly butter a 9 × 3-inch or 10½ × 2-inch springform pan. Wrap outside in foil. In large mixing bowl with electric mixer at high speed, beat cream cheese until light and fluffy. Gradually beat in 1 cup sugar, mixing until well incorporated; scrape sides of bowl. With mixer at medium speed, mix in flour, baking powder, baking soda, lemon juice and vanilla. Add yolks one at a time and whole egg, beating well after each addition. Mix in sour cream until blended.

In a separate bowl, beat egg whites until soft peaks form. Gradually beat in remaining 2 tablespoons sugar, beating until stiff but not dry peaks form. Fold into cream cheese mixture. Pour into springform pan, place in a large roasting pan in center of oven and fill halfway with hot water. Bake 15 minutes. Reduce oven temperature to 325 degrees and continue baking for 35 to 40 minutes or until puffed and brown and the center jiggles slightly. Remove to rack and cool to room temperature. Cover and freeze overnight.

∗ The cake may be frozen for up to 2 months.

Cut while frozen with a sharp knife dipped into hot water and wiped clean between each cut. Defrost 6 to 8 hours in the refrigerator. Before serving, remove sides of pan. Sift confectioners sugar over the top.

Serves 10 to 12.

M E N U

MARDI GRAS SHRIMP CREOLE

Asparagus Salad with Hard-Boiled Egg Dressing

Shrimp Creole with Rice

Cheese-Crusted Rye Bread (*Page 144*)

Fried Okra
or
Zucchini with Walnuts

Southern Pecan Pie

Edon Waycott, my assistant and an outstanding cook, brought me this down-home dinner. She grew up where the shrimp are locally caught, the fiery sauce is spiked with homegrown peppers and the nuts for pie come from the tree at the end of the drive. Asparagus Salad is my contribution to the menu.

The Waycotts' favorite dish for entertaining was Shrimp Creole, and it's little wonder why. The recipe can be doubled or tripled for a crowd, is made in one pot and tastes wonderful.

I had never tasted Fried Okra until Edon made it for me. Her grandmother's cook, Lulu Bell, could barely get a bowlful to the table past all the outstretched hands. If you'd prefer another vegetable, try Zucchini with Walnuts.

I've tasted pecan pies enhanced with chocolate, liqueur and sweet potatoes. But I agree with Edon: Southern Pecan Pie needs no embellishment.

Besides Mardi Gras, other suggestions for serving this menu are:
- **TV or Video Home Screening**
- **Games Night—Invite friends to play Trivial Pursuit, cards or charades.**
- **Post-Game Dinner**

Asparagus Salad with Hard-Boiled Egg Dressing

Since this thick, chunky mustard dressing won't run onto other food when spooned over chilled vegetables, it is a good choice to serve on the same plate with the entree. The dressing is great over broccoli, cauliflower and artichokes as well as asparagus.

1½ to 2 pounds fresh asparagus

Hard-boiled Egg Dressing

3 green onions with tops, cut into 1-inch pieces
4 hard-boiled eggs, divided
2 teaspoons Dijon mustard
1 tablespoon plus 1 teaspoon white wine vinegar
¼ cup olive oil
¼ cup plain yogurt
¼ teaspoon salt, or to taste
¼ teaspoon white pepper
1 head Boston or butter lettuce, leaves separated, optional

To cook asparagus, break off tough ends and peel lower half with a vegetable peeler. Place in a large skillet with 1 to 2 inches of boiling water; cook, covered, over moderate heat for 3 to 4 minutes or until crisp-tender when bitten into. Drain and run under ice cold water to stop the cooking. Place in dish, cover and refrigerate until chilled.

* The asparagus may be refrigerated overnight.

To make the Hard-boiled Egg Dressing, in a food processor fitted with the metal blade, finely chop green onions. Add 2 of the eggs and process until pureed. Add mustard and vinegar; process until incorporated. With motor running, pour oil slowly through feed tube until mixture thickens. Add yogurt, salt and pepper; pulse until combined. Add remaining 2 eggs and pulse until coarsely chopped and chunky.

* The dressing may be refrigerated overnight.

Arrange asparagus on dinner plates or on salad plates lined with lettuce leaves. Spoon dressing across the center. Serve chilled or at room temperature.

Serves 4 to 6.

Shrimp Creole

Smoky bacon, zesty pickling spice and hot-pepper flavoring give fresh seafood and a hearty herbed tomato sauce an unmistakable Southern accent. Although this recipe serves only four, you can make enough for six by increasing the amount of shrimp to two pounds. You can also double or triple it in one large pot. Just allow more time for the sauce to thicken, one and a half to two hours for triple the recipe.

- ½ pound sliced bacon, diced
- 1 green pepper, seeded and chopped into ½-inch pieces
- 1 onion, coarsely chopped
- 3 cloves garlic, minced
- 2 cans (28 ounces each) whole tomatoes
- 1 tablespoon bottled pickling spice
- 1 teaspoon dried tarragon
- 1 teaspoon bottled fines herbes
- 1 tablespoon red wine vinegar
- 1 tablespoon Worcestershire sauce
- 1 tablespoon hot-pepper sauce
- 1 teaspoon salt, or to taste
- ½ teaspoon celery seed
- 1½ pounds medium shrimp, raw, peeled and deveined
- 1 cup cooked long-grain white rice

In a medium soup pot or Dutch oven, cook the bacon until crisp; remove with slotted spoon to paper towels. Discard all but 2 tablespoons of the drippings. Sauté green pepper, onion and garlic until tender. Pour in tomatoes with their juice, breaking up the tomatoes. Place pickling spice, tarragon and fines herbes in the center of a 6-inch square piece of cheesecloth and tie with a string to make a small bag. Add to pot. Stir in vinegar, Worcestershire sauce, hot-pepper sauce, salt and celery seed. Simmer, uncovered, stirring occasionally, until reduced by about half and very thick, approximately 1 hour. Remove spice bag. Stir in bacon.

* The sauce may be refrigerated up to 2 days or frozen.

Before serving, bring the sauce to a simmer. Stir in shrimp and simmer, uncovered, until the shrimp turn pink, about 10 minutes. Serve over rice.

Serves 4.

Fried Okra

The okra looks like little golden nuggets of popcorn and are just as easy to munch by the handful.

- 1 pound fresh whole or frozen sliced okra
- 1 egg
- 1 cup yellow cornmeal
- ½ cup all-purpose flour
- 1 teaspoon salt, or to taste
- Vegetable oil or shortening for frying
- Salt and pepper to taste

Wash fresh okra and pat dry; cut off stems and cut into ¼-inch rounds. (Or defrost frozen okra and drain on paper towels.) In a medium bowl, beat egg lightly; add okra and toss to coat. In a plastic or paper bag, shake the cornmeal, flour and salt together. Add okra and shake until completely coated.

Pour 1 inch oil into a 10-inch skillet. Heat over moderately high heat until it reaches 335 degrees or sizzles when a piece of okra is added. Using a slotted spoon, remove okra to pan. Fry in batches without crowding until golden brown on both sides, 7 to 9 minutes, turning once. Remove with slotted spoon to paper towels to drain. Continue with remainder in same manner. Sprinkle with salt and pepper and serve immediately.

Serves 4.

Zucchini with Walnuts

Choose the smallest zucchini available. They will be more tender and cook faster when sautéed. A little walnut oil packs in a lot of nutty flavor.

6 small zucchini (about 1½ pounds)
½ teaspoon salt, or to taste
2 tablespoons butter or margarine
½ cup coarsely chopped walnuts (2 ounces)
1 tablespoon walnut oil
1 large clove garlic, minced
Freshly ground pepper to taste

Wash and dry zucchini; trim ends. Using the thin slicing blade of a food processor or a sharp knife, slice them into very thin slices, about ⅛ inch thick. Place them in a colander in the sink, toss with salt and drain for 30 minutes; pat dry.

In a large skillet, melt butter or margarine. Sauté walnuts until golden; remove with slotted spoon. Add walnut oil to butter; heat over moderately high heat until hot. Add zucchini and garlic; cook, tossing with spoon, for 3 to 5 minutes or until crisp-tender. Season with pepper. Stir in walnuts and serve immediately.

Serves 6.

Southern Pecan Pie

This recipe certainly doesn't skimp on the nuts! A thick layer of toasty brown pecans sits atop a thin layer of silky, mahogany-hued custard.

Pastry

1¼ cups all-purpose flour, chilled in freezer until cold
¼ teaspoon salt
¼ pound (1 stick) butter or margarine, cold and cut into 16 pieces
2 tablespoons vegetable shortening, chilled in freezer until firm
5 tablespoons ice water

Filling

3 eggs
½ cup sugar
1 cup dark corn syrup
1 teaspoon vanilla
⅛ teaspoon salt
2 tablespoons butter or margarine, melted
1 teaspoon lemon juice
1½ cups pecan halves and pieces (about 6 ounces)
Whipped cream or vanilla ice cream for serving, if desired

To make the Pastry, in a food processor fitted with the metal blade or in a medium bowl with a pastry blender, mix flour, salt, butter or margarine and shortening until mixture is the size of peas. Add 3 tablespoons ice water and pulse or mix only until the dough holds together when pressed with fingertips; if too crumbly, add more water 1 teaspoon at a time. Do not form into a ball. Transfer to a plastic bag and press into a disk. Refrigerate for 30 minutes or until ready to use.

* The pastry may be refrigerated up to 3 days or frozen.

On a lightly floured board, roll the pastry into an 11-inch circle. Fit into a 9-inch pie dish. Crimp the edges. Refrigerate while preparing the filling. Place oven rack on bottom rung and preheat the oven to 425 degrees.

(continued)

To make the Filling, in a medium bowl, whisk eggs until blended. Whisk in sugar, corn syrup, vanilla, salt, butter or margarine and lemon juice until incorporated. Stir in nuts. Pour into pie shell. Bake for 10 minutes. Reduce oven temperature to 350 degrees and bake for 35 to 40 more minutes or until puffed and deeply browned. Serve warm or at room temperature with whipped cream or ice cream, if desired.

* The pie may be held, covered, at room temperature overnight or frozen. Defrost, covered, at room temperature. To reheat, bake at 375 degrees for 10 minutes or until warm.

Serves 6 to 8.

M E N U

TROUT STRUTS ITS STUFF

Mixed Greens with Fried Goat Cheese

Brioche Rolls (*Page 148*)

Almond-Stuffed Trout

Spinach-Artichoke Timbales

Strawberry Nut Torte

You have two distinct serving options with Almond-Stuffed Trout. Coated with a last-minute Lemon Sabayon Sauce prepared with the poaching liquid, they make an ultra-fine dinner entree. Made ahead and garnished with lemon slices and chopped parsley, they are splendid for a buffet or elegant picnic.

You should encounter no flustered moments in either cooking or presenting this elaborate sit-down dinner menu. Toss the greens and divide them among the plates before frying the goat cheese. Substitute Warm Spinach, Brie and Mushroom Salad (page 127) or Green Garden Vegetable Soup with Mozzarella Pesto (page 68) if you like.

Put the trout in the oven before you sit down to the first course. If you opt to make the sauce, do it while reheating the Spinach-Artichoke Timbales. A bright make-ahead alternate for the timbales is Pattypan Squash with Tomatoes and Corn (page 174). This sophisticated dinner calls for a light, luscious dessert like Strawberry Nut Torte with its airy layers of ground pecans. Suggested occasions for serving this menu are:

◇ Wedding Rehearsal
◇ Bridal Shower or Engagement Party
◇ Business Entertaining
◇ Elegant Picnic

Mixed Greens with Fried Goat Cheese

Slices of goat cheese are breaded and frozen. Then, just before serving, they are fried until golden and crisp on the outside and smoothly melting within.

- 10 ounces goat cheese, such as montrachet, chilled
- 1 egg
- 1 teaspoon water
- ⅔ cup dry bread crumbs
- 2 large heads Boston or butter lettuce
- 1 head red leaf lettuce
- Vinaigrette (See below)
- Vegetable oil

Vinaigrette

- ½ cup vegetable oil
- 3 tablespoons red wine vinegar
- 1 tablespoon fruity olive oil
- 1 teaspoon Dijon mustard
- Salt and pepper to taste

Cut the cold cheese into 16 slices, about ⅓ inch thick. In a small bowl, mix egg and water with a fork until frothy. Place bread crumbs in a small bowl. Dip the cheese into egg and then into crumbs; if not completely coated, dip a second time. Place the coated slices on a baking sheet and cover with foil. Freeze for at least 30 minutes.

* The cheese may be frozen up to 2 weeks.

Wash and dry lettuce, tear into bite-size pieces; wrap in paper towels and a plastic bag and refrigerate until ready to use or overnight, if desired.

To make the Vinaigrette, mix all the ingredients together in a small bowl or jar. It may be refrigerated overnight, if desired. Stir well before using.

Before serving, toss greens with enough dressing to coat the greens lightly and divide among 8 salad plates. Heat about ¼ inch oil in a medium skillet over moderate heat to 375 degrees or until a piece of bread browns lightly in 40 seconds. Remove cheese from freezer and fry without crowding until golden brown and crisp on each side, turning with a spatula. Place 2 pieces of fried cheese on each salad and serve immediately.

Serves 8.

Spinach-Artichoke Timbales

Timbales are small dome-shaped molds commonly used for baking vegetable custards. When unmolded, they make elegant individual portions. Any small ovenproof dishes, even custard cups, may be used.

- 2 tablespoons butter or margarine
- 1 package (9 ounces) frozen artichoke hearts, thawed
- ½ cup chopped onion
- 1 clove garlic, minced
- 2 eggs
- 2 egg yolks
- 1 cup heavy cream
- ⅓ cup grated parmesan cheese
- ⅛ teaspoon grated nutmeg
- ½ teaspoon salt, or to taste
- Freshly ground pepper to taste
- Dash cayenne pepper to taste
- 1 package (10 ounces) frozen chopped spinach, thawed and squeezed dry

Butter 8 individual ½ cup timbale molds or soufflé dishes. In a medium skillet, melt butter or margarine; sauté artichoke hearts, onion and garlic until soft. Remove to a food processor fitted with the metal blade and process until pureed. Mix in eggs, egg yolks, cream, parmesan cheese and seasonings. Mix in spinach. Divide mixture among prepared dishes.

* The molds may be refrigerated, covered, overnight. Bring to room temperature before baking.

Preheat the oven to 350 degrees. Place the molds in a shallow baking pan in the oven. Pour in enough boiling water to come half way up the molds. Bake, uncovered, for 20 to 25 minutes or until the tops feel firm and a knife inserted in the center comes out almost clean. Let set 10 minutes, go around edge with tip of a sharp knife and invert onto serving plates.

Serves 8.

Almond-Stuffed Trout

Individual poached trout filled with a delectable almond stuffing make a spectacular entree. Serve warm or at room temperature, garnished with lemon slices or cloaked in an aromatic lemon sauce.

8 trout (10 to 12 ounces each), boned
Salt and pepper to taste
1½ cups blanched almonds (about 6 ounces)
2 onions, peeled and quartered
1 pound mushrooms
¼ pound (1 stick) butter or margarine
4 teaspoons grated lemon peel
½ cup chopped fresh parsley
1⅓ cups chicken broth
6 tablespoons lemon juice (2 to 3 lemons)
¼ cup imported dry vermouth or dry white wine
Lemon slices and parsley sprigs for garnish, if desired

Lemon Sabayon Sauce, optional

Reserved poaching liquid
1 cup heavy cream
4 egg yolks, at room temperature
6 tablespoons water
Salt and pepper to taste

Open the trout out on a work surface. Remove any small bones with tweezers; sprinkle with salt and pepper.

In a food processor fitted with the metal blade, grind almonds; set aside. In same processor workbowl, chop onions and mushrooms. In a large skillet, melt butter or margarine over moderate heat. Sauté almonds, stirring constantly, until lightly browned. Add onions, mushrooms and lemon peel; cook, stirring, until the onions are soft. Remove from heat, stir in parsley, salt and pepper to taste. Cool to room temperature.

Divide the stuffing over half of each trout. Fold other half over to close, pressing edges together. Place in 1 or 2 buttered shallow glass baking dishes in which they fit comfortably side by side.

* The trout may be refrigerated, covered, up to 8 hours.

Preheat the oven to 425 degrees. Pour chicken broth, lemon juice and wine over fish; cover with foil. Bake for 15 to 18 minutes or until the flesh is opaque. Remove trout; if you like, scrape off the skin. (If not served immediately, the trout may be refrigerated overnight.) Transfer to a platter and garnish with lemon slices and parsley.

If desired, make the Lemon Sabayon Sauce by pouring the poaching liquid into a deep saucepan. Stir in cream and boil rapidly over high heat until thickened slightly and reduced by about a third. Lower the heat so the sauce barely simmers. In a small bowl, whisk egg yolks and water until pale yellow and very foamy, about 45 seconds. Gradually pour the egg mixture into the simmering sauce, whisking constantly. Continue to whisk the sauce for a few seconds, until it is light and foamy, taking care not to let it boil. Season to taste with salt and pepper; spoon over trout and serve immediately.

Serves 8.

Strawberry Nut Torte

A thick layer of sweetened whipped cream and juicy sliced berries is sandwiched between airy nut cake layers. Frosted with more cream and garnished with whole glazed fruit, this is an elegant cousin to strawberry shortcake.

1½ cups chopped pecans (about 6 ounces)
3 tablespoons all-purpose flour
½ teaspoon baking powder
Dash salt
6 eggs, separated and at room temperature
¾ cup sugar, divided
1 teaspoon vanilla

Filling and Topping

1 cup heavy cream
3 tablespoons confectioners sugar
¼ cup seedless strawberry or raspberry jam, melted
½ pint strawberries, sliced (about 1 cup)
6 small strawberries, for garnish

Grease two 8 × 1½-inch round cake pans; line each bottom with a circle of parchment or waxed paper. Grease and flour the paper. Preheat the oven to 350 degrees. Place nuts and flour in a food processor fitted with the metal blade. Process until the nuts are very finely ground. Add baking powder and salt; pulse once or twice to combine. In a large mixing bowl with an electric mixer, beat egg yolks until thick. Slowly beat in ½ cup sugar, mixing on high speed until very thick and light colored, about 5 minutes. Mix in vanilla. In another mixing bowl with clean beaters, beat egg whites until soft peaks form. Beat in remaining ¼ cup sugar, 1 tablespoon at a time, until stiff but not dry peaks form. Partially fold half the nuts and whites into the yolks, then lightly fold in the other half until blended.

Spread batter into prepared pans. Bake in center of oven for 20 to 24 minutes or until a toothpick inserted in the center comes out clean. Cool 10 minutes and invert onto racks. Remove paper and cool completely.

* Cakes may be wrapped in foil and held at room temperature up to 2 days or frozen. Defrost, covered, at room temperature.

Up to 8 hours before serving, make Filling and Topping. Beat cream until thick, add confectioners sugar and mix until soft peaks form. Melt jam in a very small saucepan or butter warmer. Line a serving plate with strips of waxed paper. Place 1 cake layer on plate, brush the top with jam and spread with a thick layer of whipped cream. Place sliced strawberries over cream. Top with second cake layer. Spread top and sides with remaining whipped cream, piping a border around the top, if desired. Carefully remove waxed paper strips from platter.

Dip whole berries in warm jam and place on a plate. Refrigerate berries and cake until serving time. Before serving, place berries around top of cake.

Serves 8.

OVER THE COALS

FIRED-UP CAJUN SHRIMP

PACIFIC NORTHWEST SALMON BROIL

ALL-AMERICAN BACKYARD BARBECUE

FIVE-STAR RACK OF LAMB

FAJITA FIESTA

ORIENTAL GRILLED TUNA

Devilishly Hot Mixed Nuts, Cajun Cocktails, Green and Orange Salad, Hot and Spicy Shrimp.

MENU

FIRED-UP CAJUN SHRIMP

Cajun Cocktails

Devilishly Hot Mixed Nuts (*Page 183*)

Green and Orange Salad

Hot and Spicy Shrimp

White Cornmeal Spoonbread

Mardi Gras Ice Cream Pie with Praline Sauce

Hot and Spicy Shrimp is my kind of party. Everyone comes casually dressed, gets their spirits up and lets their hair down. Because the shrimp are so much tastier when grilled and served in the shell, guests peel their own. A very messy, but delicious job indeed. The last time I served them, I bought each guest a lobster bib at a party shop. Finger-licking is all part of the fun but if you prefer neater, more orderly dining, grill the shrimp without the shell. This recipe can be multiplied to serve any size crowd. I've thrown this Cajun bash for 20 people.

The Green and Orange Salad looks pretty and counter-balances the peppery shrimp nicely. If you would like to add or substitute another salad, try Green and Red Cabbage Salad with Peanuts (page 161). You can double the White Cornmeal Spoonbread and either bake it in a 4-quart casserole or divide it between two 2- or 3-quart dishes. If you bake it in one large dish, make sure to allow extra baking time.

To begin your party with a "kick," serve Cajun cocktails, but offer cooler long drinks too. By the time you get to dessert, your palate will welcome the cold and creamy Mardi Gras Ice Cream Pie.

Cajun Cocktails

Add zing to your party with this potent jalapeño potable. (See photograph, page 115.)

2 pickled jalapeño peppers, drained
2 cups orange juice
2 cups rum
Ice or crushed ice

Wearing rubber gloves to protect your hands, slice jalapeños into rounds. Pour orange juice into a glass container with a tight-fitting lid; stir in jalapeños with their seeds. Cover and refrigerate for 24 hours. Strain out jalapeños.

* The juice may be refrigerated for several days or frozen.

Before serving, pour orange juice into a pitcher. Stir in rum. Fill stemmed glasses half full of ice; pour cocktail over.

Makes 8 servings, 4 ounces each.

Green and Orange Salad

Pureed orange segments give the dressing such fresh taste and thick texture that it's not necessary to use much oil. (See photograph, page 115.)

1 large or 2 small heads Boston or butter lettuce
Pureed Orange Dressing (See below)
1 orange, preferably navel, peeled and divided into segments
2 small green onions with tops, thinly sliced
1 avocado, halved, pitted, peeled and sliced
¼ cup roasted and salted sunflower seeds

Pureed Orange Dressing

4 orange segments
1 teaspoon honey
2 tablespoons raspberry vinegar
¼ cup vegetable oil
¼ teaspoon salt, or to taste
Freshly ground pepper to taste

Wash and dry the lettuce and tear it into bite-size pieces. Wrap in paper towels and a plastic bag and refrigerate until serving time.

To make the Pureed Orange Dressing, in a food processor fitted with the metal blade, puree orange segments. Mix in honey and vinegar. With motor running, slowly pour oil through the feed tube. Season to taste with salt and pepper.

* The lettuce and dressing may be refrigerated overnight, if desired.

Before serving, place lettuce in a salad bowl. Add orange segments, green onions and avocado. Pour over as much dressing as needed to coat everything lightly and toss well. Sprinkle with sunflower seeds.

Serves 4 to 6.

Hot and Spicy Shrimp

Part of the fun in this dish is letting your guests peel their own shrimp—that way they get to savor every last drop of the dynamite sauce. Be sure to have lots of napkins on hand! (See photograph, page 115.)

1½ pounds jumbo shrimp (about 18)
12 tablespoons (1½ sticks) butter or margarine
2 tablespoons plus 2 teaspoons Worcestershire sauce
1½ teaspoons hot chili paste or 1½ teaspoons cayenne pepper and 1 teaspoon hot-pepper sauce
2½ teaspoons dried rosemary
2 tablespoons finely chopped fresh parsley
3 large cloves garlic, minced
1 teaspoon dry mustard
Metal or wooden skewers soaked in ice water for 15 minutes to keep them from burning

Cut shrimp down the center through the shell and remove the vein, leaving the shell intact. Pull back on the shell to loosen it slightly. Rinse the shrimp and pat dry with paper towels. Place in a shallow glass dish into which they fit snugly. In a small skillet, melt butter or margarine; stir in Worcestershire sauce, chili paste or cayenne and hot-pepper sauce, rosemary, parsley, garlic and mustard. Cook 2 minutes for the flavors to blend. Cool slightly. Pour over shrimp, turning to coat all sides, gently opening the shells so some of the mixture can get inside. Refrigerate for 1 hour. Remove to room temperature and let sit for 45 minutes to 1 hour longer. Thread shrimp on skewers.

Preheat grill. Place rack about 4 to 5 inches from hot coals. Remove shrimp from butter mixture and grill for 6 to 8 minutes, turning once, until they turn pink and are cooked through. Reheat butter mixture remaining in dish and spoon over shrimp when serving.

Serves 4 to 5.

White Cornmeal Spoonbread

White cornmeal adds fluffy texture to this delicate, moist custard. The natural sweetness of corn beautifully balances peppery and pungent entrees.

- 2 cups water
- 1 cup white cornmeal
- 4 tablespoons (½ stick) butter or margarine, cut into pieces
- 3 tablespoons sugar
- ½ teaspoon salt, or to taste
- 1¾ cups milk
- 4 eggs
- 3 teaspoons baking powder
- 1 cup fresh or frozen corn kernels

Preheat the oven to 375 degrees. Butter a 7 × 11-inch baking dish or 2-quart gratin dish. In a heavy large saucepan over moderate heat, bring water, cornmeal, butter or margarine, sugar and salt to a boil. Stir until mixture becomes a soft mush. Remove from heat and slowly whisk in milk until smooth. Whisk in eggs one at a time. Whisk in baking powder until thoroughly incorporated. Stir in corn.

Pour into prepared dish. Bake in center of oven for 45 to 55 minutes or until the top is golden brown and the center jiggles slightly. A knife inserted in the center will not test clean. Remove from oven and let sit 10 minutes before serving. Spoonbread will remain hot for at least 30 minutes.

Serves 6.

Mardi Gras Ice Cream Pie with Praline Sauce

An ice-cream sundae of a pie done Southern style with caramel pecan praline sauce poured over all.

- 2 tablespoons butter or margarine, at room temperature
- 1¼ cups flaked coconut
- 1 quart butter pecan, praline or English toffee ice cream
- 1 quart coconut or chocolate chip ice cream

Praline Sauce

- 2 cups sugar
- 1 cup buttermilk
- 2 tablespoons light molasses
- ¼ pound (1 stick) butter or margarine
- 3 tablespoons light corn syrup
- 1 teaspoon baking soda
- 1 teaspoon vanilla
- 1 cup coarsely chopped pecans

Preheat oven to 300 degrees. Spread butter on bottom and up sides of 9-inch pie dish; press coconut into butter. Bake for 14 to 18 minutes or until lightly browned; cool to room temperature.

Soften first flavor of ice cream and spread into bottom of shell. Freeze for 1 hour or until firm. Using an ice-cream scoop, place small scoops of second flavor over the first. Freeze until firm. Cover with foil and freeze until ready to serve.

∗ The pie may be frozen for several months.

To make Praline Sauce, in a deep saucepan over moderately high heat, bring sugar, buttermilk, molasses, butter or margarine, corn syrup and baking soda to a gentle boil; it will foam up and increase in volume. Reduce heat and simmer 10 minutes, stirring occasionally. Stir in vanilla and pecans. Cool to room temperature, transfer to a bowl and refrigerate.

∗ The sauce may be refrigerated up to 2 weeks. Remove from refrigerator 1 to 2 hours before serving; stir well.

Remove pie from freezer at least 10 minutes before serving or until soft enough to cut. Drizzle some sauce over top. Spoon remaining sauce over each slice.

Serves 8.

MENU

PACIFIC NORTHWEST SALMON BROIL

Seven Greens Salad (*Page 72*)

Italian Herb Toasts (*Page 146*)

Sweet Mustard-Glazed Salmon

Grilled Garden Vegetables

Blueberries and Cream Pie

Once on a trip through the Pacific Northwest, I had a taste of Sweet Mustard-Glazed Salmon that was so incredible the memory of it makes my mouth water to this day. Granted, it was grilled over a white-hot fire while men with long-handled brushes bathed the salmon in a sweet, buttery sauce. A backyard grill may lack the high drama of the original, but the taste comes pretty close. And best of all, it's amazingly easy with a simple four-ingredient glaze.

All the Grilled Garden Vegetables (except white potatoes, which must be parboiled) need only be cut up before being cooked on the grill right beside the fish. Seven Greens Salad may be made with any type or number of greens—just change the name! Serve it as a first course or with the salmon.

Blueberries and Cream Pie is full of phenomenal taste sensations. When cinnamon is blended into the crust rather than the filling, it lingers in your mouth after every bite.

Sweet Mustard-Glazed Salmon

For fish that is caramelized and crusty outside, flaky and succulent within, here is an amazingly easy means to a delicious end.

8 salmon fillets (5 to 8 ounces each) or 1 whole salmon or piece (about 6 to 8 pounds), butterflied and bones removed
¼ pound (1 stick) butter or margarine
2 tablespoons (packed) golden light brown sugar
3 tablespoons coarse-grain mustard
2 tablespoons Dijon mustard

Wipe fish dry. In a small skillet, melt butter or margarine. Stir in sugar and mustards. Dip both sides of fillets in mixture. If using whole fish or a large piece, brush the mixture on both sides and place in a hinged grill basket. Grill 4 to 6 inches from hot coals for 6 to 10 minutes depending on thickness, basting occasionally and turning once, until fish is well browned and flesh at thickest part has begun to turn opaque when flaked with the point of a knife.

Serves 8.

Grilled Garden Vegetables

Most vegetables that retain their shape when cooked can be grilled with outstanding results. Experiment with olive, walnut, sesame or plain vegetable oil to obtain different flavors. You might also try sprinkling the vegetables with chopped fresh or dried herbs.

Squash

Choose zucchini or crookneck. Cut in half lengthwise. Brush both sides with olive or walnut oil or sesame oil mixed with an equal amount of vegetable oil. Sprinkle with salt and pepper. Grill about 4 inches from hot coals, turning once and basting once with oil, until tender, 12 to 14 minutes.

Leeks

Choose youngest or smallest leeks available. Cut off and discard all but 2 inches of green. Cut in half lengthwise, leaving root end attached. Wash thoroughly under cold water, dislodging any dirt between the leaves; dry well. Brush both sides with olive or vegetable oil. Sprinkle with salt and pepper. Grill about 4 inches from hot coals for 10 minutes per side or until well browned and tender.

Maui, Vidalia or Walla Walla Sweet Onions

You will need metal skewers or wooden skewers soaked in ice water for 15 minutes to keep them from burning. Peel onions and slice ¾ to 1 inch thick. Thread a skewer sideways through each slice to hold the layers together and help turn them. Brush each side with olive or walnut oil or sesame oil mixed with an equal amount of vegetable oil. Grill about 4 inches from hot coals, turning and basting with oil, until well browned and tender, 10 to 12 minutes.

Green Onions or Scallions

Trim root and top, leaving about 3 inches of green. Brush with olive or walnut oil or sesame oil mixed with an equal amount of vegetable oil. Grill about 4 inches from hot coals, turning and basting with oil, until browned and tender, about 15 minutes.

Mushrooms

Wipe with a damp cloth; cut stems even with caps. If very large, grill them directly on rack. Thread medium mushrooms on skewers. Brush with walnut or olive oil or sesame oil mixed with an equal amount of vegetable oil. Sprinkle with salt and pepper and grill until browned and tender, about 10 minutes.

Eggplant

Choose either Japanese or a medium-size regular eggplants. Do not peel. Cut Japanese eggplant in half lengthwise. Cut regular eggplant in half lengthwise and then into ½-inch slices. Brush both sides lightly with sesame oil or olive oil. Sprinkle with salt and pepper. Grill about 4 inches from hot coals, turning and basting with oil, until browned and tender, about 10 to 15 minutes.

Red and Yellow Bell Peppers

Cut out core, cut in half through stem end and discard seeds. Cut into eighths. Brush both sides of each section with olive or walnut oil. Sprinkle with salt and pepper. Grill about 4 inches from hot coals, turning, until browned and tender, 8 to 10 minutes.

Potato Slices

Choose russet or baking potatoes. Scrub skins; do not peel. Slice ⅓ inch thick. Cook in a pot of boiling water until barely tender when pierced with the tip of a sharp knife. Drain, run under cold water and pat dry. The potatoes may be held at room temperature all day, if desired. Before grilling, brush with vegetable oil and sprinkle with salt and pepper. Grill about 4 inches from hot coals, turning and basting with oil frequently, until golden and tender, about 15 minutes.

Yam or Sweet Potato Slices

Choose either yams or sweet potatoes. (Yams are more orange in color and have a sweeter flavor, but technically both varieties are sweet potatoes.) Scrub skins; do not peel. Slice into ¾-inch rounds. Brush with vegetable oil and sprinkle with salt and pepper. Grill over hot coals, turning and basting with oil, for about 20 minutes. You may also parboil the slices in boiling water until barely tender and blot dry. Then grill for about 8 minutes, turning, until browned and tender. When parboiled, the slices can sit at room temperature until ready to grill without turning dark.

Blueberries and Cream Pie

You don't even need to to take out your rolling pin for this pie—just press the pastry in with your fingers. Juicy blueberries, tangy sour cream and a crunchy cinnamon crust add up to a sensational summer pie.

Cinnamon Cookie Pastry

- 1/4 pound (1 stick) butter or margarine, cold and cut into 8 pieces
- 1/4 cup sugar
- 1 teaspoon cinnamon
- 1 egg
- 1½ cups all-purpose flour

Blueberry Filling

- 2 pints (4 cups) fresh blueberries, picked over, rinsed and dried
- 1 cup sugar
- 2 tablespoons plus 1 teaspoon cornstarch

Cream Cheese Topping

- 6 ounces cream cheese, at room temperature
- 1 egg
- 1/4 cup sugar
- 1/4 cup sour cream

To make the Cinnamon Cookie Pastry, in a food processor fitted with the metal blade or in a mixing bowl with an electric mixer, pulse or mix butter or margarine, sugar and cinnamon until blended. Pulse or mix in egg. Add flour and process or mix until the dough holds together. Remove to a sheet of plastic wrap and flatten into a disk. Break off small pieces of dough and with your fingers, push it evenly into the bottom and up the sides of a 9-inch pie dish, crimping the edges to form a border. Prick bottom with a fork and refrigerate 30 minutes.

Place oven rack on bottom rung and preheat the oven to 400 degrees. Prebake crust for 12 to 13 minutes or until the sides are very lightly browned and the bottom is set. Cool 10 minutes.

Preheat oven to 450 degrees. While the crust cools, make the Blueberry Filling. Stir together blueberries, sugar and cornstarch in a medium bowl, breaking up some of the berries with a fork until all the sugar and cornstarch are dissolved. Pour into partially baked crust. Cover edges of pastry with strips of foil. Place on baking sheet and bake for 20 minutes; the mixture will not be bubbling. Remove from oven and cool 10 minutes. Reduce oven temperature to 350 degrees.

To make the Cream Cheese Topping, in a food processor fitted with the metal blade or a mixing bowl with an electric mixer, process or mix cream cheese until fluffy. Add egg, sugar and sour cream; process or mix until blended and smooth. Remove foil from pastry and pour topping evenly over blueberries. Bake at 350 degrees for 20 minutes or until set. Remove to rack to cool. Cool at least 1 hour before serving. Serve warm or at room temperature.

* The pie may be held, covered, at room temperature overnight.

Serves 8.

MENU

ALL-AMERICAN BACKYARD BARBECUE

Cauliflower Ranch Dip with Vegetables (*Page 181*)

Barbecued Chicken and Ribs
with Maple Barbecue Sauce

Marinated Chuck Roast

Grilled Corn in the Husk

Pasta Salad with Fresh Tomato Pesto

Napa Blue-Cheese Coleslaw

Red, White and Blueberry Pound Cake

Frozen Rainbow Yogurt Torte

An All-American Backyard Barbecue ought to be the most casual, relaxed party of the year. By precooking chicken and ribs the night before or early in the day, you can just brown them quickly on the grill before serving. If barbecuing only one type of meat, round out the menu with a hearty dish you can prepare ahead, like Spinach-Mushroom Lasagne (page 155), Pork Molé Chili with Black Beans (page 159) or Shrimp Creole (page 108). Since Marinated Chuck Roast needs lengthy marinating and last-minute carving, it's a better choice for smaller groups.

If you are hosting an all-afternoon affair, supplement your dips and spreads with some individual chilled appetizers like Marinated Mushrooms with Blue Cheese (page 177) or Pepper Wedges with Tomatoes and Basil (page 178).

Serve a large pitcher of Overnight Iced Tea (page 56) as well as an ice-filled tub brimming over with canned soft drinks, beer and wine. I've offered two desserts, but you don't need to do them both. Top either with a crown of needle-thin 6-inch colored candles or sparklers.

Barbecued Chicken

My good friend Gary Hendler makes the best barbecued chicken ever. Perhaps because he hovers over it like a hawk. When I'm busy preparing other dishes and tending to my guests, I prefer to prebake the chicken, then finish it on the grill.

1 recipe Maple Barbecue Sauce (page 123)
6 pounds assorted chicken pieces
Vegetable oil
Salt and pepper to taste

Prepare Maple Barbecue Sauce; set aside. Rinse chicken pieces and pat dry with paper towels. Brush with oil and season with salt and pepper.

To cook entirely on the grill, preheat grill, positioning rack about 4 to 6 inches from heat. Place chicken skin side down on rack. Cover, open air vents slightly and grill 10 minutes; turn and grill, covered, for 10 more minutes. Turn once again, baste with sauce and continue grilling, covered, turning the pieces and basting every 5 minutes on skin side and 8 minutes on bone side, for 40 to 45 minutes total. Uncover and grill for about 15 more minutes, basting and turning until all pieces are browned and cooked through.

To prebake, place chicken in shallow baking pans. Preheat oven to 375 degrees; bake legs and thighs 40 minutes, breasts 30 minutes. Brush with barbecue sauce.

* The chicken may be refrigerated, covered with plastic wrap, overnight, if desired. Remove from refrigerator 30 minutes before grilling.

Brush with more sauce and grill, uncovered, for about 15 minutes, basting and turning until all pieces are browned and cooked through.

Serve with any remaining sauce.

Serves 6 to 8.

Barbecued Ribs

By parboiling ribs in water on the stove, you don't need to cook them as long on the grill. When they're finished, they will be brown and crusty on the outside and moist and succulent within.

- 1 recipe Maple Barbecue Sauce
- 8 pounds pork spareribs or baby back ribs in whole slabs (3 to 4 racks), or 4 pounds country-style individual ribs (about 16) or 8 pounds meaty beef ribs (about 16)

Make Maple Barbecue Sauce; set aside. Bring a large pot of water to a boil. Add ribs (the whole slabs or individual ribs), return to a boil and simmer for 15 minutes. Drain and pat dry.

∗ The ribs may be refrigerated overnight, if desired.

One to 2 hours before serving, place ribs on baking sheets. Brush both sides generously with barbecue sauce. Let sit at room temperature until ready to grill. Preheat grill, position rack about 6 inches from the heat. Place ribs meat side down on rack. Grill, basting once or twice with sauce, until they are well browned and no longer pink inside but still juicy, about 8 minutes per side. To serve, cut slabs into individual ribs. Serve with additional sauce.

Serves 8.

Maple Barbecue Sauce

Maybe everyone thinks his or her barbecue sauce is the best, but mine really is. Three sweeteners, two vinegars and lots of zippy seasonings make it extra-special.

- 2 tablespoons vegetable oil
- 1 medium onion, chopped
- ½ cup white distilled vinegar
- ¼ cup sugar
- 1 bottle (32 ounces) ketchup (3 cups)
- ¼ cup (packed) golden light or dark brown sugar
- 1 cup maple syrup
- 1 cup water
- ½ cup red wine vinegar
- 10 cloves garlic, minced
- 4 teaspoons Worcestershire sauce
- 4 teaspoons A-1 sauce
- 1 teaspoon ground black pepper
- ½ teaspoon paprika
- ¼ teaspoon cayenne pepper
- ¼ teaspoon salt, or to taste

In a deep, heavy saucepan, heat oil; sauté onion until soft. Add distilled vinegar and sugar; bring to a boil, stirring until sugar dissolves. Stir in ketchup, brown sugar, maple syrup, water, wine vinegar and seasonings. Simmer, uncovered, stirring occasionally, 45 minutes to 1 hour or until thickened slightly. Cool to room temperature and use immediately or store in covered container in the refrigerator.

∗ The sauce may be refrigerated for several months.

Makes about 5 cups.

Marinated Chuck Roast

Marinating and grilling an inexpensive chuck roast allows you to carve it into tender slices that have a lot more flavor than most steaks. Just be sure to purchase a blade or first-cut chuck, the piece nearest the prime rib section, cut 1½ inches thick.

- 1 medium onion, chopped
- 2 tablespoons vegetable oil
- 4 cloves garlic, minced
- ⅓ cup soy sauce
- ¼ cup red wine vinegar
- 2 tablespoons chopped fresh rosemary or 1 tablespoon dried rosemary
- 2 tablespoons honey
- 1¼ cups beef broth
- 1 blade or first-cut chuck roast, cut 1½ inches thick (about 3 pounds)
- 1 recipe Maple Barbecue Sauce (page 123)

In a bowl, stir together onion, oil, garlic, soy sauce, vinegar, rosemary, honey and broth. Place the chuck roast in a nonaluminum baking dish into which it fits snugly. Pour marinade over; it should come half way up the meat. Turn meat to ensure it is all coated. Cover and refrigerate 36 hours, turning once. Continue marinating at room temperature for 1 to 2 hours, turning once. Meanwhile make Maple Barbecue sauce as directed; set aside.

Preheat grill. Remove meat from marinade and grill 4 to 6 inches from hot coals, basting with barbecue sauce and turning once or twice until cooked as desired, about 20 to 30 minutes. An instant-read thermometer inserted horizontally into the side of the meat should read 125 to 130 degrees for medium rare and 140 to 145 for medium. Remove from fire and let rest 10 minutes before serving. Carve into thin slices; pass additional barbecue sauce, if desired.

Serves 4 to 6.

Grilled Corn in the Husk

When selecting corn, look for ears with pale green stems. If they're brown, the corn is old and has already lost its sweetness.

- 8 ears fresh corn in the husk, preferably untrimmed
- ¼ pound (1 stick) butter or margarine, melted, optional
- Salt, optional

Gently pull back husks, peeling down to about 2 inches from the base but being careful not to pull husks off. Remove and discard as much silk as possible. Smooth husks back over corn and tie at top with a thin strip of husk or string. Soak the ears in water for 10 to 15 minutes; this will allow the corn to steam. Preheat grill. Squeeze out excess water and grill about 4 inches from hot coals for 20 to 30 minutes, turning until well browned on all sides. To serve, cut off strings and remove husks. Serve with butter or margarine and salt, if desired.

Serves 8.

Pasta Salad with Fresh Tomato Pesto

In the heat of summer when tomatoes are at their peak, chop them into a glorious basil-scented pesto. This crimson dressing with its bite of garlic really peps up cold pasta.

Fresh Tomato Pesto (See below)
1 pound pasta, such as penne, rotelle or small shells
¾ cup chopped celery
½ cup chopped carrot
¾ cup chopped peeled and seeded cucumber
1 can (15 ounces) artichoke hearts, drained and chopped
1 can (4¼ ounces) sliced black olives, drained

Fresh Tomato Pesto

6 large tomatoes (about 2¾ pounds)
4 cloves garlic, peeled
2 cups packed fresh basil leaves (about 2 ounces)
6 tablespoons pine nuts or walnuts
1 cup grated parmesan cheese (about 4 ounces)
½ cup olive oil
½ cup vegetable oil
¼ teaspoon cayenne pepper
Salt and pepper to taste

To make the Fresh Tomato Pesto, cut tomatoes in half, crosswise, squeeze out seeds and chop coarse. In a food processor fitted with the metal blade, mince garlic. Add basil, nuts and parmesan cheese; process until ground. Add olive and vegetable oil, process until blended. Season with cayenne and salt and pepper to taste. Add tomatoes and pulse 3 or 4 times until finely chopped, but not pureed.

To make the salad, cook the pasta until tender to the bite (al dente). Drain, rinse with cold water and place in salad bowl. Stir in celery, carrot, cucumber, artichoke hearts and olives. Pour pesto over and toss well. Refrigerate at least 1 hour for flavors to blend. Serve at room temperature.

* The salad may be refrigerated overnight. Bring to room temperature before serving.

Serves 10 to 12 as a side dish.

Napa Blue-Cheese Coleslaw

Sweet, mild-flavored Napa cabbage is a wonderful choice for coleslaw. Because it's juicier than the more common cabbage varieties, it should be tossed just before serving.

1 head Napa or Chinese cabbage (about 2 pounds)
6 ounces blue cheese, or to taste, crumbled (1½ cups)
2 cloves garlic, peeled
¼ cup coarsely chopped onion
⅓ cup cider vinegar
¼ teaspoon dry mustard
½ teaspoon celery seed
¼ teaspoon salt, or to taste
½ teaspoon white pepper
2 tablespoons sugar
¾ cup vegetable oil

In a food processor fitted with the thin slicing blade or with a sharp knife, slice the cabbage into thin shreds. Place in a large bowl, toss with blue cheese, cover and refrigerate until chilled. The cabbage may be refrigerated overnight, if desired.

To make the dressing, in a food processor fitted with the metal blade, mince garlic. Add onion and chop fine. Add vinegar, mustard, celery seed, salt, pepper and sugar; process until combined. With the motor running, slowly pour oil through the feed tube.

* The dressing may be refrigerated overnight, if desired.

Just before serving, toss cabbage and blue cheese with the dressing.

Serves 8.

Red, White and Blueberry Pound Cake

Salute patriotic holidays with this rich cream cheese pound cake with its glittering berry topping.

- ¼ pound (1 stick) butter, at room temperature
- ½ pound (2 sticks) margarine, at room temperature
- 1 package (8 ounces) cream cheese, at room temperature
- 3 cups sugar
- 6 eggs
- 3 cups all-purpose flour
- 1 tablespoon vanilla

Berry Topping

- 3 cups fresh blueberries (1½ pints)
- 3 teaspoons cornstarch
- 9 tablespoons sugar
- 2 tablespoons plus 1 teaspoon water
- 1 cup fresh raspberries
- 1 cup fresh strawberries, stemmed and halved

Preheat the oven to 325 degrees. Butter and flour a 12-cup tube pan. In a large mixing bowl with an electric mixer, cream butter, margarine and cream cheese until blended. Mix in sugar; beat until light and fluffy. Mix in 2 eggs, half the flour, remaining eggs, then remaining flour, beating well after each addition. Add vanilla and mix well. Spoon batter into prepared pan. Smooth the top. Place on a baking sheet and bake for 1 hour and 25 to 35 minutes or until the top is cracked and golden brown and a toothpick inserted in the center comes out clean. Cool in pan. Go around edges and bottom with a knife; remove sides of pan and lift cake off tube.

* The cake may be stored, tightly covered, at room temperature for 2 days or frozen.

Up to 8 hours before serving, make Berry Topping by stirring blueberries, cornstarch, sugar and water in a medium saucepan. Bring to a boil over moderately high heat, stirring occasionally. Cook, stirring until the mixture thickens and some berries pop, about 2 minutes. Place cake on platter and spoon blueberries over. Heap raspberries and strawberries on top. Refrigerate, uncovered. Bring to room temperature about 30 minutes before serving.

Serves 12 to 14.

Frozen Rainbow Yogurt Torte

I used to make this torte by layering different kinds of ice cream, but when I updated it with yogurt, I found it was fruitier, lighter and more refreshing. You can use any variety of flavors; they are best found at a frozen yogurt store.

- ¼ pound (1 stick) butter or margarine, cold and cut into 8 pieces
- ¼ cup (packed) golden light brown sugar
- 1 cup all-purpose flour
- 1 teaspoon vanilla
- ½ cup chopped pecans
- ¾ cup flaked coconut
- 3 pints assorted fruit-flavored frozen yogurt, such as raspberry, lemon, banana, strawberry, peach, lime

Preheat oven to 350 degrees. In a food processor fitted with the metal blade, pulse butter or margarine, brown sugar, flour, vanilla and pecans until crumbly. Pulse in coconut. Place the mixture on a baking sheet and bake for 15 to 20 minutes, stirring occasionally with a fork, until the crumbs are lightly toasted. Set aside to cool.

Remove yogurt from freezer to soften slightly. Sprinkle ⅓ of the crumbs into the bottom of an 8-inch springform pan. Drop tablespoonfuls of each flavor of yogurt randomly over crumbs, using half of each container. Sprinkle with another ⅓ of the crumbs and cover with spoonfuls of remaining yogurt. Top with remaining crumbs; press down with your hands. Cover with foil and freeze until firm.

* The torte may be frozen up to 1 month.

Remove from the freezer 10 to 15 minutes before serving to soften slightly. Remove sides of springform and cut into wedges.

Serves 8.

MENU

FIVE-STAR RACK OF LAMB

Warm Spinach, Brie and Mushroom Salad

Crisp Garlic French Rolls (*Page 144*)

Rack of Lamb with Mustard-Peppercorn Crust

Baked Pasta with Basil and Parmesan Cheese

Fresh Fruit Meringue Shortcake

To my mind, nothing summer dining has to offer compares with crisply grilled Rack of Lamb with Mustard-Peppercorn Crust. (The recipe also works well with chops or a butterflied leg. If you prepare chops, marinate them for only three to four hours, then spread with a thin coating of the mustard-peppercorn mixture before grilling.)

Even with food as elegant as this, there is no need to set a formal table. Warm Spinach, Brie and Mushroom Salad is spectacular and with everything prepared ahead, all you have to do is reheat the dressing. If you are putting together this menu alone, you'll especially appreciate Baked Pasta with Basil and Parmesan Cheese.

Any fresh fruit dessert stands out with this dinner, but I've chosen Fresh Fruit Meringue Shortcake, one of my favorites. An equally impressive choice would be the Fresh Strawberry Tart with Chocolate Crust (page 137).

Warm Spinach, Brie and Mushroom Salad

Small cubes of brie melt into a creamy mustard vinaigrette to coat and wilt crisp greens and mushrooms.

¾ pound bulk spinach (about 3 ounces stemmed)
1 large head romaine lettuce (about 1 pound)
8 ounces brie cheese, chilled
5 mushrooms (about ¼ pound)

Dressing
½ cup vegetable oil
¼ cup red wine vinegar
2 teaspoons Dijon mustard
2 teaspoons Worcestershire sauce
2 tablespoons mayonnaise
Salt and pepper to taste

Wash and dry spinach and lettuce; tear into bite-size pieces. Wrap in paper towels and a plastic bag and refrigerate until needed or overnight, if desired. Slice rind off cold brie and cut it into very small pieces. Bring to room temperature 1 hour before assembling the salad.

To make the Dressing, in a small saucepan whisk oil, vinegar, mustard, Worcestershire sauce and mayonnaise until combined. Before serving, slice mushrooms. Place them and the greens in a large salad bowl. Bring dressing to a simmer. Remove from heat, add brie and stir until softened, but not melted. Pour over salad, season to taste with salt and pepper and toss well, making sure the cheese is distributed throughout the salad. Serve immediately.

Serves 8.

Rack of Lamb with Mustard-Peppercorn Crust

A rack of lamb is one of the most impressive cuts of meat to barbecue. Once carved, the individual chops retain all their pink juiciness.

- 2 racks of lamb (about 1½ pounds with 8 chops each)
- 2 teaspoons plus 1 tablespoon green peppercorns packed in brine or dried green peppercorns soaked in hot water for 5 minutes, drained and divided
- 4 teaspoons seasoned pepper or coarsely ground black pepper, divided
- 2 tablespoons chopped fresh rosemary or 2 teaspoons dried rosemary
- ½ cup coarsely chopped fresh mint
- 6 cloves garlic, minced
- ½ cup raspberry or red wine vinegar
- ¼ cup soy sauce
- ½ cup dry red wine
- Salt to taste
- 4 tablespoons Dijon mustard

Trim meat of all visible fat. Place lamb in a shallow nonaluminum baking pan or dish, preferably glass, meat side down. In a small bowl, coarsely mash 2 teaspoons green peppercorns with the back of a fork. Stir in 2 teaspoons black pepper, rosemary, mint, garlic, vinegar, soy sauce, and wine. Pour over racks, spooning to cover meat and bones. Cover with plastic wrap and refrigerate for 8 to 10 hours, turning once.

Remove racks from marinade and bring to room temperature 1 hour before grilling. Preheat grill. Discard marinade and pat meat dry. Sprinkle with salt. Place on grill about 4 to 6 inches from hot coals. Grill, covered, with air vents open, for 12 to 15 minutes for medium rare and 17 to 25 for medium well, turning occasionally until browned on both sides.

Meanwhile, in a small bowl, mash remaining 1 tablespoon green peppercorns coarsely with back of a fork. Stir in mustard and remaining 2 teaspoons black pepper. Remove meat from grill and spread it with a thin layer of the marinade. Brush grill rack with oil. Return lamb to grill, meat side down. Grill, uncovered, until coating is browned, about 8 minutes. Turn and brown other side. Lamb is done when an instant-read thermometer inserted horizontally into meat from the side, not touching the bone, reads 130 degrees for medium rare, 150 degrees for medium well. Remove from heat and let rest 10 minutes. Carve between ribs.

Serves 8.

Variation:

Butterflied Leg of Lamb

A 3- to 4-pound butterflied leg of lamb may be substituted for the racks. Marinate for 24 hours. Grill, uncovered, for 10 minutes on each side. Spread outside with mustard coating and continue grilling 5 to 7 minutes per side.

Baked Pasta with Basil and Parmesan Cheese

More delicate than a traditional noodle pudding, this casserole has a light creamy sauce coating thin strands of cappellini. Don't be afraid to be generous with the garlic; the flavor dissipates as the pasta bakes.

- 1 package (16 ounces) cappellini (angel hair) pasta
- 4 tablespoons (½ stick) butter or margarine
- 6 large cloves garlic, minced
- 4 eggs
- 1½ cups half and half
- 1 cup very coarsely chopped fresh basil (about 1 ounce)
- 1½ cups grated parmesan cheese (about 6 ounces), divided
- Salt and pepper to taste

Lightly butter a 9 × 13-inch baking dish. Cook cappellini until barely tender to the bite (al dente). Drain, rinse with cold water; drain again and place in a large bowl. Meanwhile, melt butter or margarine; stir in garlic. Pour over pasta and toss well. In a medium bowl, whisk eggs and half and half until foamy. Stir in basil, 1 cup parmesan cheese, salt and pepper to taste. Pour over pasta, tossing until well distributed. Pour into prepared pan; sprinkle top with remaining ½ cup cheese.

* The casserole may be refrigerated, covered, overnight. Remove from refrigerator 2 to 3 hours before baking.

Preheat oven to 325 degrees. Bake, covered, for 30 to 35 minutes or until set. Remove from oven and let rest 10 minutes before serving. Cut into squares to serve.

Serves 8 to 10.

Fresh Fruit Meringue Shortcake

Meringue is spread over sponge cake batter and baked. Whipped cream and fruit are then sandwiched between the layers to make a very high, multi-textured torte.

Cake

- ½ cup shortening
- 1½ cups sugar, divided
- 4 eggs, separated and at room temperature
- 2 teaspoons vanilla
- 5 tablespoons milk
- 1 cup cake flour
- 2 teaspoons baking powder

Filling and Frosting

- 1 cup heavy cream
- 2 pints strawberries
- 2 ripe but firm bananas, sliced about ¼ inch thick on a diagonal
- 3 ripe but firm kiwis, peeled and sliced about ¼ inch thick

Preheat oven to 350 degrees. Grease two 8-inch round cake pans. Line the bottoms with waxed paper or parchment and grease the paper.

To make the Cake, in a large mixing bowl with an electric mixer, beat shortening and ½ cup sugar until fluffy. Beat in egg yolks and vanilla, mixing well. Add milk and mix on low speed until incorporated. Mix in cake flour and baking powder. Divide the batter between the pans, spreading evenly.

To make the meringue, beat egg whites with clean beaters on high speed until soft peaks form. Beat in remaining 1 cup sugar, 1 tablespoon at a time, until the mixture is stiff and shiny like marshmallow cream. Divide and spread evenly over cake layers. Bake for 20 to 25 minutes or until a toothpick inserted into the cake comes out clean and meringue is puffed and lightly browned. Cool in pans to room temperature; the meringues will fall and crack. Go around edges with a small knife, invert onto racks and turn meringue side up.

* The cakes may be stored meringue side up, covered with foil, at room temperature overnight or frozen.

(continued)

At least 4 hours before serving, make Filling and Frosting. Whip cream until soft peaks form. To assemble the cake, place 1 layer meringue side down on a serving plate. Reserve 6 perfect berries for top; hull and cut remainder in half and arrange a layer over entire top of cake, cut side down. Spread ⅓ of the whipped cream over berries. Top with a layer of sliced bananas. Spread with half the remaining cream. Top with a layer of sliced kiwis, reserving some for garnish. (You may not need to use all the fruit.) Place second cake layer on top, meringue side down. Spread remaining cream over the top. Refrigerate, uncovered, up to 8 hours. Before serving, garnish the top with reserved strawberries and kiwi slices.

Serves 10.

MENU

FAJITA FIESTA

White Wine Sangria

Fresh Tomato Salsa with Home-Fried Tortilla Chips
(*Pages 180 and 181*)

Avocado Gazpacho

Chicken Fajitas

Romaine Salad with Papaya, Jícama
and Toasted Pecans

Acapulco Margarita Pie

I'm not quite sure why Mexican dishes seem to shout "Fiesta!" but they are the ultimate let's-have-a-party food. Maybe it's the margaritas, or the sangria, or the chips and salsa, or the spicy, colorful food. Or perhaps it's the lively informality. Most likely it's a combination of all these.

Avocado Gazpacho is invigorating any time of the year. Serve it in bowls for a luncheon or dinner first course or in cups lined up on the buffet table.

Although fajitas are traditionally made with skirt steak, I like them filled with chicken even better. Simply cut chicken breasts into bite-size pieces, thread on skewers and marinate until ready to grill. Accompany them with warm tortillas wrapped in cloth napkins, salsa, sour cream and as many cold chopped salad vegetables as you wish. Direct your guests to push the chicken off the skewer into the center of a tortilla, sprinkle with condiments, roll up and dig in. If you have any fajitas left over, wrap them in foil and freeze. Later, when the urge strikes, reheat in the microwave for a terrific impromptu meal or snack. For dessert, savor Mexico's popular cocktail in a unique pie—creamy margarita custard in a saltine-meringue crust.

White Wine Sangria

Serve this refreshing, clear cooler as an aperitif or along with your meal.

- 1 cup water
- 1 cup sugar
- 2 bottles (¾ liter each) Chablis wine
- ½ cup orange liqueur, such as curaçao, Triple Sec or Cointreau
- 2 cups sparkling mineral water, chilled
- 1 lemon, halved and sliced
- 2 limes, halved and sliced
- 2 oranges, halved and sliced
- Ice for serving

In a small saucepan over moderate heat, bring water and sugar to a boil. Simmer 5 minutes or until the sugar is dissolved. Cool to room temperature. Stir sugar syrup, wine and liqueur together, cover and refrigerate until chilled.

∗ The mixture may be refrigerated overnight.

Before serving, pour wine mixture into a large pitcher or punch bowl. Stir in sparkling water and fruit. Serve over ice in wine goblets, adding a few slices of fruit to each glass.

Makes 12 servings, about 6 ounces each.

Avocado Gazpacho

This icy green, cucumber-based avocado soup is distinctly Latin with its splash of lime and flash of jalapeños.

- 1½ large hothouse or European cucumbers, unpeeled, or 3 regular cucumbers, peeled and seeded (1½ pounds)
- 3 large avocados, peeled, pitted and coarsely chopped
- 3 large green onions with tops, cut into 1-inch pieces
- ½ cup plus 1 tablespoon fresh lime juice (about 6 limes)
- 3 cups chicken broth
- 1½ teaspoons salt, or to taste
- 1½ cups sour cream
- 3 tablespoons salsa jalapeña or diced pickled jalapeño peppers to taste
- Chopped avocados, cucumbers, cilantro, green onions and jalapeño chilies for serving

In a food processor fitted with the metal blade, process half the cucumber, avocado and green onion until pureed. Process in lime juice. Remove to a large bowl. Repeat with remaining ingredients. Stir in chicken broth, salt, sour cream and salsa or jalapeños to taste. Cover and refrigerate until chilled.

∗ The gazpacho may be refrigerated overnight.

Pass assorted condiments.

Serves 8 to 10.

Chicken Fajitas

Fajitas are soft tortillas rolled around strips of seared meat, salsa and vegetables. Offer a choice of condiments and let your guests assemble their own.

1 recipe Avocado Salsa (page 180)
3 pounds boneless, skinless chicken breasts, cut in 1½-inch cubes
8 metal or bamboo skewers (about 9 inches)
½ cup lime juice
4 cloves garlic, minced
1 teaspoon dried oregano or 1 tablespoon fresh chopped oregano
1 cup olive oil
Salt and pepper to taste
⅓ cup hot jalapeño jelly, melted
16 flour tortillas

Condiments for Serving

1 cup sour cream
4 medium tomatoes, chopped
⅓ cup chopped fresh cilantro
⅓ cup finely diced pickled jalapeños
1 can (4¼ ounces) sliced black olives
½ cup chopped green onions with tops
½ cup sliced radishes

Make Avocado Salsa as recipe directs. Thread chicken on bamboo skewers. Place in a shallow nonaluminum baking dish into which they fit snugly in 1 or 2 layers. In a bowl, make marinade by stirring together lime juice, garlic, oregano and oil. Pour over chicken. Cover with plastic wrap and marinate at room temperature for 1 to 1½ hours or in the refrigerator for 3 to 4 hours, turning once. Preheat grill. Remove chicken from marinade; sprinkle one side with salt and pepper. Brush both sides with jelly. Brush grill rack with oil. Grill 4 inches from hot coals, basting often with the jelly and turning once, until browned on the outside and cooked through, 6 to 8 minutes.

Meanwhile, divide the tortillas into 2 stacks. Wrap in foil and bake at 325 degrees for 10 minutes or cover with plastic wrap and heat in a microwave for 1 to 2 minutes or until soft and steaming. Do not overcook or they will fall apart. Serve chicken with tortillas, salsa and condiments.

Serves 8.

Romaine Salad with Papaya, Jícama and Toasted Pecans

Velvety smooth papaya and avocado play against crisp jícama and toasted pecans in this delightful salad. The papaya has a dual role: it is chopped and mixed into the lettuce and pureed in a sunshiny, low-oil dressing.

2 large heads romaine lettuce
1 cup pecan halves or large pieces (about 4 ounces)
Papaya Vinaigrette (See below)
1 papaya, peeled, seeded and coarsely chopped
1 cup chopped jícama (about 4 ounces)
2 avocados, peeled, pitted and coarsely chopped
¼ cup chopped green onions with tops

Papaya Vinaigrette

2 small green onions, white part only
¾ cup chopped papaya (about ½ papaya)
2 tablespoons lime juice
3 tablespoons white wine vinegar
5 tablespoons vegetable oil
Salt and pepper to taste

Wash and dry lettuce and tear into bite-size pieces. Wrap in paper towels and a plastic bag and refrigerate until ready to use or overnight, if desired. Toast nuts on a baking sheet at 350 degrees, stirring once or twice, until very brown and toasted, about 12 to 15 minutes; set aside.

To make the Papaya Vinaigrette, in a food processor fitted with the metal blade, finely chop green onions. Add papaya and process until pureed. Pulse in lime juice and vinegar. With the motor running, slowly pour oil through the feed tube. Season to taste with salt and pepper.

* The dressing may be refrigerated up to 2 days. Bring to room temperature and stir before serving.

Before serving, place lettuce in a large salad bowl. Add papaya, jícama, avocados, green onions and toasted nuts. Toss with as much dressing as desired.

Serves 8.

Acapulco Margarita Pie

Just like the cocktail, this pie's both slightly salty and silky smooth. Although the strawberries on top may be omitted, I really like the balance their juicy sweetness brings.

Saltine-Meringue Crust

- 3 egg whites, at room temperature
- 1 cup sugar
- ¼ teaspoon baking powder
- 1 teaspoon vanilla
- 16 single saltine crackers, broken into 1-inch pieces

Filling

- 4 egg yolks
- ½ cup sugar
- ⅛ teaspoon salt, or to taste
- ¼ cup lime juice
- 1 tablespoon grated lime peel
- 2 tablespoons tequila
- 2 tablespoons orange liqueur, such as curaçao, Triple Sec or Cointreau
- 1 teaspoon cornstarch
- 1 cup heavy cream
- 1 pint strawberries, stemmed, optional

Preheat oven to 325 degrees. To make the Saltine-Meringue Crust, in a small mixing bowl with an electric mixer on high speed, beat egg whites until soft peaks form. Add 1 tablespoon sugar; mix 2 minutes. Beating continuously, add 2 tablespoons sugar, baking powder and vanilla. Mix in remaining sugar, 2 tablespoons at a time, beating until very stiff and shiny like marshmallow cream. Fold in crackers. Spoon into a heavily greased 9-inch pie dish, spreading up the sides and forming a rim around the edge. Bake for 20 to 22 minutes or until puffed, beige and beginning to crack. Remove from oven and cool to room temperature; crust will crack as it cools.

To make the Filling, in a small, heavy saucepan, whisk yolks, sugar, salt, lime juice, peel, tequila, liqueur and cornstarch until combined. Cook over moderate heat, whisking constantly until custard is thickened and very hot to the touch, and steam is coming from the top. Do not boil. Remove from heat and cool to room temperature, stirring occasionally.

In a small mixing bowl with an electric mixer, beat cream until soft peaks form; fold into cooled custard. Spoon into shell, cover with plastic wrap and refrigerate until set.

* The pie may be refrigerated overnight.

If desired arrange strawberries over the top before serving.

Serves 8.

MENU

ORIENTAL GRILLED TUNA

Chinese Coleslaw

Oriental Tuna with Julienne of Peppers and Zucchini

Crusty Potato Casserole

Grilled Tofu

Fresh Strawberry Tart with Chocolate Crust

Perfectly grilled Oriental Tuna circled with glistening strips of red, yellow and green vegetables is the type of artfully arranged plate you would expect to find at a very chic restaurant, and it's not at all difficult to create at home. Have the vegetables and oil ready in the kitchen. Finish grilling the fish and tofu, cover lightly with foil and keep warm in a low oven (250 degrees) while you stir-fry the vegetables. The remainder of the menu should require no last-minute work.

The refreshing Chinese Coleslaw can be served on lettuce leaves right along with the tuna, but if you prefer a first course salad, substitute Sesame Spinach Salad (page 98). The tuna, grilled tofu and salad are really all you need for a complete menu, but Crusty Potato Casserole adds a terrific plus to the meal. Put it in the oven and forget about it while you prepare the other dishes. If you like chocolate-dipped strawberries, you'll love the Fresh Strawberry Tart with its candy-coated chocolate cookie crust.

Chinese Coleslaw

Sweet mandarin oranges and crunchy water chestnuts are tossed in a soy-ginger dressing full of zip. It's made in a flash with a food processor to chop and shred the vegetables and blend the dressing.

- 1 medium head green cabbage (about 2 pounds)
- 2 carrots, peeled
- 4 green onions with tops, cut into 1-inch pieces
- 1 can (8 ounces) water chestnuts, drained and sliced
- 2 cans (11 ounces each) mandarin oranges, drained

Dressing

- 3 cloves garlic, peeled
- 1 piece (1 inch) fresh ginger, peeled
- 2 tablespoons soy sauce
- ⅓ cup honey
- ¼ cup red wine vinegar
- ¼ teaspoon dried red pepper flakes
- ½ cup vegetable oil

Cut core from cabbage. Shred cabbage using the thin or medium slicing blade of a food processor; remove to medium bowl. Shred carrots using shredding blade; add to cabbage. With the metal blade, chop green onions; add to cabbage. Stir in water chestnuts. Cover and refrigerate until ready to serve.

To make the Dressing, mince garlic and ginger in the food processor fitted with the metal blade. Add remaining dressing ingredients; process until blended. Toss cabbage and other vegetables with dressing. Gently toss in oranges. Refrigerate at least 1 hour before serving.

* The coleslaw may be refrigerated overnight. Stir well before serving.

Serves 8.

Oriental Tuna with Julienne of Peppers and Zucchini

Buttery, dark meat and a high fat content make tuna an exceptionally good choice for barbecuing. Served on a bed of red, green and yellow vegetables, this dish is particularly colorful.

Ginger Marinade (See below)
6 tuna steaks, cut about 1 inch thick (2½ to 3 pounds)
2 tablespoons vegetable oil
2 red bell peppers, cut into ¼-inch strips
2 yellow bell peppers, cut into ¼-inch strips
2 medium zucchini, cut into ¼-inch strips
¼ cup coarsely chopped fresh cilantro, optional

Ginger Marinade
1 piece (4 inches) fresh ginger, peeled and cut into 1-inch pieces
2 cloves garlic, peeled
½ cup rice wine or sake
½ cup white rice wine vinegar
1 tablespoon dry mustard
2 teaspoons sugar
⅔ cup vegetable oil
2 tablespoons sesame oil

To make the Ginger Marinade, in a food processor fitted with the metal blade, mince ginger and garlic. Add wine or sake, vinegar, dry mustard, sugar, vegetable and sesame oil; process until well blended.

Place fish steaks in a shallow nonaluminum pan in a single layer. Pour 1¼ cups of the marinade over, cover with plastic wrap and refrigerate for 3 to 4 hours, turning once. Refrigerate remaining marinade to use on vegetables.

Remove fish from refrigerator 30 minutes before grilling. Preheat grill; place rack 4 to 6 inches from coals. Remove fish from marinade, reserving marinade; pat fish dry. Grill for 7 to 9 minutes, turning once and basting with marinade from fish, until the fish is beginning to turn from translucent to opaque when tested with the tip of a knife.

While fish cooks, heat 2 tablespoons oil in a medium skillet. Sauté peppers over moderately high heat, stirring occasionally, for 3 minutes. Add zucchini and continue cooking for another 3 minutes or until vegetables are crisp-tender. Remove from heat and toss with ¼ cup reserved marinade. Arrange vegetables like spokes of a wheel in the center of 6 dinner plates. Top with grilled fish. Sprinkle with chopped cilantro, if desired.

Serves 6.

Variation:
Shark or swordfish steaks may be substituted for the tuna.

Crusty Potato Casserole

This exceptional recipe comes from Flo Baker, a talented pastry chef from Palo Alto and a good friend. Thin layers of sliced potatoes bake in a small amount of water to become soft on the inside and crisp and crunchy on top.

2 pounds baking potatoes (about 4 large)
Salt and pepper
1 cup water
6 tablespoons butter or margarine

Peel potatoes; place in a bowl of cold water to cover until ready to use. Preheat oven to 375 degrees. Thinly slice potatoes in a food processor with the thin slicing blade or with a sharp knife. Arrange slices in layers in a heavily buttered 9 × 13-inch casserole, sprinkling each layer lightly with salt and pepper. Pour water over top; dot with small pieces of butter. Bake, uncovered, for 1½ hours or until the top is brown and crisp and potatoes are tender. Serve immediately.

Serves 6.

Grilled Tofu

For years I tried unsuccessfully to get my vegetarian daughter, Caryn, to eat tofu. Then one day I barbecued it. She's eaten it ever since! If the tofu you find is not firm, weigh it down with a plate and several tin cans in the refrigerator overnight. Baste with either this sauce or the Ginger Marinade from Oriental Tuna (page 135).

Oriental Basting Sauce (See below)
1 package (1 pound) firm fresh tofu
12 wooden or bamboo skewers (about 9 inches), soaked in ice water for 15 minutes to keep them from burning

Oriental Basting Sauce

2 tablespoons salad oil
1 tablespoon sesame oil
3 tablespoons rice wine
1 tablespoon white rice wine vinegar
1 tablespoon honey
3 tablespoons soy sauce
1 tablespoon finely chopped green onion with tops

To make Oriental Basting Sauce, whisk all ingredients together in a small bowl. Cut tofu into 6 slices, each about 1 inch thick. Cut each slice in half, forming approximately 2½-inch squares. Insert a skewer sideways through each piece. Brush tofu with basting sauce. Grill about 4 inches from hot coals for about 20 minutes, using the skewers to help you turn them once and basting often, until golden brown.

Serves 6 as a side dish; 4 as a vegetarian main dish.

Fresh Strawberry Tart with Chocolate Crust

Picture a crisp, chocolaty cookie crust painted with melted chocolate and filled with ruby red berries. Each one sparkles with a rosy glaze and is drizzled with ribbons of lacy chocolate. If this vision doesn't inspire you to run in the kitchen and bake, I don't know what will.

Chocolate Pastry

- 1 cup plus 2 tablespoons all-purpose flour
- 3 tablespoons unsweetened cocoa
- ¼ cup (packed) golden light brown sugar
- ¼ pound (1 stick) butter or margarine, cold and cut into 8 pieces
- 1 egg
- 3 teaspoons ice water

Filling and Glaze

- 4 ounces semisweet chocolate, chopped
- 1 teaspoon vegetable oil
- 3 pints fresh strawberries, stemmed
- 2 tablespoons sugar
- 1 tablespoon cornstarch
- ½ cup water
- ¼ cup seedless strawberry jam or currant jelly
- 3 drops red food coloring, optional

To make the Chocolate Pastry, in a food processor fitted with the metal blade, pulse flour, cocoa and sugar. Add butter or margarine and pulse to small pieces. Process in egg and 1 teaspoon ice water. If dough does not hold together, add more water a teaspoon at a time. There will be small pieces of butter in the dough. Press into bottom and up the sides of an 11-inch tart pan with a removable bottom or a rectangular flan mold, dusting your fingers with flour, if needed. Prick bottom with a fork; refrigerate 30 minutes.

Preheat oven to 400 degrees. Place oven rack on lowest rung. Bake the crust on a baking sheet for 13 to 14 minutes; the edges will be set and the pastry will begin to crack. Remove to a rack and cool before filling.

∗ The crust may be held at room temperature, covered, up to 2 days or frozen.

To make the Filling, melt chocolate and oil in top of double boiler or microwave. Spread a thin layer over bottom of crust, reserving a small amount for garnishing. Cut a small slice off stem end of strawberries and place them stem side down on chocolate.

To make the Glaze, in a small saucepan, mix sugar and cornstarch. Stir in water and jam or jelly. Bring to a boil over moderately high heat, stirring constantly; cook 1 minute. Stir in red food coloring, if desired. Cool until lukewarm, about 5 minutes, and brush over berries, letting the glaze fall between them. Reheat reserved chocolate if it has hardened and drizzle over the top in a lacy pattern. Refrigerate tart for at least 1 hour. Bring to room temperature 15 minutes before serving; remove pan sides.

∗ The tart may be refrigerated, uncovered, up to 8 hours.

Serves 8.

FROM THE SOUP KETTLE & THE BOUNTIFUL BREAD BASKET

***Clockwise from top right:** No-Knead Onion Bread, Cheese-Crusted Rye Bread, Cheddar-Garlic Twist, Cajun Meatball Gumbo, Chicken Soup with Rice and Vegetables.*

RECIPES

THE SOUP KETTLE

Split Pea Soup with Sausage

Chicken Soup with Rice and Vegetables

New England Clam Chowder

Cajun Meatball Gumbo

During the cold winter months, few foods are more appreciated than steaming hot soup. It's hearty, nourishing, economical and easy to prepare. All you need is bread and butter to round out the meal.

Split Pea Soup with Sausage is a great dish to serve in front of the roaring fire. The aroma of Chicken Soup with Rice and Vegetables wafts enticingly out of the kitchen as it simmers slowly on the stove.

The authenticity of my New England Clam Chowder recipe may be debatable, but it is one of the most clam-packed ever. And even though Cajun Meatball Gumbo is simpler to make than most gumbos, it would still do a Southern cook proud. Suggested Soup Kettle occasions:

- ◇ **Halloween Carve-A-Pumpkin Party—Everyone brings a pumpkin to carve.**
- ◇ **Soup and View—Invite your friends to watch a video movie or TV special.**
- ◇ **Super Bowl Sunday—Or any football game get-together.**
- ◇ **Snowmania—Snowman-building party.**
- ◇ **Christmas Tree-Trimming Party—Serve soup in mugs.**
- ◇ **After-Theater Get-together**

Split Pea Soup with Sausage

This is one of those hearty, stick-to-the-ribs soups made with good old-fashioned ingredients like ham hocks and sausage. It will warm you from head to toe.

2 pounds green split peas, rinsed
2 ham hocks
4 ribs celery, chopped
4 leeks, white part only, sliced
3 large carrots, cut into ¼-inch slices
5 onions, chopped
4 cloves garlic, minced
1 tablespoon dried marjoram
1 teaspoon dried thyme
2 cups dry white wine
1 teaspoon salt, or to taste
¼ teaspoon pepper
1 pound Polish kielbasa or smoked sausage
Salt and pepper to taste

Place peas in a large bowl. Add enough water to cover by several inches and soak overnight; drain. Make 3 cuts in skin of each ham hock. In a very large soup pot (about 16 quarts) over moderate heat, bring peas, 3½ quarts water, ham hocks, celery, leeks, carrots, onions, garlic, marjoram, thyme, white wine, salt and pepper to a boil; skim off foam that rises to the top. Lower heat, cover and simmer for 1 hour. Uncover and continue simmering for 1½ hours, stirring occasionally, until peas are tender. Remove ham hocks and separate meat from bones; return meat to soup and discard bones and fatty skin. Slice sausage in half lengthwise and then into ¼-inch slices. Add to soup and cook 15 more minutes or until heated through. Season to taste with salt and pepper, if needed.

∗ The soup may be refrigerated up to 2 days or frozen.

Makes 8 to 10 main dish servings.

Chicken Soup with Rice and Vegetables

You don't really need a recipe for this catch-all soup. Once you've made the basic stock, any type of vegetables, pasta or legumes may be cooked in it. (See photograph, page 139.)

Stock

1 whole chicken fryer, 3½ to 4 pounds
2 pounds chicken backs and necks
1 teaspoon salt, or to taste
2 yellow onions, unpeeled and quartered
2 medium parsnips, peeled and coarsely chopped (about 1 pound)
1 bay leaf
8 sprigs parsley

Vegetables

2 onions, peeled and chopped
3 stalks celery, cut into ½-inch pieces
6 small carrots, peeled and thinly sliced
¾ cup long-grain white rice
2 small zucchini, chopped into ½-inch pieces
1½ cups fresh or frozen peas
½ pound fresh mushrooms, sliced
1 teaspoon dried thyme
1 teaspoon poultry seasoning
2 tablespoons chopped fresh parsley
Salt and pepper to taste

Remove giblets from fryer and reserve liver for another use. Rinse giblets and chicken and place in a large soup pot. Rinse backs and necks; add to pot with barely enough water to cover (3½ to 4 quarts). Bring to a boil; boil 5 minutes, skimming foam from the top as it rises. Add salt, unpeeled onions, parsnips, bay leaf, parsley sprigs and enough water to cover chicken by 1 inch. Bring to a boil, reduce heat to low and simmer, partially covered, skimming occasionally, for 2½ hours. Do not allow the broth to boil or it will be cloudy. Remove whole chicken, backs and necks and strain broth into a large pot. Chill the broth in refrigerator or freezer for several hours or until fat rises to the surface; skim off fat. Tear meat from chicken and backs and chop it into 1-inch pieces; refrigerate, covered.

Place broth over moderate heat and add chopped onions, celery, carrots and rice. Simmer until rice and vegetables are almost tender, 20 to 25 minutes. Stir in zucchini, peas, mushrooms, thyme, poultry seasoning, parsley and reserved chicken. Season with salt and pepper to taste. Simmer 10 minutes.

* The soup may be refrigerated overnight or frozen.

Serves 8.

New England Clam Chowder

This snowy chowder is thick, creamy and swimming with clams.

3 cans (6½ ounces each) minced clams
1 can (10½ ounces) whole shelled clams
½ pound sliced bacon, diced
4 tablespoons (½ stick) butter or margarine
1 medium onion, chopped
½ cup all-purpose flour
2 cups bottled clam juice
2 all-purpose potatoes, scrubbed but not peeled
1½ cups half and half

Drain liquid from clams and reserve. In a medium soup pot, cook bacon until crisp; remove and set aside. Measure ¼ cup drippings back into pot. Add butter or margarine, heat until sizzling and sauté onion until soft. Reduce heat to low, stir in flour and cook, stirring for 2 to 3 minutes until incorporated. Slowly stir in reserved and bottled clam juice. Chop potatoes into ¼-inch pieces; stir into soup. Bring to a boil, reduce heat and simmer, uncovered, until potatoes are tender, about 15 to 20 minutes. Stir in reserved clams, half the reserved bacon and the half and half. Cook until heated through; do not boil.

* The chowder may be refrigerated overnight or frozen. Reheat gently before serving.

Sprinkle each serving with remaining bacon.

Serves 8.

Cajun Meatball Gumbo

Served with a loaf of homemade bread and a glass of cold beer to help douse the internal fires, this makes a splendid meal. *(See photograph, page 139.)*

1 meaty ham hock (about 1 pound)
1 large onion, unpeeled and sliced
3 sprigs parsley
2 bay leaves
1 teaspoon seasoned black pepper
3 cups chicken broth
4 cups water
1 can (28 ounces) whole tomatoes
1 onion, chopped
4 large cloves garlic, minced
1½ teaspoons dried thyme
2 green peppers, seeded and finely chopped
¼ cup long-grain white rice
½ teaspoon cayenne pepper
1½ cups sliced fresh okra or 1 package (10 ounces) frozen sliced okra
1 package (10 ounces) frozen corn
½ teaspoon salt, or to taste

Meatballs

1½ pounds hot pork sausage in bulk
⅓ cup dry bread crumbs
1 egg, lightly beaten

Cut 3 gashes in skin of ham hock and place it, onion slices, parsley, bay leaves, pepper, broth and water in a deep soup pot. Bring to a boil. Reduce heat to low, cover pot and simmer for 2 to 2½ hours or until meat is very tender and falling off the bone. Strain liquid and return it to pot. Remove meat from bones and cut it into bite-size pieces; cover and set aside. Discard bones and fatty skin.

Drain juice from tomatoes into liquid; chop tomatoes and stir them, chopped onion, garlic, thyme, green peppers, rice and cayenne into stock. Bring to a boil, skim foam off top, cover and simmer over low heat until rice is tender, about 30 minutes.

Meanwhile, make Meatballs by mixing sausage, bread crumbs and egg in a medium bowl until combined. Shape into approximately 75 balls, ¾ inch each. Place on a rimmed baking sheet and bake at 500 degrees for 12 to 15 minutes or until cooked through. Remove to paper towels to drain.

Reduce heat to low, add okra, corn, reserved ham and meatballs. Simmer, uncovered, for 10 minutes or until okra is tender. Season to taste with salt.

* The gumbo may be refrigerated up to 2 days or frozen.

Makes 6 main dish servings.

RECIPES

THE BOUNTIFUL BREAD BASKET

Crisp Garlic French Rolls

Cheese-Crusted Rye Bread

Whole Wheat Banana Bread

Drop Biscuits with Chives

Buttermilk Crescent Rolls

Italian Herb Toasts

Ricotta Cheese Herb Rolls

Cheddar-Garlic Twist

Brioche Rolls

Lemon-Glazed Brioche with Lemon-Honey Butter

No-Knead Onion Bread

My own initial attempts at bread-baking were disastrous, but my failures taught me more than success would have done. If only I had let the dough rise longer, all would have been fine. The important factor is not the time but the texture. Dough has risen enough when 2 fingers pressed into it leave an imprint. The ideal temperature for rising is 85 to 90 degrees. This is the average temperature in a gas oven with a constant pilot light. If you have an electric oven, set it on warm (about 110 degrees), put the dough in, then turn the oven off after about 10 minutes.

You have a lot more flexibility with bread-baking than you might imagine. Dough left in a cooler place will rise slower, giving you extra time before you get back to it. Using rapid-rise yeast cuts back on the rising time by about a third. Dough can be refrigerated or frozen at almost any point. Of course, it will take much longer to reach room temperature and then its needed volume if it starts cold.

Crisp Garlic French Rolls

Aromatic olive oil sparked with garlic and herbs lends a new taste to ever popular garlic bread.

½ cup fruity olive oil
4 cloves garlic, minced
1 teaspoon dried oregano
½ teaspoon dried rosemary
4 French rolls (5 to 7 inches long)

In a small bowl, whisk together the olive oil, garlic and herbs. Slice the rolls in half lengthwise; place on a baking sheet. Brush tops with herbed oil.

∗ The rolls may be covered with foil and held at room temperature overnight or frozen. Bring to room temperature before baking.

Preheat oven to 375 degrees. Bake for 8 to 12 minutes or until lightly browned with crusty edges. Serve immediately.

Serves 8.

Cheese-Crusted Rye Bread

An unsliced loaf of bakery rye infused with herbed garlic butter and swiss cheese upstages the ever-popular Italian garlic bread. My son Kenny is always first to the table when this is served. *(See photograph, page 139.)*

2 cloves garlic, peeled
¼ cup loosely packed parsley sprigs
2 green onions with tops, cut into 1-inch pieces
12 tablespoons (1½ sticks) butter or margarine, at room temperature
½ teaspoon dried basil
1½ cups shredded swiss cheese
1½ to 1¾ pounds oval loaf rye bread, unsliced

In a food processor fitted with the metal blade, mince garlic and parsley. Scrape down sides, add green onions, butter or margarine and basil; process until combined. Remove about two-thirds to a bowl. Add cheese to butter mixture in food processor; pulse until incorporated.

Make diagonal cuts about 2 inches apart through the loaf, cutting almost to the bottom but leaving bottom crust intact. Spread herbed butter in bowl between cuts. Spread butter and cheese mixture over top and sides.

∗ Bread may be wrapped in foil and refrigerated up to 2 days or frozen. Bring to room temperature before baking.

Preheat oven to 400 degrees. Wrap bread in foil and place on a baking sheet. Bake, covered, for 25 minutes. Remove foil and bake, uncovered, for 10 minutes or until top is crusty. Remove to cutting board and slice through bottom crust. Serve immediately.

Serves 8.

Whole Wheat Banana Bread

The recipe for this wholesome sugar-free and dairy-free bread comes from one of my testers, Carole Magness. If you store overripe bananas in the freezer, you'll be able to whip up a loaf on a moment's notice.

½ cup vegetable oil
½ cup honey
1 teaspoon vanilla
2 eggs
3 ripe bananas, mashed
1½ teaspoons baking soda
1 teaspoon salt, or to taste
1¾ cups whole wheat flour
1 cup chopped walnuts (about 4 ounces)
Butter for serving, if desired

Grease a 9 × 5-inch loaf pan. Preheat oven to 350 degrees. In a medium bowl, stir together the oil, honey, vanilla and eggs until combined. Mix in bananas. Stir in soda, salt and flour. When thoroughly incorporated, stir in nuts. Transfer to prepared pan and bake for 50 to 60 minutes or until a toothpick inserted in the center comes out clean. Remove to rack and cool to room temperature. To remove from pan, go around edges with a knife and invert. Slice and serve with butter, if desired.

* The bread may be kept, tightly covered, at room temperature for up to 2 days or frozen.

Makes 1 loaf.

Drop Biscuits with Chives

Make these chive-studded baking powder biscuits while your soup simmers.

1½ cups all-purpose flour
2 teaspoons baking powder
1 cup heavy cream
1 egg
½ teaspoon salt, or to taste
2 tablespoons finely chopped chives
Butter for serving

Preheat the oven to 425 degrees. In a medium bowl, stir together flour and baking powder. Stir in heavy cream, egg, salt and chives. The batter will be very sticky. Drop by heaping tablespoonfuls 3 inches apart onto ungreased baking sheet. Bake in center of oven for 10 to 15 minutes or until golden brown. Immediately remove to rack to cool slightly. Serve warm with butter.

* Biscuits may be held, in an airtight container or wrapped in foil, at room temperature overnight or frozen. Reheat, uncovered, at 375 degrees for 3 to 5 minutes before serving.

Makes 10 to 12 biscuits.

Buttermilk Crescent Rolls

Baking powder, soda and yeast combine to produce these ultra-tender, no-knead rolls. (See photograph, page 67.)

- 5 cups all-purpose flour
- ¼ cup sugar
- 3 teaspoons baking powder
- 1 teaspoon baking soda
- 1½ teaspoons salt, or to taste
- ½ pound (2 sticks) unsalted butter or margarine, cold and cut into 16 pieces
- 2 tablespoons warm water (110 to 115 degrees)
- 1 package dry yeast
- 2 cups buttermilk
- 1 egg mixed with 1 teaspoon water for glaze
- Butter for serving, if desired

In a food processor fitted with the metal blade or a large mixing bowl with a pastry blender, mix flour, sugar, baking powder, soda, salt and butter or margarine until mixture resembles coarse meal. If using processor, transfer mixture to a large bowl. Place warm water and yeast in a small bowl and stir with a fork to dissolve the yeast; stir in buttermilk. Make a well in the center of the dry ingredients and pour in the buttermilk/yeast mixture. Stir with a wooden spoon until dry ingredients are moistened and a stiff dough is formed. Knead lightly by hand to combine ingredients. Form dough into a ball and place in a large oiled bowl. Turn to grease all sides, cover with plastic wrap and refrigerate until cold enough to roll. The dough may be refrigerated overnight, if desired.

To shape the rolls, divide the dough in half; it will be soft. Roll half on a lightly floured board into a 12-inch square; trim edges even. Cut the square in half lengthwise and then across, making 4 equal squares. Cut each diagonally, making 8 triangles. Beginning with the outside edge, roll each triangle up towards the opposite point. Place on greased baking sheet at least 2 inches apart with tips underneath, curving the ends to form a crescent. Repeat with remaining dough.

Let the rolls rise, uncovered, in a warm place not over 85 degrees (do not put them in a warm oven) for 45 minutes to 1 hour, or until they are puffed slightly; they should not double in bulk. After about 35 to 50 minutes, preheat oven to 400 degrees. Brush risen rolls lightly with egg glaze. Bake in center of oven for 10 to 14 minutes or until golden. Serve warm with butter, if desired.

* Rolls may be frozen. Defrost at room temperature and reheat before serving.

Makes 16 to 18 rolls.

Italian Herb Toasts

Herbed olive oil permeates crisp, thin slices of toast. These are splendid with spreads, soups and salads.

- ½ cup fruity olive oil
- 2 large cloves garlic, minced
- 2 teaspoons dried rosemary
- 2 teaspoons dried basil
- ⅛ teaspoon dried red pepper flakes
- ¼ teaspoon seasoned salt
- 1 long Italian or French bread, baguette type (8 ounces)

Preheat oven to 375 degrees. In a small bowl stir together oil, garlic, rosemary, basil, red pepper flakes and salt. Slice bread diagonally ⅓ inch thick. Brush one side of each with the oil mixture. Place on baking sheet oiled side up and bake for 10 minutes or until lightly browned. Serve warm or at room temperature.

* The toast may be kept in an airtight container or tightly wrapped in foil and held at room temperature overnight or frozen. Reheat at 350 degrees for 3 to 5 minutes or until warm.

Makes about 26 toasts.

Ricotta Cheese Herb Rolls

Six herbs and ricotta cheese impart Italian gusto to these light-textured rolls.

¼ cup milk
6 tablespoons (¾ stick) butter or margarine
2 packages dry yeast
1 tablespoon sugar
2 eggs
1 teaspoon salt, or to taste
1½ cups ricotta cheese
2 tablespoons chopped fresh parsley
2 tablespoons chopped chives or green onion tops
½ teaspoon dried marjoram
1 teaspoon dried basil
1 teaspoon dried rosemary
1 teaspoon dried oregano
3¼ cups bread flour, plus extra for kneading
1 egg yolk, mixed with 2 tablespoons milk for glaze
Butter for serving, if desired

Scald milk and butter or margarine; cool to 115 degrees. It will feel very hot on your wrist. In a large bowl with an electric mixer or in a food processor fitted with the metal blade, combine milk, butter, yeast and sugar. Let stand until foamy, about 5 minutes. Mix in eggs and salt. Mix or process in ricotta and herbs. Add 3 cups flour; mix or pulse until incorporated. The dough can be kneaded in a mixing bowl with dough hook for 3 minutes or on a floured board by hand for 5 minutes, adding more flour as needed. Place in a greased bowl, turn so all sides are coated, cover with a sheet of oiled plastic wrap and a damp towel. Set in a warm place until doubled in bulk, about 1½ hours. Punch dough down.

Grease 18 medium 2½-inch muffin cups. With lightly floured hands, shape the dough into 54 balls, 1 inch in diameter. Place 3 balls in each cup (1 will sit atop the others). Let rise, uncovered, until double in size, about 1 hour. Brush lightly with egg glaze. Preheat oven to 375 degrees. Bake for 18 to 22 minutes or until golden. Immediately remove from muffin cups to cool slightly. Serve warm with butter, if desired.

* The rolls may be kept in an airtight container or wrapped in foil and kept at room temperature or refrigerated up to 2 days or frozen. Reheat before serving.

Makes 18 rolls.

Cheddar-Garlic Twist

A simple technique of rolling and twisting the dough produces a very flaky, beautifully braided wreath. (See photograph, page 139.)

- 1/4 cup warm water (110 to 115 degrees)
- 1 package dry yeast
- 1/2 teaspoon sugar
- 3/4 cup milk
- 2 tablespoons butter or margarine
- 3 1/2 cups bread flour
- 1 teaspoon salt, or to taste
- 3/4 cup shredded sharp cheddar cheese (about 3 ounces)
- 1 egg, at room temperature
- Filling (See below)
- 1 egg mixed with 1 teaspoon water for glaze

Filling

- 4 tablespoons (1/2 stick) butter or margarine
- 3 cloves garlic, minced
- 1 teaspoon dried basil
- 3/4 cup shredded sharp cheddar cheese (about 3 ounces)

Pour water into a large electric mixer bowl; stir in yeast and sugar and let stand until foamy, about 3 minutes. In a small saucepan, heat milk and butter or margarine until warm and butter is almost melted. Add to yeast mixture with 1 cup of the flour, salt, cheese and egg. Beat at low speed until incorporated. Increase speed to medium and beat 3 minutes. Add as much of the remaining flour as necessary to make a soft dough. Knead with dough hook for 3 to 4 minutes or on a well-floured board by hand for 6 to 8 minutes or until smooth. Shape dough into a ball and place in an oiled bowl; turn to coat all sides. Cover loosely with a piece of oiled plastic wrap and a damp towel; let rise in a warm place until doubled in bulk, about 1 1/2 hours.

Meanwhile prepare the Filling. In a small saucepan, melt butter or margarine; add garlic and basil. Cool to room temperature. Punch dough down and place on a heavily floured board. Let rest 5 to 7 minutes. Roll into a rectangle, 24 × 9 inches. Spread with melted butter and sprinkle with cheese. Starting at a long side, roll the dough up jelly-roll fashion. Cut roll in half lengthwise, making two 24-inch portions. Place the pieces side by side with cut edges up. Pinch one end of each portion together. Twist the 2 pieces together by lifting one over the other several times. Place twist on a greased baking sheet and shape into a ring, overlapping the ends. Let rise in a warm place, uncovered, for 30 minutes or until puffed and slightly risen. Do not let rise until double. Do not be concerned if some of the butter oozes out; it will bake back into the bread.

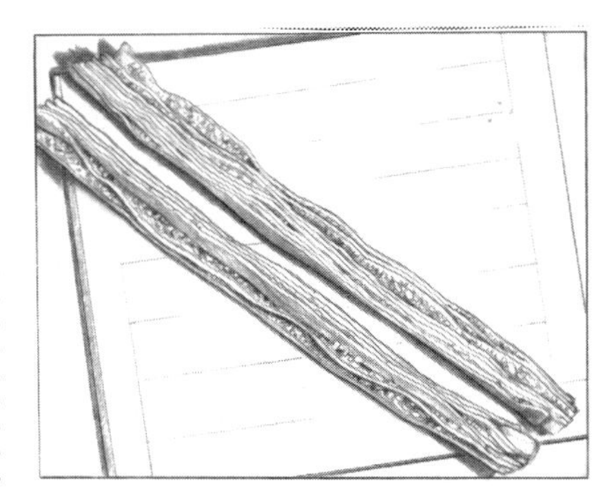

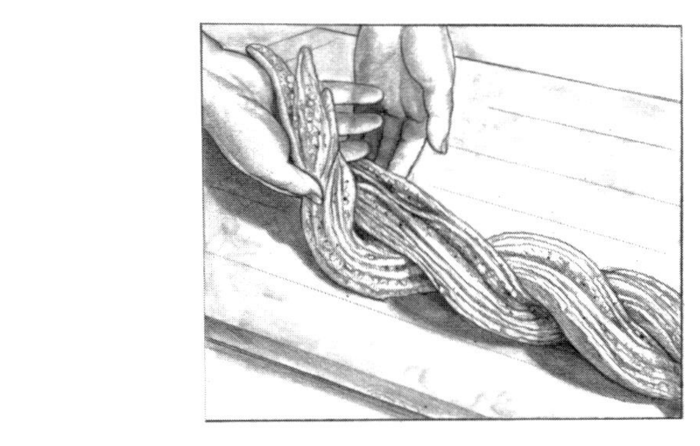

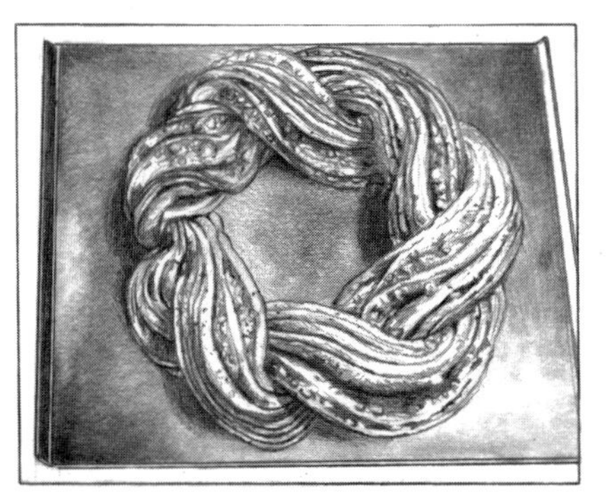

Preheat oven to 350 degrees. Brush top of bread with beaten egg. Bake for 35 to 40 minutes or until golden brown. Immediately loosen from baking sheet with spatula. Cool slightly and remove to rack. Serve warm.

∗ The bread may be stored, tightly wrapped, at room temperature overnight or frozen. To reheat, bake at 350 degrees until warm.

Makes 1 loaf.

Brioche Rolls

These jaunty little rolls with topknots are prettiest when baked in fluted brioche molds. If you don't have any, shape the rolls in muffin or custard cups instead. (See photograph, page 89.)

1 recipe Brioche Dough (page 151), refrigerated overnight
1 egg yolk mixed with 1 teaspoon milk, for glaze
Butter for serving, if desired

Make Brioche Dough as recipe directs. To make the rolls, brush 12 individual brioche tins (1½ inches across the bottom and 3 inches across the top) or 12 medium 2½-inch muffin or custard cups generously with butter. Work with half the dough at a time, keeping remainder refrigerated until needed. With floured hands, make 6 balls, using about ¾ of the dough. Place a ball in each tin or cup; with a buttered finger or spoon handle, make an indentation in the top of each. Make 6 small balls from remaining dough; pinch one end, elongating it to form a pear shape. Lightly press the tapered end into the indentation. Repeat with remaining dough.

Place individual tins on a baking sheet. Lightly cover with a piece of buttered plastic wrap and let rise in a warm place until doubled in bulk, about 1½ hours.

Preheat oven to 425 degrees. Lightly brush tops of rolls with egg yolk glaze, being careful not to let it run down the tins. Bake for 5 minutes. Reduce oven temperature to 350 degrees and bake for 6 to 8 minutes longer or until a toothpick inserted in the center comes out clean. Turn out and cool slightly on racks. Serve warm with butter, if desired.

∗ The rolls may be refrigerated, tightly covered, up to 2 days or frozen. Reheat at 350 degrees for 3 to 5 minutes or until warm.

Makes 12 rolls.

Lemon-Glazed Brioche with Lemon-Honey Butter

Lemon in the batter, in the glaze and in the butter. It takes most of the juice and all the rind from 5 to 6 lemons to produce this lavish loaf. (See photograph, page 46.)

1 recipe Brioche Dough (page 151), refrigerated overnight
2 tablespoons grated lemon peel

Lemon-Honey Butter

¼ pound (1 stick) butter or margarine, at room temperature
2 tablespoons honey
2 teaspoons lemon juice
1 tablespoon finely grated lemon peel

Lemon Glaze

½ cup sugar
¼ cup lemon juice
2 tablespoons grated lemon peel

Make Brioche Dough as directed in the recipe, mixing the lemon peel into batter with the eggs. It must be refrigerated overnight.

To make the Lemon-Honey Butter, beat butter or margarine in a small mixing bowl with electric mixer until fluffy. Add honey, lemon juice and peel, mixing until well blended.

* The butter may be refrigerated up to 1 week or frozen. Bring to room temperature before serving.

To make the Lemon Glaze, stir sugar, lemon juice and peel in a small saucepan over moderate heat until the sugar is melted, about 3 minutes; set aside.

Grease bottom and sides of a 9 × 2½- or 9 × 3-inch springform or heart-shaped pan. Cut foil to fit bottom and grease. Press the cold brioche dough into pan. Brush top with half the glaze, being careful not to let it drip down into the pan. Let rise, uncovered, in a warm place until doubled in bulk, about 1½ hours. Brush top again with remaining glaze.

Preheat oven to 375 degrees. Bake loaf for 20 to 30 minutes or until the top is deep golden brown. Remove pan from oven and immediately go around the sides with a sharp knife; invert the loaf onto a rack and turn right side up. Serve warm or at room temperature with Lemon-Honey Butter.

* The bread may be refrigerated, tightly wrapped in foil, for up to 2 days or frozen. Defrost covered; reheat, uncovered, at 350 degrees for 10 minutes or until warm.

Makes 1 loaf.

Brioche Dough

This rich, buttery dough can be used for both Brioche Rolls (page 149) and Lemon-Glazed Brioche (page 150). Make sure you allow time to refrigerate the dough overnight.

- ¼ cup warm water (110 to 115 degrees)
- 1 package dry yeast
- ¼ teaspoon plus 2 tablespoons sugar
- 2¼ cups all-purpose flour
- 1 teaspoon salt, or to taste
- 3 eggs, at room temperature
- 12 tablespoons (1½ sticks) butter or margarine, melted and cooled to lukewarm

Pour water into a large electric mixer bowl. Stir in yeast and ¼ teaspoon sugar; let stand until foamy, about 5 minutes. With electric mixer at low speed, mix in 2 tablespoons sugar, flour, salt, and eggs. Mix until thoroughly incorporated. Beating continuously at medium speed, slowly add the butter until it is thoroughly incorporated. Continue mixing for 3 to 4 minutes. The dough will be shiny and sticky.

Scrape the dough down and cover the bowl loosely with a piece of oiled plastic wrap and a damp towel and let rise in a warm place until light and spongy and tripled in bulk, about 3 hours. Punch dough down, cover the bowl tightly with plastic wrap and refrigerate overnight.

No-Knead Onion Bread

Lots of onion soup mix and dill lace this tender, even-grained peasant loaf. A perfect partner to hearty soups and entrees. (See photograph, page 139.)

- ¼ cup warm water (110 to 115 degrees)
- 1 package dry yeast
- ¼ teaspoon sugar
- 1 cup small curd cottage cheese
- 2 tablespoons butter or margarine, cut into small pieces
- 3 tablespoons honey
- 3 tablespoons dry onion soup mix
- 1 tablespoon dried dillweed
- ¼ teaspoon baking soda
- ¾ teaspoon salt, or to taste
- 1 egg, lightly beaten
- 2½ cups bread flour
- 1 egg mixed with 1 teaspoon water for glaze
- Butter for serving, if desired

Pour water into a large bowl. Stir in yeast and sugar; let sit 5 minutes or until foamy. In a medium saucepan, heat cottage cheese, butter or margarine, honey and onion soup mix until butter melts and mixture is warm to the touch. Stir in dill, baking soda, salt and egg. Stir into yeast mixture. Stir in flour; the batter will be stiff. Cover with a piece of oiled plastic wrap and a damp towel. Set in a warm place and let rise 1 hour or until doubled in bulk. Punch dough down and place in a well greased 9 × 5 × 3-inch loaf pan. Cover and let rise 1 hour.

Preheat the oven to 350 degrees. Brush the top of the loaf lightly with egg glaze. Bake for 30 to 40 minutes or until the top is browned. Remove from oven, immediately go around edges with a knife and invert loaf. Turn right side up and cool on rack. Serve with butter, if desired.

* The bread may be wrapped in foil and stored at room temperature up to 2 days or frozen.

Makes 1 loaf.

SPECTACULARS

GALA ITALIA

SANTA FE CHILI BLOWOUT

OLYMPIAN GREEK FEAST

SYMPHONY IN BLACK AND WHITE

THE CONSUMMATE COCKTAIL PARTY

Antipasto All'Italiana, including Hearts of Palm in Spinach-Walnut Pesto, Marinated Mushrooms with Blue Cheese, Pepper Wedges with Tomatoes and Basil; Marinated Shrimp in Italian Bread, Pesto-Topped Appetizer Cheesecake, Campari Slush.

M E N U

GALA ITALIA

Campari Slush

Antipasto All'Italiana

Pesto-Topped Appetizer Cheesecake (*Page 179*)

Spinach-Mushroom Lasagne

Marinated Shrimp in Italian Bread

Praline Cassata with Raspberry Sauce

Perhaps it is because the people of Italy are so spirited, earthy, adventurous and creative that their food has the same wonderful attributes. This is a menu specially designed to be served buffet style.

Start with invitations written with a red or green felt-tip pen on raw lasagne noodles. ("The time is half-pasta seven!") Slip them into padded manila envelopes. Create an original centerpiece by scooping out a loaf of Italian bread. Line the bread with foil or plastic wrap and fill with floral sponge. Insert stems of fresh flowers interspersed with bunches of dry spaghetti. Then string the spaghetti with an assortment of pasta shapes. Turn empty wine bottles into trattoria candlesticks with multicolored drip candles.

You might want to serve the Antipasto All'Italiana and Shrimp in Italian Bread as appetizers with drinks or substitute Shrimp Brochettes with Feta (page 168). The Spinach-Mushroom Lasagne can be prepared ahead and refrigerated for up to 2 days, but I don't recommend freezing it. Seven Greens Salad (page 72) could be added to the menu if desired.

There probably isn't an easier, tastier dessert for a large gathering than Praline Cassata with Raspberry Sauce, but Cappuccino Nut Torte (page 78) is hard to resist, too.

Campari Slush

As vivid as a summer sunset, this cool smoothie also goes great with brunch. (See photograph, page 153.)

- 2 cans (6 ounces each) frozen orange juice, not defrosted
- 2½ cups sparkling mineral water, chilled
- 1 cup Campari
- 4 cups ice cubes or crushed ice
- 5 orange slices, cut in half, for garnish

Place half the orange juice, mineral water and Campari in a blender container. Add 2 cups ice and process until mixture is slushy. Repeat with remaining ingredients. Serve in stemmed glasses with a slice of orange curled over the rim.

Makes 12 servings, about 6 ounces each.

Spinach-Mushroom Lasagne

The great Italian classic reinvented vegetarian-style. This version has no meat or tomato sauce and is assembled with uncooked noodles.

- 2 pounds fresh bulk spinach (about 10 ounces stemmed)
- 4 tablespoons vegetable oil
- 1 onion, chopped
- 3 cloves garlic, minced
- 2 pounds fresh mushrooms, sliced
- ¼ teaspoon dried red pepper flakes
- 2 cups (1 pint) ricotta cheese
- 1 cup grated parmesan cheese (4 ounces)
- 3 tablespoons fresh chopped basil or 1 tablespoon dried basil, crumbled
- ¼ teaspoon pepper
- 1¼ cups shredded extra-sharp cheddar cheese (about 5 ounces)
- 4 cups shredded mozzarella cheese (about 1 pound)
- 8 ounces lasagne noodles, uncooked
- 1 jar (4 ounces) roasted sweet red peppers or pimientos, drained and cut into ½ × 1-inch strips

Discard stems from spinach and wash leaves. Shake off excess water and tear into 2-inch pieces. Heat oil in a large skillet; sauté onion and garlic until soft. Add mushrooms and red pepper flakes; cook, stirring over moderately high heat, until barely tender. Pile spinach on top and stir by turning the mixture over until the spinach is wilted.

In a medium bowl, stir together ricotta, parmesan, basil and pepper. To assemble the casserole, spread a third of the spinach-mushroom mixture with some of its liquid into the bottom of a 9 × 13-inch casserole. Top with half the lasagne noodles. Spoon half the remaining spinach mixture over. Spread entire ricotta mixture over the vegetables, smoothing it as evenly as possible. Sprinkle with half the cheddar and half the mozzarella cheese. Place red pepper or pimiento strips over cheese. Cover with remaining noodles, overlapping them if necessary. Cover noodles with remaining spinach mixture and pour over any liquid left in the pan.

Place on a baking sheet and bake at 350 degrees for 15 minutes. Sprinkle with remaining cheddar and mozzarella cheese and bake for 15 to 20 more minutes or until juices are bubbling and cheese is golden brown. Let sit 15 minutes before serving.

* The baked lasagne may be refrigerated, covered, up to 2 days. Bring to room temperature at least 2 hours. To reheat, bake, covered, at 350 degrees for 20 minutes; uncover and bake 10 more minutes. Or reheat in microwave until sides are bubbling.

Serves 8 to 10.

Marinated Shrimp in Italian Bread

A long loaf of Italian bread is scooped out, toasted and filled with marinated shrimp. Cut into small slices and eaten with the fingers like an open-face sandwich, it makes an outstanding buffet accompaniment. The marinated shrimp can also be served as an hors d'oeuvre with crackers. *(See photograph, page 153.)*

- ⅔ cup vegetable oil
- 4 cloves garlic, minced
- 1½ teaspoons salt, or to taste
- ⅓ cup lemon juice
- 3 tablespoons finely chopped chives or green onion tops
- ¼ cup chopped jarred pimiento
- ¼ cup finely chopped fresh parsley
- ¼ cup finely chopped fresh dill or 1 tablespoon dried dill
- 1 pound large shrimp, cooked, shelled and deveined (about 40)
- 1 or 2 long loaves Italian, French or sourdough bread

In a medium nonaluminum bowl, whisk together oil, garlic, salt, lemon juice, chives or green onion, pimiento, parsley, and dill. Add shrimp, toss to coat, cover with plastic wrap and marinate in the refrigerator for 1 to 4 hours.

As close to serving as possible, preheat the oven to 400 degrees. Cut a small slice off top of bread. Using your fingers, pull out bread from the base, leaving a ½-inch shell; reserve the bread for another use. Remove shrimp from marinade; set shrimp aside.

With a pastry brush, coat inside and top edges of bread boat liberally with the marinade. Place on a baking sheet and bake for 10 to 12 minutes or until lightly toasted. Cut across into ½- to ¾-inch slices. Place 1 shrimp around the curve of each slice as pictured on page 153, or arrange 3 or 4 shrimp across each slice.

Serves 10.

Antipasto All'Italiana

I've never made antipasto the same way twice. Use as many or as few of my suggestions as you like—and throw in a couple of favorites of your own. *(See photograph, page 153.)*

- 1 medium cantaloupe or ½ large honeydew or Cranshaw melon or 12 fresh figs
- 12 slices prosciutto
- 1 recipe Hearts of Palm in Spinach-Walnut Pesto (page 177)
- 1 recipe Marinated Mushroom with Blue Cheese (page 177)
- 1 recipe Pepper Wedges with Tomatoes and Basil (page 178)
- 8 ounces cotto or Genoa salami, thinly sliced
- 8 ounces mortadella, thinly sliced, at room temperature
- 8 ounces mozzarella cheese, thinly sliced, at room temperature

Cut melon into 12 thin wedges; if using figs, leave whole. Wrap 1 slice of prosciutto around each piece of fruit. Cover with plastic wrap and refrigerate until serving, or overnight, if desired.

Prepare Hearts of Palm, Marinated Mushroom and Pepper Wedges as recipes direct. Place in serving dishes.

Roll meat and cheese into logs or cones. Cover with plastic wrap and refrigerate until serving. Arrange all ingredients decoratively on a large platter.

Serves 12.

Praline Cassata with Raspberry Sauce

Crushed storebought nut brittle folded into whipped cream and egg whites makes a big crunch with very little work.

- ½ pound nut brittle, almond, cashew, peanut or mixed
- 6 egg whites, at room temperature
- 2 cups heavy cream
- 3 tablespoons Amaretto
- 2 recipes Raspberry Sauce (page 53)
- ½ pint raspberries or strawberries stemmed and halved, optional

In a food processor fitted with the metal blade, process brittle until ground; you should have about 1¾ cups. In a small mixing bowl with an electric mixer, beat egg whites until stiff peaks form. In a large mixing bowl with the electric mixer, whip cream until soft peaks form. Add Amaretto and beat until stiff. Fold brittle and egg whites into cream. Pour into a lightly oiled 9 × 5 × 3-inch loaf pan. Cover with foil and freeze overnight.

∗ The cassata may be frozen up to 2 weeks.

Make the Raspberry Sauce as directed. Refrigerate until ready to use. Several hours before serving, go around edge of cassata with the tip of a sharp knife, dip pan into warm water and invert onto a platter. Return cassata to freezer.

To serve, spoon several tablespoons Raspberry Sauce onto each dessert plate, twirling to coat the bottom. Slice the cassata and place a slice in the center of each plate. Garnish with a cluster of sliced strawberries or raspberries, if desired. Serve immediately.

Serves 12.

MENU

SANTA FE CHILI BLOWOUT

Iced or Papaya Margaritas

Red Wine Sangria

Avocado Salsa with Home-Fried Tortilla Chips
(*Pages 180 and 181*)

Pork Molé Chili with Black Beans

Aztec Corn Crêpes

Green and Red Cabbage Salad with Peanuts

Café Olé Caramel Flan

Flamboyant Tex-Mex parties seem to generate contagious fun. This is a time to bring out your colorful glazed pottery. Wrap the silverware in bright napkins and tie with yarn—don't worry about matching. Decorate with large paper flowers and a multicolored piñata from the party shop. Write the invitations with a felt-tip pen on 6-inch tortillas. Spray with fixative or lacquer and slip into padded envelopes for mailing.

Absolutely everything here is made ahead. The Pork Molé Chili and Aztec Corn Crêpes can both be frozen, allowing you to make batches when time permits. The chili condiments can be chopped a day ahead and refrigerated. If your kitchen is a comfortable place for guests to congregate, set up the buffet there and serve the chili right from the stove. Serve Green and Red Cabbage Salad and the crêpes from large wooden and ovenproof earthenware dishes. Instead of the crêpes you could serve White Cornmeal Spoonbread (page 118).

Café Olé Caramel Flan adds the right light touch to this menu. The recipe doubles beautifully, but don't try baking it in one large container. You might even add Acapulco Margarita Pie (page 133). If space permits, hire strolling mariachis or a guitar player. If not, pipe up-tempo Mexican music throughout the house.

Iced Margaritas

To serve this classic concoction the traditional Mexican way, frost the rim of each glass with coarse salt.

- Coarse salt
- 1 lime, cut in wedges
- 2 cans (6 ounces each) frozen limeade concentrate, not defrosted
- ½ cup orange liqueur such as curaçao, Triple Sec or Cointreau
- 1½ cups tequila
- ¼ cup lemon juice
- 2 egg whites
- 4 cups ice cubes or crushed ice

Place salt on a small plate. Run lime around the rim of stemmed glasses; dip into salt and coat evenly. If desired, freeze glasses.

Place half the limeade, orange liqueur, tequila, lemon juice and 1 egg white in blender container. Add 2 cups ice and blend until slushy. Repeat with remaining ingredients. Pour into prepared glasses.

Makes 10 servings, about 6 ounces each.

Papaya Margaritas

A fresh fruity variation on the traditional citrus version.

- 2 cans (6 ounces each) frozen margarita mix, not defrosted
- 1½ cups tequila, divided
- 2 ripe papayas, peeled, seeded and chopped
- Ice cubes or crushed ice
- 2 limes, halved and sliced

Place 1 can margarita mix, ¾ cup tequila and 1 papaya in blender jar. Blend until pureed. Fill blender jar to within 1 inch of top with ice cubes or crushed ice. Blend until slushy. Repeat. Garnish each glass with a half slice of lime.

Makes 12 servings, about 6 ounces each.

Variation:

Banana Margaritas

Substitute 3 ripe bananas for the papayas.

Red Wine Sangria

This fruity party punch is festive for the cocktail hour as well as with dinner.

- ½ cup water
- ½ cup sugar
- 2 bottles (⅘ quart each) dry red wine
- ½ cup (4 ounces) brandy
- ½ cup orange juice
- 2 bananas, cut in half
- 2 limes, halved and thinly sliced
- 1 lemon, halved and thinly sliced
- 1 orange, halved and thinly sliced
- 2 cups club soda, chilled
- Ice cubes

In a small saucepan, bring water and sugar to a boil. Cook over moderate heat for 3 minutes or until sugar is dissolved. Cool to room temperature. If not using immediately, pour into a covered container and refrigerate.

In a large pitcher or bowl, stir together red wine, brandy, orange juice, sugar syrup and bananas. Refrigerate, covered, overnight. Two hours before serving, remove bananas. Stir in sliced fruit. Refrigerate until ready to serve. Add club soda and pour over ice cubes into large glasses or wine goblets, adding a few slices of fruit to each glass.

Makes 12 servings, about 6 ounces each.

Pork Molé Chili with Black Beans

Chocolate adds rich deep color. Cinnamon and sugar add sweetness. Chili powder, cumin and cayenne add spice. Corn tortillas add texture. This will be the most intensely flavored chili you've ever tasted. Two 16-ounce cans of black beans, rinsed and drained, may be substituted for the cooked dried beans.

1½ cups dried black beans (10 ounces)
4 tablespoons vegetable oil, divided
2 onions, finely chopped
6 cloves garlic, minced
4 pounds pork butt or shoulder, fat removed and cut into ½-inch cubes
⅓ cup chili powder
1 tablespoon plus 1 teaspoon ground cumin
1 tablespoon plus 1 teaspoon dried oregano
1 teaspoon cinnamon
1 tablespoon sugar
½ teaspoon cayenne pepper, or to taste
1 teaspoon salt, or to taste
1 can (14½ ounces) whole tomatoes, with their liquid
4½ cups chicken broth
1½ ounces (1½ squares) unsweetened chocolate, chopped
2 corn tortillas, torn into bite-size pieces

Condiments

3 medium tomatoes, chopped
½ cup chopped fresh cilantro
1 large onion, finely chopped
10 radishes, finely chopped
1 cup sour cream

Rinse beans and pick through to remove pebbles and other foreign matter. Place beans in a large saucepan; add enough water to cover by 2 inches. Bring to a boil over high heat and cook 1 minute; drain. Add fresh water to cover by 3 inches, bring to a boil over high heat, reduce heat to moderately low, and simmer, partially covered, stirring once or twice, until tender, about 45 minutes to 1 hour. Drain and set aside to cool.

In a wide large nonaluminum saucepan, heat 2 tablespoons oil. Add onions and garlic and cook, covered, over low heat, stirring once or twice, until the onions are soft, about 20 minutes. Remove to a bowl and set aside. Heat remaining 2 tablespoons oil and add the pork. Cook over moderate heat, stirring occasionally, for 20 minutes or until all the pink is gone; pour off drippings. Stir in cooked onions, chili powder, cumin, oregano, cinnamon, sugar, cayenne pepper and salt. Cook 5 minutes. Break up tomatoes roughly with a spoon and add them with their juice, the chicken broth and chocolate. Bring to a boil, lower heat and simmer, uncovered, stirring occasionally, for 1 hour 30 minutes or until pork is nearly tender. Add beans and continue simmering 30 minutes until pork is tender and chili has thickened. Stir in tortillas; simmer until they have dissolved into sauce, about 10 minutes.

* The chili may be refrigerated up to 2 days or frozen. Reheat slowly in a saucepan on the stove or in a glass dish in the microwave, stirring occasionally.

Serve with condiments.

Serves 8.

Aztec Corn Crêpes

Corn and cornmeal crêpes wrap up a filling of sweet creamed corn and caramelized onion. Turn them into a fantastic luncheon entree by topping with sour cream and shredded cheddar cheese.

Corn Crêpes

- ½ cup water
- ¾ cup buttermilk
- 2 tablespoons vegetable oil
- 2 eggs
- ¾ cup all-purpose flour
- ⅓ cup yellow cornmeal
- 2 tablespoons canned creamed corn
- ¼ teaspoon sugar
- ¼ teaspoon salt, or to taste

Creamed Corn Filling

- 2 tablespoons butter or margarine
- 1 medium onion, chopped
- Rest of can (17 ounces) creamed corn from crêpes

To make the Corn Crêpes, in a medium bowl, whisk water, buttermilk, oil, eggs, flour, cornmeal, 2 tablespoons canned creamed corn, sugar and salt until blended; do not use a food processor. To make 5-inch crêpes, you will need a 7-inch crêpe pan measuring 5 inches across the bottom. If the pan is not nonstick, brush it with butter or oil. Heat pan over moderately high heat, lift from heat and pour in 3 tablespoons batter, tilting the pan in all directions so the batter covers the bottom in a very thin layer. Return to heat and cook crêpe over moderately high heat until underside is golden brown. Slip onto waxed paper, browned side down, and continue with remaining batter, separating the crêpes with sheets of waxed paper.

To make the Creamed Corn Filling, melt butter or margarine in a small skillet; sauté onion over moderately high heat stirring occasionally until golden, about 20 minutes. Stir in the rest of the can of creamed corn.

Place crêpe, browned side down, on a work surface. Spread 2 tablespoons filling over uncooked side and roll up. Place in a buttered baking dish, seam side down.

* The crêpes may be refrigerated overnight or frozen. Defrost, covered, at room temperature.

Before serving, preheat oven to 350 degrees. Cover with foil and bake for 15 minutes or until heated through.

Makes 12 to 13 crêpes.

Green and Red Cabbage Salad with Peanuts

No one can guess the mysterious crunchy green of this refreshing, light salad is cabbage. That's because it's cut into bite-size pieces like lettuce, not shredded as for coleslaw.

- 1 small head green cabbage (about 2 pounds)
- ½ head red cabbage (about ¾ pound)
- ¾ cup vegetable oil
- 3 tablespoons olive oil
- 3 tablespoons red wine vinegar
- 3 tablespoons coarse-grain mustard
- 1 tablespoon lemon juice
- ¼ teaspoon salt, or to taste
- 1 cup skinless salted peanuts
- Salt and pepper to taste

Cut core from cabbages. Cut into quarters. Cut each quarter in half across and then into ½-inch pieces. Make the dressing in a small bowl by whisking the oils, vinegar, mustard, lemon juice and salt until blended.

* The cabbage and dressing may be refrigerated, separately, overnight.

Before serving, place cabbage in large bowl. Add peanuts, pour dressing over and toss well. Season with salt and pepper to taste.

Serves 8 to 10.

Café Olé Caramel Flan

Steeping coffee beans in cream releases their aromatic flavor without altering the color of the cream. The first taste of this ivory custard, full of wake-up coffee flavor, comes as a complete surprise.

- 1 quart (4 cups) half and half
- 1¾ cups sugar, divided
- 4 ounces (1½ cups) whole coffee beans, preferably French roast
- 3 tablespoons water
- 5 eggs
- 2 teaspoons vanilla

In a medium saucepan, bring the half and half and ¾ cup of sugar to a boil. Remove from heat and stir in coffee beans. Cover and steep for 3 hours.

In a heavy small saucepan, stir together remaining 1 cup sugar and the water. Bring to a boil over moderately high heat. Boil without stirring until the mixture turns caramel color, about 8 minutes. Immediately pour into a 6-cup soufflé mold or deep baking dish. Using pot holders to protect your hands, tilt the dish to coat the bottom and partially up the sides. Set aside to cool.

Preheat the oven to 350 degrees. Place a roasting pan large enough to hold the baking dish in the oven; fill half full with water. In a medium bowl, whisk eggs and vanilla until frothy. Reheat cream and coffee beans until hot (do not boil); pour through a strainer into the eggs. Whisk until blended; discard the beans. Pour the custard through a strainer into the caramel-lined dish. Place in roasting pan. Bake for 50 to 60 minutes or until a knife inserted in the center comes out clean. The top will be browned, but the custard will jiggle when the pan is shaken. Remove from water, empty roasting pan and refill with ice water; set the custard in to cool. Cover with plastic wrap and refrigerate until chilled.

* The custard may be refrigerated up to 2 days.

Before serving, go around edges of custard with the tip of a sharp knife. Invert onto a rimmed platter. Cut into wedges, spooning some of the caramel sauce over each slice.

Serves 10.

M E N U

OLYMPIAN GREEK FEAST

Roasted Eggplant Dip with Toasted Pita Chips
(*Page 182*)

Great Greek Salad

Lemon Tabbouleh Stuffed Vegetables

Moussaka in Phyllo

Shrimp Brochettes with Feta

Honey-Drenched Baklava

Butter-Crust Date Bars

Sesame Seed Cookies (*Page 45*)

The mildly exotic, hauntingly subtle flavors of Greek cuisine lend themselves to an exciting and high-spirited buffet gathering. Splash your table with vivid colors, the more the better. Gather all the brass serving pieces you can and set oversize candles in brass holders on each side of the table.

Moussaka in Phyllo is the star of the party. These flaky strudel rolls will remain hot for at least 30 minutes after baking. If you have a large cutting board, serve them right on it, garnishing the border with parsley. Unless you're entertaining 16 or more, it isn't necessary to prepare the entire menu. Shrimp Brochettes with Feta can serve as a second entree for a crowd or be doubled for a solo main course. Vegetables stuffed with Lemon Tabbouleh can be served with or without the Great Greek Salad. For dessert, offer an assortment of fresh fruit along with the sweet pastries.

Surprise your guests with a belly dancer. Make this Olympian Greek Feast an event they'll remember for years!

See photograph on previous page. *Clockwise from top right: Honey-Drenched Baklava, Moussaka in Phyllo, Lemon Tabbouleh Stuffed Vegetables, Roasted Eggplant Dip, Toasted Pita Chips.*

Great Greek Salad

Lettuce, feta cheese, cucumbers and tomatoes are the essential elements of Greek salad; I add other ingredients as well. Kalamata olives are available at Middle Eastern and Italian markets and some supermarkets.

1 large head romaine lettuce (about 1½ pounds)
2 heads red leaf lettuce (about 1 pound)
2 bunches watercress (about 1 pound)
2 cucumbers, peeled, seeded and coarsely chopped
16 radishes, thinly sliced
8 large green onions with tops, chopped
2 cans (15½ ounces each) chickpeas (garbanzo beans), drained
24 kalamata olives, pitted and halved, or ¾ cup halved ripe black olives
1 pound feta cheese, cut into ½-inch cubes
1 can (2 ounces) anchovy fillets, drained, dried and finely chopped, optional
6 tomatoes, cut in wedges
Salt and pepper to taste

Dressing
1 cup fruity olive oil
⅔ cup red wine vinegar
3 cloves garlic, minced
1½ teaspoons dried oregano, crumbled
⅓ cup chopped fresh parsley

Wash greens, break off stems and tear leaves into bite-size pieces. Wrap in paper towels and a plastic bag; refrigerate until crisp or overnight.

In a medium bowl, gently toss cucumber, radishes, green onions, chickpeas, olives, feta and anchovies, if using.

To make the Dressing, in a small bowl or jar, combine olive oil, vinegar, garlic, oregano, parsley, and pepper until blended. Pour over vegetables and marinate, covered, in the refrigerator for 4 to 12 hours.

Before serving, place greens in a very large salad bowl. Pour vegetables with their dressing over. Add tomatoes and toss well. Season with salt and pepper to taste.

Serves 16.

Lemon Tabbouleh Stuffed Vegetables

Lemon bulgur is an offbeat filling for colorful vegetable cups and grape leaves. Presented on a fancy platter or in a shallow wicker basket, they make a stunning centerpiece. (See photograph, page 163.)

Lemon Tabbouleh

- 2 cups bulgur
- ½ cup olive oil
- ½ cup lemon juice
- ½ cup chopped parsley
- 1 cup coarsely chopped fresh mint
- 2 cloves garlic, minced
- 1 teaspoon salt, or to taste
- 1 teaspoon sugar
- 2 teaspoons ground coriander
- 2 teaspoons ground cumin
- 2 teaspoons dry mustard
- ¼ teaspoon hot-pepper sauce

Vegetables

- 4 bell peppers, red, yellow or green
- 4 Japanese eggplants or 2 small eggplants
- 4 Italian plum tomatoes, cut in half and scooped out
- 32 grape leaves (8-ounce jar)
- 1 lemon, thinly sliced
- Curly endive or red leaf lettuce for lining platter or basket

To make Lemon Tabbouleh, place bulgur in a large bowl; add enough water to cover by at least 1 inch. Soak for 1 hour or until bulgur has doubled in bulk and most of the liquid is absorbed. Drain in a colander, pushing down to remove excess water. To make the dressing, whisk oil, lemon juice, herbs, garlic, salt, sugar, spices and hot-pepper sauce in a small bowl. Place bulgur in a bowl, pour dressing over, toss well and let stand at room temperature for 1 hour for the flavors to blend.

∗ Tabbouleh may be refrigerated up to 1 week.

To prepare the Vegetables, place peppers and eggplants in a shallow baking dish. Pour in ½ inch water; cover with foil. Bake at 350 degrees until the vegetables give slightly when lightly pressed with fingers. The peppers will take about 35 minutes; the eggplants, 40 to 60 minutes, depending on their size. Do not overbake, as they will continue softening after they are removed from the oven. Set aside until cool enough to handle.

Cut out core from peppers and scoop out seeds. Cut eggplants in half, scoop out insides, leaving a thin shell. Chop eggplant flesh into small dice and add to tabbouleh, if desired. Spoon tabbouleh into peppers, filling them to about ½ inch from the top. Cut in eighths. Fill eggplant halves, mounding the tops slightly. If large, cut into quarters or eighths. Fill tomato halves, mounding the tops.

Remove grape leaves from jar and drop into a saucepan of boiling water. Bring back to a boil and drain. Place leaves shiny side down on paper towels; cut out stems. Spoon 1 tablespoon tabbouleh onto each grape leaf, about 1 inch in from the stem. Fold stem end over, turn in sides and roll up tight. Place seam side down in 2 or 3 layers in an ovenproof casserole or saucepan. Arrange lemon slices over each layer. Invert a plate and place it directly on top of the leaves to hold them down. Pour in water to within 1 inch of top of pan. Bake at 350 degrees or simmer on top of stove for 40 minutes or until leaves are tender. Cool to room temperature.

∗ The stuffed vegetables may be refrigerated, covered, overnight. Bring to room temperature several hours before serving.

Line a platter or shallow basket with lettuce leaves. Arrange vegetables on lettuce, keeping each type together.

Serves 16.

Moussaka in Phyllo

In the Middle East, moussaka is prepared in accordance with a family's income. Poorer people use potatoes, while the more affluent use meat. Although not expensive to prepare, this is a rich American version, with two kinds of meat, eggplant and tomatoes all rolled up in layers of buttery phyllo pastry. *(See photograph, page 163.)*

Meat Mixture

- 4 tablespoons olive oil
- 2 large onions, finely chopped (about 2 cups)
- 4 cloves garlic, minced
- 3 medium eggplants (about 3 pounds), unpeeled and chopped into ½-inch cubes
- 1½ pounds lean ground lamb
- ½ pound lean ground beef
- 4 tablespoons tomato paste
- 2 cups canned tomato puree
- ¾ cup dry red wine
- ¾ teaspoon cinnamon
- 1 tablespoon dried oregano, crumbled
- 1 tablespoon dried basil, crumbled
- 2 teaspoons salt, or to taste
- Pepper to taste
- ¼ teaspoon sugar
- 1 teaspoon dried red pepper flakes or ½ teaspoon hot-pepper sauce
- ½ cup coarsely chopped parsley leaves

White Sauce

- 4 tablespoons (½ stick) butter or margarine
- 4 tablespoons all-purpose flour
- 1¾ cups milk, at room temperature
- ¾ teaspoon salt, or to taste
- ¼ teaspoon pepper
- ⅛ teaspoon cayenne pepper
- ½ cup grated parmesan cheese
- 1 cup ricotta cheese
- 2 egg yolks, lightly beaten

Pastry

- 1 pound phyllo, approximately 12 × 16 inches, defrosted if frozen (about 16 sheets)
- ½ pound (2 sticks) butter or margarine, melted
- 1 cup dry bread crumbs

To make Meat Mixture, heat olive oil in a heavy wide nonaluminum saucepan or Dutch oven; sauté onions and garlic until soft. Add eggplants, cover and cook over moderate heat, stirring often, until soft, about 15 minutes. Add ground lamb and beef and cook, uncovered, stirring and breaking meat up, until it loses its red color. Drain off excess juices if necessary. Stir in tomato paste, puree, wine, cinnamon, oregano, basil, salt, pepper, sugar and pepper flakes or hot-pepper sauce. Simmer, uncovered, over moderately low heat, stirring often, until juices have evaporated, 15 to 20 minutes. Stir in parsley. Divide meat into 3 portions, 1 portion to be used for each of the 3 strudel rolls.

To make White Sauce, in a medium saucepan, melt butter or margarine over moderately low heat. Stir in flour and cook 1 minute, stirring constantly. Slowly whisk in milk. Increase heat to moderately high and cook, whisking constantly, until mixture comes to a boil and thickens. Remove from heat and stir in salt, pepper, cayenne pepper, parmesan cheese, ricotta and egg yolks. Cover and refrigerate until cold.

To make the first roll, remove about a third of the sheets of phyllo; cover remaining sheets with waxed paper and a damp towel. Place a lightly dampened towel on the work surface. Place sheets one at a time on the towel with the long side toward you. Brush each sheet of phyllo with butter or margarine and sprinkle every other sheet lightly with bread crumbs, using about ⅓ cup. Spoon half of one of the meat portions down one long side of the pile of phyllo, about 2 inches in from the edge, leaving a 1½-inch border on each of the short ends. Spread a third of the white sauce over the meat; top with remainder of meat portion, mounding the mixture into a log shape. Fold the long 2-inch edge over the filling, fold in the two sides and then fold the remaining phyllo over the top to enclose the filling. Place the roll, seam side down, on a lightly buttered rimmed baking sheet. Make 2 other rolls in the same manner. Place on baking sheet at least 3 inches apart. Brush tops and sides of rolls with butter or margarine.

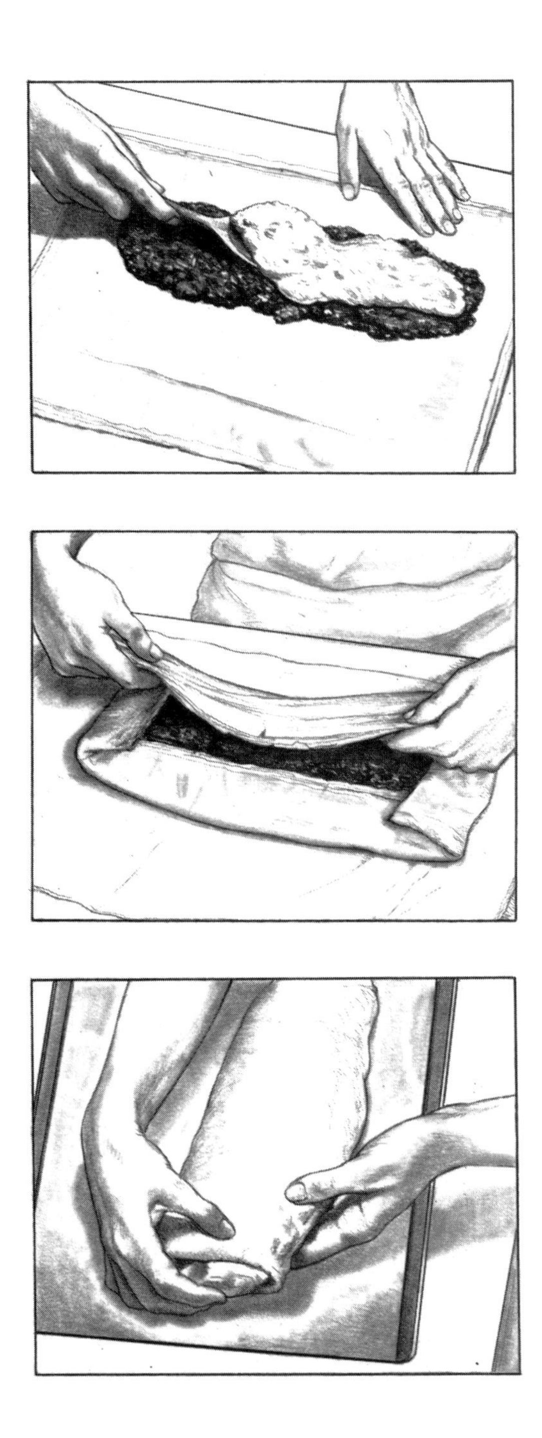

* The rolls may be refrigerated overnight or frozen. Refrigerate or freeze, uncovered, until firm, about 1 hour, then cover tightly with foil. Defrost, uncovered, at room temperature for several hours.

Preheat oven to 400 degrees. Brush tops and sides of rolls with butter. Bake 35 to 45 minutes or until golden. If the rolls are cold, they will take longer. If baking 2 sheets in one oven, reverse their positions half way through the baking time. Let rolls sit 20 to 30 minutes at room temperature before serving. Transfer to a serving platter by inserting 2 spatulas or a flat baking sheet underneath. To serve, cut into 1½-inch slices.

Makes 18 slices (serves 12 to 18).

Shrimp Brochettes with Feta

Shrimp flavored with Pernod and tarragon are capped with snowy white feta cheese and baked on skewers. They look great on a buffet table and are easy to pick up and eat.

2 pounds large or jumbo raw shrimp, peeled and deveined, with the tails left on (about 24)
Metal or wooden skewers soaked in ice water for 15 minutes to keep them from burning
½ cup fruity olive oil
⅓ cup lime juice
3 tablespoons lemon juice
2 tablespoons Pernod
2 teaspoons dried tarragon
¼ teaspoon pepper
6 cloves garlic, minced
½ cup feta cheese, shredded or finely crumbled (about 2 ounces)

Thread 2 shrimp on each skewer. Place in a shallow nonaluminum dish, preferably glass. To make the marinade, in a small bowl stir together oil, lime and lemon juice, Pernod, tarragon, pepper and garlic. Pour over shrimp; turn to coat both sides. Cover with plastic wrap and marinate in refrigerator for 1 hour. Turn and marinate at room temperature for 30 to 60 more minutes.

Preheat oven to 450 degrees. Line a rimmed baking sheet with foil. Remove shrimp from marinade; do not dry. Place on baking sheet and sprinkle with feta cheese, pressing it in lightly with your hands. Bake large shrimp for 7 to 8 minutes, jumbo for 9 to 11 minutes or until firm and just turned pink. Take care not to overcook. Serve immediately.

Serves 12, allowing 2 per person.

Honey-Drenched Baklava

When I asked the chef from a taverna on Crete for his marvelous baklava recipe, he was only too willing to oblige. Little did I know he would give it to me in Greek! *(See photograph, page 163.)*

1 pound walnut halves and pieces (about 4 cups)
1 tablespoon plus 2 teaspoons cinnamon
1 pound phyllo, approximately 12 × 16 inches, defrosted if frozen (about 16 sheets)
½ pound (2 sticks) butter or margarine, melted

Syrup
1 cup sugar
½ cup water
½ cup light corn syrup
1 cup honey

In a food processor fitted with the metal blade, chop nuts and cinnamon fine; set aside. Butter a 9 × 13-inch baking pan. Unwrap phyllo leaves and place on work surface. Place pan over dough and trim to fit. Cover phyllo with waxed paper and a damp towel to prevent drying out.

Remove 8 phyllo sheets and brush them one at a time with butter or margarine and place in bottom of pan. Sprinkle with a third of the nut mixture. Top with 2 sheets of buttered phyllo, sprinkle with half of the remaining nuts, 2 more buttered sheets of phyllo and the rest of the nuts. Top with remaining sheets of phyllo, buttering each one before putting it in place. Using the tip of a sharp knife, tuck in the edges. Butter top sheet and sprinkle lightly with water to prevent it from curling.

Preheat oven to 325 degrees. Using a very sharp knife, cut into diagonal parallel strips about 1½ inches apart, making about 40 diamond-shaped pieces. Be sure to cut all the way through the bottom layer. Bake for 1 hour or until golden brown.

Meanwhile, make Syrup. In a medium saucepan, combine sugar, water, corn syrup and honey. Bring to a boil over moderate heat, stirring to dissolve sugar; cool to room temperature.

When baklava is done, remove from oven and cool 5 minutes. Slowly pour cool syrup over warm pastry, allowing syrup to run between cut pieces. Let sit, uncovered, at room temperature for 6 to 8 hours. Serve at room temperature.

* Baklava may be kept, covered, at room temperature up to 3 days or frozen. Defrost, uncovered, at room temperature.

Makes about 40 pieces.

Butter-Crust Date Bars

A thick, sweet date-nut mixture bakes atop a buttery cookie crust. These bars are a date you're sure to remember.

Butter-Crust Layer

1¼ cups all-purpose flour
⅓ cup sugar
¼ pound (1 stick) butter or margarine, cold and cut into 8 pieces

Date-Nut Layer

½ cup (packed) golden light brown sugar
¼ cup granulated sugar
2 eggs
1 teaspoon vanilla
2 tablespoons all-purpose flour
1 teaspoon baking powder
¼ teaspoon salt, or to taste
¼ teaspoon ground nutmeg
1 cup chopped walnuts (about 4 ounces)
1 cup chopped pitted dates (about 4 ounces)
Confectioners sugar for sprinkling on top

Preheat the oven to 350 degrees. Line a 9 × 13-inch baking pan with heavy foil, letting it extend at least 1 inch over the sides. Butter the bottom. To make the Crust, pulse or mix flour, sugar and butter or margarine in a food processor fitted with the metal blade or in a mixer until crumbly. Press into bottom of the prepared pan. Bake for 16 to 18 minutes or until the edges are lightly browned.

While the crust bakes, make the Date-Nut Layer. Using the same food processor workbowl and metal blade or the same mixing bowl, process or mix both sugars, eggs and vanilla until frothy. Add flour, baking powder, salt and nutmeg; mix until incorporated. Pulse or mix in nuts and dates only until combined. Spread topping over the hot pastry. Return to oven and bake 15 to 18 more minutes or until the top is golden. Remove from oven and cool to room temperature. Lift out the foil, place on a flat surface and cut into 1¼ × 2-inch bars.

* The bars may be stored at room temperature in an airtight container for several days or frozen.

Before serving, sift confectioners sugar over the top.

Makes 42 bars.

MENU

SYMPHONY IN BLACK AND WHITE

Black Caviar Musical Note

Seafood Tourtière

Pattypan Squash with Tomatoes and Corn

Marinated Vegetables in Raspberry-Walnut Vinaigrette (*Page 50*)

Chocolate Hazelnut Rhapsody

Celebrating the fine art of music through the grand art of cooking is a lyrical experience. Announce the occasion by sending invitations written on a musical score sheet. Playing further upon the theme, arrange flowers in a black top hat with a pair of white opera gloves attached to the rim.

Prelude for this symphony is an Egg, Avocado and Caviar Mold shaped into a musical note and served with crackers. For the grandezza, present the pastry-wrapped Seafood Tourtière. If the occasion heralds a birthday or anniversary, embellish the top with pastry cut-outs of the guest of honor's initials, hearts or flowers.

Orchestrating all the details needn't be a big production. The Seafood Tourtière must sit for two hours after baking. The pattypan squash cups need only to be reheated and the Marinated Vegetables in Raspberry-Walnut Vinaigrette (page 50) can be arranged in a basket or platter at least an hour before.

For the grand finale, take a deep bow and prepare for a standing ovation when the curtain rises on Chocolate Hazelnut Rhapsody, a dulcet rendition of the piano keyboard.

See photograph on previous page. Pattypan Squash with Tomatoes and Corn, Seafood Tourtière with Lemon Butter Sauce, Chocolate Hazelnut Rhapsody.

Black Caviar Musical Note

Don't shy away from creating an hors d'oeuvre as impressive as this one. With easy-to-mold layers of egg and avocado to work with, it's quite simple to assemble.

1 recipe Egg, Avocado and Caviar Mold (page 178), with black caviar
Crackers or bread rounds, for serving

Make egg and avocado layers as recipe directs. On a large oval or rectangular platter, spread the egg mixture into a musical note as follows: Begin at bottom left of platter. Spread a 5-inch circle. Make the stem up the right side, 11 inches high and ¾ inch wide. Make curved part of stem, starting at top and spreading a 1¼-inch arc. Spread avocado layer over egg layer, smoothing the top and sides. Spread sour cream evenly over top and sides, covering them completely. Refrigerate until serving.

* The mold may be refrigerated, covered, with plastic wrap overnight.

Before serving, spread black caviar carefully over the top. Serve chilled with crackers or bread rounds.

Serves 12.

Seafood Tourtière

This is the pièce de résistance. Layers of pink seafood, green herbs, creamy white sauce—and more—are wrapped in a blanket of flaky pastry. Preparation is lengthy, but the tourtière can be assembled weeks in advance. And the bravos you receive will more than compensate for the time it takes to compose it. (See photograph, page 171.)

Pastry

- 12 tablespoons (1½ sticks) butter or margarine, cold and cut into 12 pieces
- 6 ounces cream cheese, cold and cut into 4 pieces
- 3 tablespoons sour cream
- 2 cups all-purpose flour
- ¾ teaspoon salt, or to taste

Filling

- 3 medium cloves garlic, peeled
- ½ cup (loosely packed) parsley sprigs
- 6 green onions with tops, chopped into 1-inch pieces
- 2 tablespoons chopped fresh dill or 2 teaspoons dried dill
- 4 tablespoons (½ stick) butter or margarine
- ¼ cup all-purpose flour
- 1⅔ cups milk
- 1½ teaspoons Dijon mustard
- Cayenne and white pepper to taste
- Salt to taste
- ¾ pound cooked crab meat or 1 pound cooked salmon
- 1 pound very small shrimp, cooked
- 2 cups shredded swiss cheese (about 8 ounces)
- 4 hard-boiled eggs, peeled and chopped
- 1 cup sour cream
- 1 egg yolk mixed with 1 tablespoon milk for glaze
- Lemon wedges and parsley for garnish, if desired

Lemon Butter Sauce

- ½ pound (2 sticks) butter or margarine
- 5 teaspoons fresh lemon juice
- 3 tablespoons chopped fresh parsley
- ⅛ teaspoon salt, or to taste

To make the Pastry, in a food processor fitted with the metal blade, process butter or margarine, cream cheese and sour cream until blended. Add flour and salt; pulse until the mixture is crumbly and the consistency of coarse meal. Remove from bowl and shape a third of the dough into a disk. Shape remaining dough into another disk. Wrap them in plastic wrap and refrigerate until ready to assemble tourtière.

* The pastry may be refrigerated overnight or frozen.

To make Filling, in a food processor fitted with the metal blade, mince garlic. Add parsley, green onions and dill; process until finely minced. Remove to small bowl and set aside. Melt butter or margarine in a medium saucepan. Stir in flour, cook over low heat for 1 minute. Slowly stir in milk, whisking over moderate heat until mixture comes to a boil and thickens. Whisk in mustard and season generously with cayenne, white pepper and salt. The mixture will be very thick. If not using immediately, place a piece of plastic wrap directly on the surface of the sauce. Flake crab or salmon in a medium bowl, removing all bones; gently toss in shrimp.

To assemble the tourtière, on a lightly floured board, roll the large disk of pastry into a 16-inch circle; it should be large enough to cover the bottom and sides of a 9 × 3- or 9½ × 2½-inch springform pan and extend about 1 inch over the rim. Transfer to pan and press into bottom and up the sides. Trim edges of pastry so they extend over the rim by ½ inch. Do not be concerned if pastry tears just patch it with scraps. Reserve all scraps for decorations.

Sprinkle half the cheese over bottom. Top with half the seafood, half the white sauce, half the chopped eggs, half the herb mixture and half the sour cream. Repeat layers ending with sour cream.

Roll remaining pastry into a 10-inch circle about ⅛ inch thick. Place on top of tourtière and trim to fit the top. Fold ½-inch edge of bottom pastry over the top, making a border. Brush pastry with egg glaze. Reroll scraps and cut out desired decorations: musical notes, base and treble clef, etc. Place on pastry and brush with egg glaze.

(continued)

* Tourtière may be covered with foil and refrigerated overnight or frozen for 2 weeks. Defrost in refrigerator overnight. Bring to room temperature 4 to 6 hours before baking.

About 3 hours before serving, preheat oven to 400 degrees. Place oven rack on bottom rung. Place tourtière on rimmed baking sheet and bake for 55 to 70 minutes or until top is golden brown and sides are bubbling. Remove to rack placed over a baking sheet and cool for 2 hours; juices may seep out of the springform as it cools, but tourtière will still be warm after 2 hours.

To make Lemon Butter Sauce, melt butter or margarine over low heat in a small saucepan. Stir in remaining ingredients. Do not allow sauce to get too hot or it will separate. Serve from sauceboat.

Before serving, remove sides of springform. Place tourtière on platter and garnish with lemon and parsley, if desired. Cut into wedges and serve with Lemon Butter Sauce.

Serves 10.

Pattypan Squash with Tomatoes and Corn

Pale green scalloped summer squash make lovely containers for a bright yellow filling flecked with red and green. (See photograph, page 171.)

16 pattypan squash (about 2½ pounds)
Salt
1 medium tomato, seeded and finely chopped
½ package (10 ounces) frozen corn, thawed (about 1 cup)
¼ cup chopped fresh basil or ¼ cup chopped fresh parsley and 1½ teaspoons dried basil
Pepper to taste

Wash squash. Bring a large saucepan of salted water to a boil. Add squash, cover and simmer for 7 to 12 minutes or until barely tender when pierced with a knife. Drain, run under ice water to stop the cooking. Cut a slice off bottom so squash sits flat. Cut out rounded side, leaving a ¼- to ½-inch shell. With a spoon, scoop out the center. Discard the stem and chop the pulp; reserve about ¾ cup. Lightly salt the squash. Place cut side down on paper towels to drain for 30 minutes or longer; pat dry.

In a small bowl, stir together tomato, corn and basil. Stir in reserved ¾ cup squash and add pepper to taste. Spoon filling into squash, mounding the tops. Place on baking sheet.

* The squash may be refrigerated, covered, overnight. Bring to room temperature before baking.

Before serving, preheat oven to 350 degrees. Bake, covered with foil, for 10 minutes or until heated through.

Serves 10 to 12.

Chocolate Hazelnut Rhapsody

You bake this feather-light hazelnut cake in a jelly-roll pan, then cut it into three long strips and fill it with chocolate whipped cream. Then you frost it with ivory whipped cream and decorate with strips of ebony chocolate. With a little imagination you have created a grand piano keyboard. (See photograph, page 171.)

Hazelnut Cake

- 4 eggs, separated
- ½ cup sugar, divided
- 1 teaspoon vanilla
- ⅓ cup all-purpose flour
- ½ cup finely ground hazelnuts
- Confectioners sugar

Chocolate Filling

- 1½ cups heavy cream
- ½ cup unsweetened cocoa powder
- ¾ cup confectioners sugar
- ¼ cup Frangelico (hazelnut liqueur) or Kahlúa

Frosting and Optional Garnish

- 3 ounces semisweet chocolate, melted for piano keys, optional
- 1 cup heavy cream
- 2 tablespoons confectioners sugar
- 1 cup finely chopped hazelnuts, toasted at 350 degrees for 8 to 10 minutes, stirring occasionally

To make the Hazelnut Cake, preheat oven to 375 degrees. Grease a 15½ × 10½ × 1-inch jelly-roll pan. Line with parchment or waxed paper; grease bottom and sides of paper. In a small mixing bowl with an electric mixer at high speed, beat egg yolks with ¼ cup of the sugar until light and creamy, about 2 minutes. Mix in vanilla. Clean beaters. In a large mixing bowl with the electric mixer at high speed, beat egg whites until soft peaks form. Mix in remaining ¼ cup sugar, 1 tablespoon at a time, beating continuously until stiff, but not dry, peaks form. Partially fold yolks into whites; add flour and nuts and fold until incorporated. Spread batter evenly in prepared pan. Bake for 10 to 13 minutes or until cake is lightly browned and a toothpick inserted in the center comes out clean.

Meanwhile, place a dish towel on a flat surface; sift confectioners sugar over to cover lightly. Invert cake onto towel, remove baking pan and peel off the paper. Cool completely.

To make the Chocolate Filling, in a large mixing bowl with the electric mixer, beat cream on medium speed until soft peaks form. Add cocoa, confectioners sugar and liqueur. Beat on medium speed until of spreading consistency.

To assemble the loaf, cut cake lengthwise into 3 strips, each about 3 inches wide. Cut a piece of heavy poster board or cardboard about 5 × 18 inches; cover with heavy foil. Place 1 cake layer on the board. Spread with half the filling, top with second layer, spread with remaining filling and top with third layer.

* The torte may be covered with plastic wrap and foil and refrigerated up to 2 days or frozen. Defrost, covered, in the refrigerator.

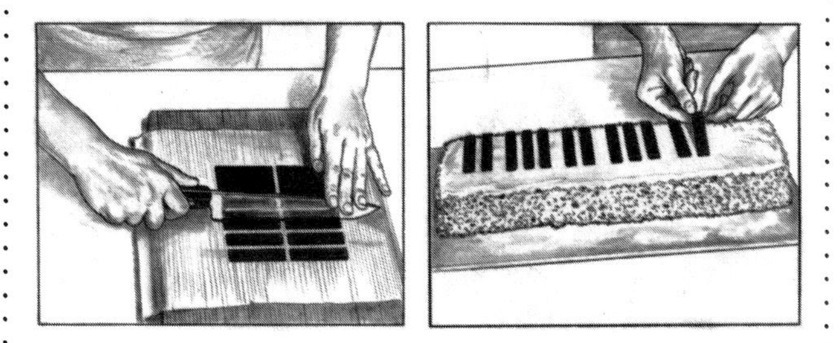

To make chocolate keys, place a sheet of waxed paper on a small tray. Spread all the melted chocolate into a 6-inch square. Freeze until firm. Bring to room temperature until soft enough to cut without shattering, 3 to 5 minutes. If the chocolate gets too soft, it may be refrozen. Trim edges, making a 5-inch square. Cut in half. Cut each half into ten ½-inch strips. You will need only 12 or 13; the extra ones are in case of breakage. Freeze until ready to decorate.

To make the Frosting, up to 8 hours before serving, whip cream until thick. Add confectioners sugar and beat until stiff peaks form. Spread as smoothly as possible over top and sides of the cake. Press hazelnuts onto the sides and ends; brush excess off foil. Place chocolate strips on cake to resemble piano keys: 2 keys ½ inch apart; 1½-inch space; 3 keys ½ inch apart; 1½-inch space; repeat 2 and 3 key groupings. Refrigerate until serving.

Serves 12.

M E N U

THE CONSUMMATE COCKTAIL PARTY

Cold Appetizers

Hearts of Palm in Spinach-Walnut Pesto

Marinated Mushrooms with Blue Cheese

Pepper Wedges with Tomatoes and Basil

Egg, Avocado and Caviar Mold

Pesto-Topped Appetizer Cheesecake

Lox and Cream Cheese Roll

Fresh Tomato Salsa

Avocado Salsa

Home-Fried Tortilla Chips

Cauliflower Ranch Dip

Roasted Eggplant Dip

Toasted Pita Chips

Cucumber Cups with Mock Crab

Devilishly Hot Mixed Nuts

Hot Appetizers

Flaky Parmesan Pesto Pinwheels

Lamb Turnovers with Yogurt Sauce

Miniature Frittatas in Whole Wheat Toast Cups

Crab Nachos

Brie Quesadillas

Italian-Style Quesadillas

Petite Pastries

Double Currant Bars

Lemon Tarts in Almond Paste Crust

White and Dark Chocolate Tartlets

Raspberry Cake Brownies

Handsomely dressed people, drinks in one hand, hors d'oeuvres in the other, stand in closely knit groups. Food is elegantly displayed on a lavishly appointed buffet table while bite-size appetizers are passed on beautifully garnished platters. Participants enter and exit the scene making new friends and meeting old ones. Overseeing the entire event with seemingly effortless ease is the host: greeting guests, introducing them to one another, keeping an eye on food and drink and making everyone feel welcome. Such is the Consummate Cocktail Party.

One of the biggest dilemmas in planning this type of event is how much to make for how many. A good rule of thumb is to allow 8 dishes for the first 24 people, adding another selection for every 10 to 12 persons. For example, at a party for 50 people, offer a total of 10 or 11 dishes. For the buffet table you will want an assortment of dips and spreads in different shapes, colors and textures, perhaps four in all. Supplement these with two or three kinds of bite-size finger foods. You'll also want to pass four or five hot appetizers.

For dessert, I prefer delicate, individual confections that can be picked up to those requiring a plate and fork, even though tiny pastries take time and patience to prepare. Don't count the hours when undertaking an affair as opulent as this. When it is a labor of love, the giver is truly rewarded.

Hearts of Palm in Spinach-Walnut Pesto

Chunks of hearts of palm are marinated in a spinach pesto, surprisingly lighter in texture and flavor than its more familiar basil cousin. Serve with frilly toothpicks or forks as an appetizer or part of an antipasto. (See photograph, page 153.)

- 2 cloves garlic, peeled
- ¼ cup walnuts (about 1 ounce)
- 1 cup chopped fresh basil or ⅓ cup dried basil
- ⅓ cup (packed) chopped spinach leaves
- ⅓ cup (packed) chopped fresh parsley leaves
- ¼ cup grated parmesan cheese
- ¼ cup white wine vinegar
- ¼ cup olive oil
- ½ cup vegetable oil
- ½ cup water
- ½ teaspoon salt, or to taste
- Pepper to taste
- 3 cans (14 ounces each) hearts of palm

To make the pesto, in a food processor fitted with the metal blade, mince garlic and walnuts. Scrape down sides and add basil, spinach and parsley; process until finely minced. Add parmesan cheese, vinegar, oils and water; process until well combined. Add salt and pepper to taste.

∗ The pesto may be refrigerated up to 3 days.

Drain and rinse hearts of palm. Slice into approximately ½- to 1-inch, bite-size pieces; they will vary in size. Place in a medium bowl, pour pesto over and toss to coat. Refrigerate several hours for flavors to blend. Serve at room temperature.

∗ Hearts of palm may be refrigerated overnight.

Serves 10 to 12.

Marinated Mushrooms with Blue Cheese

Once you taste mushrooms paired with blue cheese, you'll wonder why this compatible duo doesn't get together more often. (See photograph, page 153.)

- 1 cup vegetable oil
- 2 tablespoons lemon juice
- ¼ cup white wine vinegar
- 2 cloves garlic, minced
- 2 teaspoons seasoned salt
- 1 teaspoon sugar
- ½ teaspoon dry mustard
- Several dashes hot-pepper sauce to taste
- ¼ cup crumbled blue cheese (1 ounce)
- 2 pounds small fresh mushrooms

In a large bowl, whisk oil, lemon juice, vinegar, garlic, seasoned salt, sugar, dry mustard and hot-pepper sauce until blended. Stir in blue cheese.

∗ The dressing may be refrigerated overnight, if desired.

Rub mushrooms with a damp cloth and cut stems even with cap; save stems for another use. Stir caps into vinaigrette. Refrigerate, covered, for 4 to 6 hours before serving.

∗ The mushrooms may be refrigerated overnight.

Serves 12.

Pepper Wedges with Tomatoes and Basil

Red and yellow pepper wedges are piled high with chopped tomatoes, capers, anchovies and basil and baked until crisp-tender. Their sparkling color and flavor liven up an antipasto or hors d'oeuvre platter. (See photographs, title page and page 153.)

- 2 medium cloves garlic, peeled
- 2 small green onions with tops, cut into 1-inch pieces
- 4 Italian plum or 2 medium tomatoes, seeded and coarsely chopped (1 cup)
- 3 tablespoons chopped fresh basil or 1 tablespoon dried
- 2 anchovy fillets, drained, dried and chopped
- 3 tablespoons olive oil
- 2 tablespoons capers, rinsed
- Freshly ground pepper to taste
- 2 large bell peppers, 1 red and 1 yellow if available

Preheat the oven to 375 degrees. In a food processor fitted with the metal blade, mince garlic. Add green onions and chop fine. Add tomatoes, basil and anchovies and pulse until the mixture is chopped into small pieces; do not puree. Remove to small bowl and stir in olive oil, capers and pepper.

Cut peppers in half through stem end, remove seeds and cut each half into quarters, making 8 wedges per pepper. Fill each wedge with tomato mixture. Place in a shallow baking dish, cover with foil and bake for 15 minutes. Uncover and bake for 10 to 15 minutes longer, or until the peppers are tender, but not limp. Cool to room temperature.

* The peppers may be refrigerated overnight. Bring to room temperature before serving.

Makes 16 wedges.

Egg, Avocado and Caviar Mold

A regal spread for crackers. Creamy avocado is layered over hard-boiled eggs, coated with sour cream and capped with glistening caviar.

Egg Layer

- 4 hard-boiled eggs, peeled and chopped
- ¼ cup finely chopped onion
- 2 tablespoons sour cream
- ¼ teaspoon salt, or to taste
- Pepper to taste

Avocado Layer

- 1 small avocado or ½ large avocado
- 2 ounces cream cheese, at room temperature
- 1 tablespoon finely chopped onion
- 1 teaspoon lemon juice
- Salt and pepper to taste

Topping

- ¾ cup sour cream
- 2 ounces black, gold or red caviar
- Assorted crackers and bread rounds for serving

To make the Egg Layer, stir together eggs, onion, sour cream, salt and pepper until combined.

To make the Avocado Layer, mash avocado with cream cheese until smooth. Stir in onion, lemon juice, salt and pepper to taste.

Spread egg layer in a 6-inch circle in the center of a round platter; flatten the top. Spread avocado mixture over the egg layer, making a slight dome. Spread sour cream over top and sides. Refrigerate until firm.

* The mold may be refrigerated, covered with plastic wrap, overnight.

As close to serving as possible, cover the top with caviar. Surround with crackers or bread rounds.

Serves 12.

Pesto-Topped Appetizer Cheesecake

We tend to think of cheesecake as dessert, but when cream cheese and ricotta are combined with a tangy goat cheese, the three bake into a mild and savory spread. The emerald green pesto frosting is a contrast in color, taste and texture. (See photograph, page 153.)

Pesto

- 2 large cloves garlic, peeled
- 2 cups (packed) basil leaves (2 ounces)
- ⅔ cup grated parmesan cheese
- ⅔ cup chopped walnuts (about 3 ounces)
- ¼ cup olive oil

Cheesecake

- 11 ounces cream cheese, at room temperature
- ¾ cup ricotta cheese, about 6 ounces
- 8 ounces goat cheese, such as montrachet
- 3 eggs, at room temperature
- ½ cup sour cream
- Crackers for serving

To make the Pesto, in a food processor fitted with the metal blade, process garlic until minced. Add basil, parmesan cheese and walnuts; process until ground. Add oil and process to a thick paste.

∗ The pesto may be refrigerated in an airtight container up to 1 month. (Makes about 1 cup.)

To make the Cheesecake, butter an 8- or 8½-inch springform pan. Preheat oven to 350 degrees. In a food processor fitted with the metal blade or in a mixing bowl with an electric mixer, process or mix cream cheese, ricotta and goat cheese until well blended, scraping sides. Pulse or mix in eggs until thoroughly incorporated. Add sour cream; process or mix until well blended. Pour into springform. Bake for 45 to 55 minutes or until top is puffed and golden; the middle portion will still jiggle. Remove to rack and cool completely.

∗ The cake may be refrigerated up to 3 days or frozen. Defrost in refrigerator.

As close to serving as possible, remove sides of springform. Spread pesto evenly over top of cake; cover with plastic wrap and refrigerate until serving. Serve with crackers.

Serves 14 to 16.

Lox and Cream Cheese Roll

Smoked salmon and seasoned cream cheese are rolled up and sliced into pretty pinwheels. Serve them on bagel chips or sliced mini-bagels. (See photograph, title page.)

- 4 green onions with tops, cut into 1-inch pieces
- ¼ cup chopped fresh dill or 1 tablespoon dried dillweed
- 2 packages (8 ounces each) cream cheese, at room temperature
- 2 tablespoons lemon juice
- Pepper to taste
- 8 ounces smoked salmon or lox sliced ⅛-inch thick, about 10 slices
- 2 tablespoons capers, rinsed and drained
- Bagel chips, mini-bagels sliced in half or sliced cocktail rye or pumpernickel for serving

In a food processor fitted with the metal blade, finely chop green onions and dill. Add cream cheese, lemon juice and pepper and process until combined. Place a sheet of waxed paper on a work surface. Arrange salmon slices close together to form a 7 × 16-inch rectangle. Spread cream cheese mixture over salmon, covering it completely. Sprinkle with capers. Roll up as for a jelly roll, starting at a long side; lift the paper to help you roll. Tightly wrap the roll in the paper and refrigerate for several hours or until firm enough to slice.

∗ The roll may be refrigerated up to 2 days or frozen.

Before serving, using a serrated knife, slice chilled roll as thin as possible, pushing the slices back into rounds. Either place them overlapping on a serving plate surrounded by bagels or bread rounds or put them directly on the bread.

Makes about 40 slices.

Fresh Tomato Salsa

A great dip for chips, this salsa can also be ladled over grilled fish or chicken, stirred into sauces or salads, spooned over tacos or fajitas. One strict criterion for this recipe: the tomatoes must be good quality and ripe.

- 2½ pounds large ripe tomatoes (4 to 5)
- ⅔ cup cilantro leaves
- 2 cloves garlic, peeled
- 2 teaspoons jarred salsa jalapeña or 3 or 4 jalapeño chilies, fresh or bottled, stems and seeds removed
- 6 green onions with tops, cut into 1-inch pieces
- 1½ teaspoons salt, or to taste
- ½ teaspoon dried oregano or 2 teaspoons chopped fresh oregano
- Home-Fried Tortilla Chips (page 181) for serving

Cut tomatoes in half horizontally like a grapefruit and squeeze out seeds; cut into quarters. In a food processor fitted with the metal blade, mince cilantro, garlic and salsa or chilies. Scrape down sides, add green onions and process until chopped. Add tomatoes, salt and oregano; pulse until coarsely chopped. Remove to a bowl, cover and refrigerate 1 hour or overnight. Drain excess liquid before using.

* The salsa may be refrigerated up to 2 weeks.

Makes about 2¾ cups.

Avocado Salsa

My daughter Margi often spoons this vibrant green salsa over fish steaks. With its refreshingly pure taste and mild heat, it is a vigorous alternative to guacamole. (See photograph, page 28.)

- 2 large cloves garlic, peeled
- 2 large green onions with tops, coarsely chopped (about ¼ cup)
- ½ cup (packed) cilantro leaves
- 1 can (13 ounces) tomatillos, drained, or 6 fresh tomatillos, simmered in water to cover for 5 minutes and drained
- 4 teaspoons jarred salsa jalapeña or jarred hot picante salsa
- 4 teaspoons fresh lime juice
- ½ cup chicken broth
- ½ teaspoon sugar
- 1 large avocado, peeled and pit removed
- Salt to taste
- Home-Fried Tortilla Chips (page 181), for dipping

In a food processor with the metal blade, mince garlic and onions. Add cilantro and process until chopped. Add tomatillos and salsa jalapeña and process until pureed. Process in lime juice, chicken broth and sugar. Add avocado and pulse until it is finely chopped. Season to taste. Serve with chips.

* The salsa may be refrigerated up to 1 week.

Makes about 2½ cups.

Home-Fried Tortilla Chips

Once you taste these freshly fried chips, you'll never settle for the storebought variety again. *(See photograph, page 28.)*

8 corn tortillas (6 inches in diameter)
Vegetable oil for frying
Salt, if desired

Leave tortillas out at room temperature for 1 hour to dry slightly. With scissors, cut each one into 8 triangles. Pour ¼ inch of oil into a medium skillet. Heat to 365 degrees or until it sizzles when tortilla is added. Fry tortillas in batches in hot oil until crisp and lightly browned. Drain on paper towels. If desired, sprinkle with salt.

* The chips may be held at room temperature in an airtight container for 2 days or frozen. Reheat at 375 degrees for 3 to 5 minutes or until warm.

Makes 64 chips.

Cauliflower Ranch Dip

The heart of this healthful, creamy dip—cauliflower—remains a mystery to all who taste it. When it is pureéd with a dab of sour cream and a sprinkling of ranch dressing, its flavor becomes subtle and very muted.

½ head cauliflower (about 1 pound)
1 green onion with top, chopped into 1-inch pieces
3 tablespoons sour cream
3 tablespoons ranch salad dressing mix (from a 2-ounce package)
Raw vegetables for dipping, such as carrots, celery, broccoli, zucchini, cucumbers, cherry tomatoes, jícama

Break cauliflower into florets. In a medium saucepan, bring about 1½ inches of water to a boil. Add cauliflower, cover and simmer until tender, about 15 minutes. Run under cold water to stop the cooking; drain well.

In a food processor fitted with the metal blade, puree cauliflower and green onion until smooth. Scrape down sides, add sour cream and dressing mix; process 1 minute or until creamy. Remove to serving bowl and refrigerate until chilled. Serve with fresh vegetables.

* The dip may be refrigerated up to 8 hours. The flavors intensify too much if refrigerated longer.

Makes 1½ cups.

Roasted Eggplant Dip

Broiling whole eggplants until soft and charred produces the subtle flavor of this unique dip. *(See photograph, page 163.)*

Toasted Pita Chips for dipping
2 medium eggplants (about 1¼ pounds each)
1 large clove garlic, peeled
1 teaspoon sugar
¼ teaspoon cayenne pepper
½ teaspoon cumin
3 tablespoons red wine vinegar
1½ teaspoons salt, or to taste
3 tablespoons fruity olive oil
1 Italian plum or small tomato, cut into wedges, for garnish
2 tablespoons chopped parsley for garnish

Prepare Toasted Pita Chips as directed; set aside. Line a baking sheet with heavy foil. Broil whole eggplants about 3 inches from the broiler flame or element, turning once, until blackened, wrinkled and soft when pressed, about 30 minutes. The eggplants may also be roasted on a grill, turned occasionally until charred, about 45 minutes. Remove from heat; cover with foil and set aside for 15 minutes. Holding the stem, gently peel off the skin with a sharp knife and your fingers. Discard stem, tear the flesh into pieces and place in a strainer; drain for 10 minutes.

In a food processor fitted with the metal blade, mince garlic. Add eggplant, sugar, cayenne, cumin, vinegar and salt. Process until finely chopped. Add oil all at once and process until mixture is pureed. Adjust seasonings to taste. Remove to a bowl, cover and refrigerate several hours.

* The dip may be refrigerated up to 2 days.

Serve in bowl; garnish outer edge with tomato wedges and sprinkle with chopped parsley. Surround with pita chips.

Makes about 3 cups.

Toasted Pita Chips

Use these in place of crackers or bread rounds for a change of pace with dips and spreads. *(See photograph, page 163.)*

6 pita breads (about 6 to 8 inches in diameter)
3 tablespoons olive oil
Sesame seeds or poppy seeds for topping, optional

Preheat oven to 325 degrees. Slip scissors into edge of pita breads and cut them in half horizontally, making 2 rounds. Brush inside with oil. Sprinkle with sesame or poppy seeds, if desired, pressing them in with your hands. Cut each round into 4 triangles. Place on baking sheets and bake for 10 to 15 minutes or until lightly browned and crisp.

* The chips may be held at room temperature in an airtight container for several days or frozen.

Serve warm or at room temperature.

Makes 48 chips.

Cucumber Cups with Mock Crab

This recipe was created one day when I bought imitation crab by accident. When I tried substituting the real thing, it came out too watery. Look for top-quality artificial crab with about 30 percent snow crab. This is one time when a mistake really paid off. (See photograph, title page.)

- 8 ounces mock or imitation crabmeat
- 2 teaspoons jarred salsa jalapeña
- 4 teaspoons sour cream
- 2 teaspoons finely chopped fresh cilantro
- 2 teaspoons lemon juice
- Salt
- 1 hothouse or European cucumber, unpeeled (about 10 ounces), or 2 regular cucumbers, peeled
- Cilantro sprigs, for garnish

In a small bowl, stir together crab, salsa, sour cream, cilantro and lemon juice. Slice cucumber into ½-inch rounds. Using a melon baller, hollow out the center, being careful not to go through the bottom. Sprinkle the tops lightly with salt and let stand 30 minutes; wipe dry with paper towels. Spoon about 1 teaspoon crab mixture into center, mounding slightly. Refrigerate until serving.

∗ The cucumber cups may be refrigerated, covered, overnight.

Before serving, garnish tops with small sprigs of cilantro.

Makes about 24 cups.

Devilishly Hot Mixed Nuts

They say appetizers should awaken the palate. These hot, peppery nuts will definitely rouse it. (See photograph, page 115.)

- 4 tablespoons (½ stick) butter or margarine
- 1 teaspoon seasoned salt
- 1 teaspoon seasoned pepper
- 1½ teaspoons cayenne pepper, divided
- 1 teaspoon hot-pepper sauce
- 1 cup whole pecan halves
- 1 cup whole almonds, blanched or in the skin
- 1 cup roasted peanuts
- 1 cup roasted cashews

Preheat oven to 300 degrees. In a medium skillet, melt butter or margarine. Stir in seasoned salt and pepper, 1 teaspoon cayenne and hot-pepper sauce. Add nuts and toss to coat. Place on rimmed baking sheet. Bake for 20 to 25 minutes, tossing with a spatula every 10 minutes until lightly toasted. Toss with remaining ½ teaspoon cayenne. Cool and store in airtight container.

∗ The nuts may be stored airtight at room temperature up to 3 weeks or frozen.

Makes 1 pound.

Flaky Parmesan Pesto Pinwheels

Always keep at least one of these pastry logs ready in the freezer. Then when surprise guests come, you have an impressive instant hors d'oeuvre to offer them.

- 12 ounces cream cheese, at room temperature
- 1 cup grated parmesan cheese (about 4 ounces)
- 2 green onions with tops, cut into 1-inch pieces
- ¼ cup Pesto (page 179)
- 1 package (1 pound) frozen puff pastry, thawed until cold enough to roll, but still very cold

In a food processor fitted with the metal blade, process cream cheese and parmesan until blended. Add green onions and pulse until finely chopped. Add Pesto and process until thoroughly incorporated.

On a lightly floured board, roll half (1 sheet) of the puff pastry into a 10 × 16-inch rectangle. Spread half the cheese mixture over pastry, covering it completely. Roll lengthwise like a jelly roll, starting at a long side, to make a log approximately 1¼ inches in diameter. Wrap tightly in plastic wrap. Repeat with remaining pastry and cheese mixture. Freeze logs until solid, several hours or for several months.

Remove logs from the freezer about 15 minutes before baking. Place oven racks in upper third of oven and preheat to 375 degrees. Slice logs into ¼-inch rounds; you should get about 50 slices per roll. Place on ungreased baking sheets about 1½ inches apart. Bake for 10 to 13 minutes or until the pastry is lightly browned. If baking 2 sheets in the oven at one time, reverse their positions half way through the baking time.

∗ The baked pinwheels may be stored in an airtight container at room temperature for several days or frozen. Defrost at room temperature and reheat at 400 degrees for 3 to 5 minutes or until heated through.

Makes 100 pinwheels.

Lamb Turnovers with Yogurt Sauce

Ground lamb and chopped raisins, sweetly scented with cinnamon and mint, are enveloped in a very tender pastry. The hot turnovers are dipped into a cool yogurt sauce.

Yogurt Pastry

- ½ pound (2 sticks) butter or margarine, at room temperature
- 1 cup plain yogurt
- 3 cups all-purpose flour
- 1¼ teaspoons salt, or to taste

Lamb Filling

- 2 tablespoons olive oil
- ¾ cup chopped onion
- ¾ pound ground lamb
- ½ cup finely chopped fresh parsley
- ¼ cup chopped raisins
- 2 tablespoons lemon juice
- 2 tablespoons chopped fresh mint
- 2 tablespoons tomato paste
- ½ teaspoon salt, or to taste
- ¼ teaspoon pepper
- ¼ teaspoon cayenne pepper
- ¾ teaspoon cinnamon
- ⅓ cup dry red wine
- 3 tablespoons pine nuts, toasted at 350 degrees until golden
- 1 egg mixed with 1 teaspoon milk for glaze

Yogurt Dipping Sauce

- 1 cup plain yogurt
- ½ cup sour cream
- 2 tablespoons chopped fresh mint
- ¼ teaspoon salt, or to taste
- ¼ teaspoon pepper

To make the Yogurt Pastry, in a large mixing bowl or a food processor fitted with the metal blade, mix or process butter or margarine and yogurt until blended. Add flour and salt and mix or process until thoroughly incorporated. Divide the dough in half, shape each into a disk, wrap in plastic wrap and refrigerate for at least 3 hours or overnight.

To make the Lamb Filling, heat oil in a large skillet. Sauté onion over moderate heat until golden, about 20 minutes. Add lamb and sauté until all pink is gone; pour off fat. Stir in parsley, raisins, lemon juice, mint, tomato paste, salt, pepper, cayenne, cinnamon and wine. Simmer over low heat for 5 minutes or until the liquid has evaporated. Stir in pine nuts; cool to room temperature.

On a lightly floured board, roll half the pastry into a 10 × 15-inch rectangle. Keep remaining pastry refrigerated. Using a 3-inch round biscuit cutter, cut out 25 rounds, rerolling and cutting scraps. Place 1 teaspoon filling in center of each round. Fold pastry over to enclose filling, forming a half moon. Press edges together with tines of a fork. Repeat with remaining pastry and filling.

∗ The turnovers may be refrigerated, covered, overnight or frozen. Defrost, covered, in a single layer at room teperature.

To make the Yogurt Dipping Sauce, stir all the ingredients together in a medium bowl. Refrigerate until serving or up to 3 days.

Before serving, preheat oven to 400 degrees. Place turnovers on lightly greased baking sheets. Brush tops lightly with egg glaze being careful not to let it drip onto baking sheet. Bake for 15 to 20 minutes or until golden. If baking 2 sheets in the same oven, rotate their positions half way through the baking time.

∗ The baked turnovers may be kept at room temperature overnight or frozen. Bring to room temperature and reheat at 400 degrees for 5 minutes.

Serve with Yogurt Dipping Sauce.

Makes about 50 turnovers.

Miniature Frittatas in Whole Wheat Toast Cups

These bite-size gems are simple toasted bread cups filled with a colorful vegetable and cheese batter and baked. (See photograph, title page.)

- 20 slices (not extra thin) whole wheat bread
- 6 tablespoons (3/4 stick) butter or margarine
- 3 cloves garlic, minced
- 2 medium zucchini (10 ounces)
- 1/2 small red bell pepper
- 1/2 cup ricotta cheese
- 2/3 cup grated parmesan cheese
- 1/2 teaspoon dried oregano
- 1/4 teaspoon salt, or to taste
- 1/8 teaspoon pepper
- 1/4 teaspoon dried red pepper flakes
- 1 egg

Preheat the oven to 400 degrees. Cut crusts from bread and discard. With rolling pin, roll slices as thin as possible. Using a 2-inch round biscuit cutter, cut 2 circles from each slice. Melt butter or margarine and garlic in small saucepan. Brush 1 side of each round with butter. Press the rounds against the bottom and sides of ungreased 1½-inch muffin cups, buttered side against the pan. Bake for 8 to 10 minutes or until toasted and crisp. Remove from oven, leave toast in muffin tins and reduce oven temperature to 375 degrees.

To make the filling, in a food processor with a fine shredding disk, shred zucchini. If you do not have a fine shredding disk, chop medium shreds into small pieces by pulsing them with the metal blade. Remove to a bowl. With the metal blade in place, chop red pepper into small dice; add to zucchini. Stir in ricotta, parmesan, spices and egg. Spoon into toast cups, stirring often, mounding the tops slightly. Bake at 375 degrees for 12 to 15 minutes or until the filling is set. Remove from tins with tip of a sharp knife.

∗ The frittatas may be refrigerated up to 2 days or frozen. Place on baking sheet and freeze, uncovered, until solid. Layer in covered containers separated by sheets of waxed paper. Defrost on baking sheets, covered, at room temperature. To reheat, bake at 375 degrees for 5 to 7 minutes or until hot.

Makes 40 cups.

Crab Nachos

Tortilla triangles are brushed lightly with oil and baked until crisp, rather than fried. They make a delicious base for these cheese nachos with a seafood twist.

- 4 corn tortillas (6 inches in diameter)
- About 2 tablespoons vegetable oil
- Salt, if desired
- 8 ounces crabmeat, flaked
- 2 tablespoons plus 2 teaspoons jarred salsa jalapeña or jarred hot picante salsa
- 1½ cups jack cheese, shredded (about 6 ounces)

Preheat the oven to 400 degrees. Brush both sides of the tortillas lightly with oil; cut each into 8 triangles. Place on baking sheets and sprinkle lightly with salt, if desired. Bake for 10 minutes or until lightly browned. Turn, and bake 2 to 3 more minutes or until crisp and golden. Remove and set aside.

* The chips may be kept in an airtight container at room temperature for several days or frozen.

Top each tortilla with a small mound of crab. Drizzle with ¼ teaspoon salsa and cover with cheese.

* The nachos may be refrigerated overnight or frozen. Place on a baking sheet and freeze, uncovered. When firm, layer in covered containers separated by sheets of waxed paper. Do not defrost before baking.

Before serving, preheat oven to 400 degrees. Bake on greased baking sheets for 5 minutes if at room temperature, 8 to 10 minutes if frozen, or until heated through and cheese is melted.

Makes 32 nachos.

Brie Quesadillas

Traditionally quesadillas are filled with jack cheese and fried in lard. My version, which is made with brie and cooked with no oil at all, is richer tasting and lighter at the same time. *(See photograph, title page.)*

- 8 flour or whole wheat tortillas (8 inches in diameter)
- 12 ounces brie cheese, rind removed, at room temperature
- 1 can (4 ounces) diced green chilies
- 4 teaspoons salsa jalapeña
- ½ can (4¼ ounces) sliced black olives, drained (scant ½ cup)
- 4 tablespoons chopped green onions with tops

Place 4 tortillas on work surface. Spread each with about 3 ounces of brie, leaving a ½-inch border all around. Sprinkle cheese with 1½ to 2 tablespoons diced chilies, 1 teaspoon salsa and 1 tablespoon olives and green onions. Top each with a tortilla.

Heat a large skillet or griddle over high heat until hot; reduce heat to medium. Cook quesadillas one at a time until lightly browned, about 2 minutes per side, turning with a spatula. Remove to cutting surface and if not serving immediately, cool to room temperature. With pizza cutter, scissors or sharp knife, cut each quesadilla in quarters, then cut each quarter into thirds, making 12 triangles.

* The quesadillas may be held at room temperature, covered, overnight or frozen. Place on a baking sheet and freeze, uncovered. When firm, layer in a covered container separated by sheets of waxed paper. Defrost or reheat frozen. Bake on greased baking sheets at 400 degrees for 3 to 5 minutes if at room temperature, 7 to 9 minutes if frozen, or until the cheese begins to melt out the sides.

Makes 48 triangles.

Italian-Style Quesadillas

I love experimenting with unusual combinations. Here's an Italian version of the Mexican classic.

- 10 flour or whole wheat tortillas (8 inches in diameter)
- 5 ounces gorgonzola or blue cheese, at room temperature
- 12 ounces sliced provolone cheese
- 1 jar (7 ounces) roasted red peppers or pimientos, coarsely chopped
- 1 can (8½ ounces) artichoke hearts, drained and coarsely chopped

Place 5 tortillas on a work surface. Spread each with a thin layer of gorgonzola, leaving a ½-inch border all around. Cover gorgonzola with 2 slices of provolone, cutting it as needed. Sprinkle about 1 tablespoon red peppers or pimientos and 1 tablespoon artichokes over the cheese (you will have some artichokes left over). Top each with a tortilla.

Heat a large skillet over high heat until hot; reduce heat to medium. Cook quesadillas one at a time until lightly browned, about 2 minutes per side, turning with a spatula. Remove to cutting surface and if not serving immediately, cool to room temperature. With pizza cutter, scissors or sharp knife, cut each quesadilla in quarters, then cut each quarter into thirds, making 12 triangles.

✻ The quesadillas may be held at room temperature, covered, overnight or frozen. Place on baking sheets and freeze, uncovered. When firm, layer in a covered container separated by sheets of waxed paper. Defrost or reheat frozen. Bake on greased baking sheets at 400 degrees for 3 to 5 minutes if at room temperature, 7 to 9 minutes if frozen, or until the cheese begins to melt out the sides.

Makes 60 triangles.

Double Currant Bars

Both dried currants and currant jelly go into creating this luscious bar. (See photograph, page 54.)

Pastry Layer

- 1¼ cups all-purpose flour
- ⅓ cup sugar
- ¼ pound (1 stick) butter or margarine, cold and cut into 8 pieces

Currant Layer

- 6 tablespoons (¾ stick) butter or margarine, at room temperature
- ¾ cup sugar
- 2 eggs
- 2 teaspoons white distilled vinegar
- 1 cup flaked or shredded coconut
- ¾ cup dried currants
- ¾ cup chopped walnuts (about 3 ounces)
- ½ cup currant jelly

Preheat the oven to 350 degrees. Line a 9 × 13-inch baking pan with heavy foil, letting it extend at least 1 inch over the sides. Butter lightly. To make the Pastry Layer, in a food processor fitted with the metal blade or in a mixing bowl with the electric mixer, mix flour, sugar and butter or margarine until crumbly. The mixture will feel dry. Press into bottom of the prepared pan. Bake in center of oven for 15 to 18 minutes or until lightly browned.

While pastry bakes, make the Currant Layer. In the same food processor workbowl or mixing bowl, cream butter or margarine and sugar until well blended. Pulse in eggs and vinegar. Pulse in coconut, currants, and nuts until combined. Stir currant jelly to soften and spread over hot pastry layer. Pour topping over, smooth the top and return to oven for 20 to 25 minutes or until golden brown. Cool to room temperature. Lift out the foil, place on a flat surface and cut the cookies into 1¼ × 2-inch bars.

✻ The bars may be stored at room temperature in an airtight container for several days or frozen.

Makes 42 bars.

Lemon Tarts in Almond Paste Crust

Each crisp almond cup filled with tangy lemon custard is a little bit of heaven. Regardless of the competition, these golden jewels are always the first to disappear from a dessert tray.

Almond Paste Pastry

½ package (7 or 8 ounces) almond paste
¼ pound (1 stick) butter or margarine, cold and cut into 16 pieces
1 egg
1 cup plus 2 tablespoons all-purpose flour
⅛ teaspoon salt, or to taste
¼ teaspoon almond extract

Lemon Filling

3 eggs
¾ cup sugar
¼ cup plus 2 tablespoons lemon juice (2 to 3 lemons)
1 tablespoon grated lemon peel
6 tablespoons (¾ stick) butter or margarine, at room temperature
Candied violets or whipped cream for garnish, optional

To make the Almond Paste Pastry, in a food processor fitted with the metal blade, process almond paste until softened. Add butter or margarine and process until distributed. Add egg and process until blended. Add flour and salt and pulse until incorporated. Pulse in almond extract. Remove dough to a sheet of plastic wrap and shape into a ball. It may be used immediately or refrigerated up to 2 days.

Preheat the oven to 375 degrees. Spray 1½-inch muffin cups or 2- to 3-inch tartlet tins with nonstick vegetable-oil cooking spray. Break off small pieces of dough and press a thin layer into the bottom and up the sides of the tins. If pastry is at room temperature, it will be sticky. Run your finger around the rim to make a smooth border. Place individual tins on a baking sheet. Bake the shells for 10 to 14 minutes or until the edges are very brown and the bottoms are golden. Do not underbake, as the pastry is tastier when golden. Remove from oven, cool slightly and remove from tins by inserting the tip of a sharp knife into one edge. Cool completely. It is not necessary to wash the tins between each use; brush off crumbs and spray lightly.

∗ The shells may be held, covered, at room temperature up to 2 days or frozen.

To make Lemon Filling, in a heavy medium saucepan, whisk eggs, sugar, lemon juice and peel until blended. Cook over moderate heat, whisking constantly, until the mixture comes to a full boil. Immediately remove from heat and pour into a bowl. Cut butter or margarine into bits and whisk in until melted. Refrigerate, covered, or place bowl in a pan of ice water and stir occasionally until chilled. Spoon into shells, mounding the tops. Refrigerate until serving.

∗ The filled tarts may be refrigerated, covered, up to 2 days or frozen. Defrost at room temperature for 15 to 30 minutes, depending on size.

If desired, several hours before serving, garnish each tartlet with a candied violet or a small rosette of whipped cream.

Makes 34 to 36 (1½-inch) or 18 (3-inch) tarts.

White and Dark Chocolate Tartlets

Bite-size dark chocolate shells hold rosettes of creamy, white chocolate filling.

Chocolate Pastry

1 cup plus 2 tablespoons all-purpose flour
⅓ cup sugar
3 tablespoons unsweetened cocoa
¼ pound (1 stick) butter or margarine, cold and cut into 8 pieces
1 egg
½ teaspoon vanilla

White Chocolate Cream

6 ounces white chocolate, preferably Tobler Narcisse or Lindt Blancor, chopped
¼ pound (1 stick) butter or margarine, at room temperature
⅓ cup confectioners sugar
1 egg, at room temperature
2 teaspoons light Crème de Cacao
1 teaspoon vanilla
Raspberries or strawberries for garnishing tarts, optional

To make Chocolate Pastry, in a food processor fitted with the metal blade or in a mixing bowl with a pastry blender, mix flour, sugar and cocoa powder. Add butter or margarine and pulse or mix until it is in small pieces. Add egg and vanilla and pulse or mix until the dough holds together and resembles wet sand; small pieces of butter will be visible. Remove to a sheet of plastic wrap and shape into a ball. Pastry may be used immediately or refrigerated up to 2 days.

Spray 1½-inch muffin cups or 2- to 3-inch tartlet tins with nonstick vegetable-oil cooking spray. Break off small pieces of dough and press thinly into bottom and up sides of tins. If the dough is at room temperature, it will be very sticky. Place individual tins on baking sheets. Preheat oven to 375 degrees. Bake pastry for 12 minutes or until set. Remove from oven and immediately place a plate or baking sheet over muffin tins and invert. Invert individual tarts separately. Turn shells right side up and cool. It is not necessary to wash the tins between each use; wipe out crumbs and spray lightly.

∗ The pastry shells may be held, tightly covered, at room temperature up to 2 days or frozen.

To make White Chocolate Cream, melt chocolate over hot water or in a microwave; cool slightly. In a small mixing bowl with an electric mixer, beat butter or margarine until fluffy. Mixing at high speed, slowly add sugar; beat 2 minutes. Mix in chocolate. Add egg; mix on high speed for 2 more minutes. Scrape sides of bowl, mix in Crème de Cacao and vanilla, beating until the mixture is very thick and smooth. Spoon or pipe cream through a rosette tip into baked shells. Refrigerate until serving.

∗ The tarts may be covered and refrigerated overnight or frozen. Defrost at room temperature for 10 to 30 minutes, depending on size.

Garnish the tops of large tarts with raspberries or strawberries, if desired.

Makes about 30 (1½-inch) or 15 (3-inch) tartlets.

Raspberry Cake Brownies

Not fudge, not cake and not quite a brownie, these chocolaty squares combine the best of all three.

2 ounces unsweetened chocolate, chopped
¼ pound (1 stick) butter or margarine, cut into 8 pieces
2 eggs
⅔ cup sugar
½ cup seedless raspberry jam
2 teaspoons kirsch, Chambord or framboise, optional
⅔ cup all-purpose flour
¼ teaspoon salt, or to taste
½ teaspoon baking powder
⅓ cup semisweet chocolate chips
Confectioners sugar for dusting the top, optional

Line an 8- or 9-inch square pan with a sheet of foil, letting it extend 1 inch over the sides; butter the foil. Preheat the oven to 350 degrees. In a medium saucepan over low heat or in a medium microwave-safe bowl, melt unsweetened chocolate and butter or margarine, stirring until smooth; cool slightly. Whisk eggs in. Whisk in sugar, jam and liqueur, if using. Stir in flour, salt, baking powder and chocolate chips until incorporated. The mixture will be thin. Pour into prepared pan. Bake for 25 to 30 minutes or until a toothpick inserted in the center comes out clean and the top springs back when lightly pressed with fingertips. Let cool in pan 5 minutes; lift foil out of pan and cool completely.

* The cake may be wrapped and held at room temperature for up to 3 days or frozen.

Before serving, cut into squares, approximately 1½ inches each. Dust the tops lightly with confectioners sugar, if desired.

Makes 25 squares.

INDEX

A

B

C

D

E

F

G

H

I

N

O

P

Q

R

S

T

V

W

Y

Z

PHOTO CREDITS

Mexican Brunch
Glass, Tin Box, Plate, Small Bowl
Pan-American Phoenix Shop in the Citicorp Center
153 East 53rd Street
New York, NY 10022

Cajun Shrimp
Rattan Chaise
Ann-Morris Antiques, Inc.
239 East 60th Street
New York, NY 10022

Gala Italia
Plate, Napkins, Forks
Frank McIntosh at Henri Bendel
10 West 57th Street
New York, NY 10019

Here Comes the Bride
Brass Wine Cooler
Hoffman-Gampetro Antiques
68 at The Place des Antiquaires
125 E. 57th Street
New York, NY 10022

Packing the Picnic Basket
Antique Sterling Silver Milk Can
Samuel H. Mintz Straus, Inc.
Antique Center, Shop 50D
1050 2nd Avenue
New York, NY 10022

Antique Biscuit Tin
Joe Stamps
Antique Center, Shop 65
1050 2nd Avenue
New York, NY 10022

Stand-out Sit-down Chicken Dinner
Plates, Flatware, Ceramic Basket
Lord & Taylor
Connoisseur Collections
424 Fifth Avenue
New York, NY 10036

Antique Beaten Silver Bowl
Hoffman-Gampetro Antiques
68 at The Place des Antiquaires
125 E. 57th Street
New York, NY 10022

Consummate Cocktail Party
Glasses
Leah's Gallery
Antique Center, Gallery 42
1050 2nd Avenue
New York, NY 10022

Cocktail Shaker
Betty Korn
Antique Center, Shop 32
1050 2nd Avenue
New York, NY 10022

Silver Warming Dish,
Crystal-and-Silver Pick Holder
The Geneva Galleries
Antique Center
1050 2nd Avenue
New York, NY 10022

Salmonchanted Evening
Pillivuyt Ovenproof Ceramic Tureen
Dean and Deluca
121 Prince Street
New York, NY 10012

Symphony in Black and White
Black Plates, Black-and-White Swid Powell Plates, Stainless Steel Tray, Glass Bowl
The Home at Bergdorf Goodman
754 5th Avenue
New York, NY 10019

*Cover Photo
Tablecloth, Napkins, Glasses
Frank McIntosh at Henri Bendel
10 West 57th Street
New York, NY 10019

Mother-of-Pearl Table, Glass Candelabra, Pierced Creamware Covered Compote
John Rosselli, Ltd.
255 East 72nd Street
New York, NY 10021

Brass Wine Cooler, Bronze Tazza
Hoffman-Gampetro Antiques
68 at The Place des Antiquaires
125 E. 57th Street
New York, NY 10022

Mother-of-Pearl Dish
Bob Pryor
1023 Lexington Avenue
New York, NY 10021

Flowers
Madderlake
25 East 73rd Street
New York, NY 10021

Large Beaten Brass Bowl
Fil Caravan Inc.
Antique Center
1050 2nd Avenue
New York, NY 10022